POWER PLAYERS

POWER PLAYERS

SPORTS, POLITICS, and the AMERICAN PRESIDENCY

CHRIS CILLIZZA

TWELVE

New York   Boston

Twelve
Hachette Book Group
1290 Avenue of the Americas, New York, NY 10104
twelvebooks.com
twitter.com/twelvebooks

First edition: April 2023

Twelve is an imprint of Grand Central Publishing. The Twelve name and logo are trademarks of Hachette Book Group, Inc.

The publisher is not responsible for websites (or their content) that are not owned by the publisher.

Twelve books may be purchased in bulk for business, educational, or promotional use. For information, please contact your local bookseller or the Hachette Book Group Special Markets Department at special.markets@hbgusa.com.

Photographs by Getty Images.

Library of Congress Cataloging-in-Publication Data

Names: Cillizza, Chris (Christopher Michael), 1976– author.
Title: Power players : sports, politics, and the American presidency / Chris Cillizza.
Description: First edition. | New York : Twelve, 2023.
Identifiers: LCCN 2022053153 | ISBN 9781538720608 (hardcover) | ISBN 9781538720622 (ebook)
Subjects: LCSH: Presidents—United States—Biography. | Presidents—Sports—United States. | United States—Politics and government—1945–1989. | United States—Politics and government—1989–
Classification: LCC E176.1 .C55 2023 | DDC 973.09/9—dc23/eng/20221206
LC record available at https://lccn.loc.gov/2022053153

ISBNs: 9781538720608 (hardcover), 9781538720622 (ebook)

Printed in Canada

MRQ-T

10 9 8 7 6 5 4 3 2 1

To Charlie and Will
May you never stop playing

Contents

Introduction

It's Way More Than a Game

In 1905, football was on the verge of being canceled entirely.

The sport was ludicrously violent, with eighteen players having died in just that year alone. Almost fifty people had perished in the five years since the turn of the century. Broken backs and necks were common. Concussions were legion. One player—Harold Moore of Union College—died in November 1905 of a cerebral hemorrhage after being kicked in the head while trying to make a tackle. (Helmets wouldn't become mandatory in college football until 1939.)

Enter Teddy Roosevelt, the president of the United States and an avowed fan not just of football but of violent play, more generally speaking.

"I believe in rough games and in rough, manly sports," Roosevelt once said. "I do not feel any particular sympathy for the person who gets battered about a good deal so long as it is not fatal."

Roosevelt brought the presidents of Yale, Harvard, and Princeton together twice in the fall of 1905 to see if they could agree on a series of reforms that would keep football going while making it safer for its participants. (The Ivy League was, at the turn of the twentieth century, the center of the college football universe.)

By the start of the 1906 season, a series of new rules had been adopted—including the forward pass, which led to the evolution of modern football.

Roosevelt's interest in saving football was about a lot more than his enjoyment of the game; he believed that young men engaged in (at times) brutal physical combat was the proper training for a future as a soldier in the service of the country.

Wrote Roosevelt: "There is a certain tendency...to underestimate or overlook the need of the virile, masterful qualities of the heart and mind...There is no better way of counteracting this tendency than by encouraging bodily exercise, and especially the sports which develop such qualities as courage, resolution and endurance."

(Dwight Eisenhower would put it even more bluntly: "The true mission of American sports is to prepare young people for war.")

Roosevelt then is rightly understood as our first sporting president—in both the sense that he wrestled, boxed, hunted, and fished, and that he understood that sports and politics had a symbiotic relationship that could be exploited by leaders. As historian John Sayle Watterson noted, Roosevelt was "the first president to use sports extensively for political purposes."

Of course, while Roosevelt was the first president to meld sports and politics, the fact is that the two pursuits have been intertwined for thousands of years.

In 776 BC, the first Olympics were held as both a tribute to the Greek god Zeus and a way for the various city-states of the country to prove their superiority over one another. It was a showcase for champions of each island and city-state.

"We know there was total chaos for a week because anyone who wanted to raise their profile, this was the place and time to do it," said Paul Christesen, a professor of ancient Greek history at Dartmouth.

By the time of the Roman Empire, the notion of using sports as a way to placate and pacify the people had been officially codified into a phrase: "bread and circuses."

It comes from a line from the poet Juvenal:

Already long ago, from when we sold our vote to no man, the People have abdicated our duties; for the People who once upon a time handed out military command, high civil office, legions—everything, now restrains itself and anxiously hopes for just two things: bread and circuses.

The idea went like this: To keep the people of Rome happy—and pliant—emperors did two things: (1) they gave out free wheat to keep citizens fed; and (2) they staged gladiatorial contests in the Coliseum that slaked people's more primal urges.

"Paying for spectacular games, blood sports, parades, religious festivals, and chariot races became a standard tool for politicians to win Roman elections during the Republic," wrote Dr. Linda Ellis, a professor at San Francisco State University. "Even in the absence of elections, Roman emperors and provincial governors continued to sponsor lavish entertainment events to demonstrate their generosity and justify their retention of power."

Since the end of the Second World War—and especially since the advent of television—presidents have leaned more and more on sports to cast a positive image of their presidency and speak to audiences they might not be able to reach any other way.

No one epitomized that notion better than John F. Kennedy. Despite a sickly childhood—and a series of illnesses throughout his presidency— the prevailing image of Kennedy for most Americans was of him and his extended family engaged in games of touch football at their compound in Hyannis Port. That Kennedy was often barely able to walk due to back issues—much less able to fully participate in quasi-tackle football—was glossed over. He was regarded as a hale and hearty presence by the public— thanks in large part to his purposeful close associations with sports.

The man Kennedy beat in 1960—Richard Nixon—was an awkward presence on the football field, effectively used as a tackling dummy during his collegiate years. But the future president was a rabid fan, quoting facts and figures about players and games to anyone who would listen. For the socially challenged Nixon, sports talk was a way to humanize him—and for him to talk to regular joes with whom he felt as though he had little else in common.

If Kennedy was the first modern president to grasp the power of sports to make myths, it was Ronald Reagan who took the mixing of sports and politics to the next level. Reagan was, by all accounts, a decent young athlete—he claimed to have saved seventy-seven people from drowning during his years as a lifeguard. But Reagan's real genius was in his understanding that being next to great athletes—and, as important, winners— was just as good as being one himself. While championship sports teams had, on occasion, visited the White House before Reagan's term, the Gipper formalized the process—welcoming in winners and flashing the showmanship that had made him a successful actor. (After the New York Giants won the Super Bowl in 1987, Reagan allowed members of the team to dump a Gatorade bucket full of popcorn—one of his favorite foods— over his head.)

The best overall athlete—in terms of the breadth of the sports he played and the longevity with which he continued to play them—to ever grace the White House was George H. W. Bush. (Yes, Gerald Ford was the best football player—obviously—to ever serve as president. But Bush was more well-rounded. He played tennis. Golfed. Parachuted. Played baseball in college. Did almost any sport that could reasonably be called a sport—and did it well.) Bush grew up playing tennis with his mother, who was a skilled and competitive player. He was a light-hitting and slick-fielding first baseman on the Yale baseball team, and even got to meet Babe Ruth just weeks before the Sultan of Swat's untimely death. In office, Bush's competitive fires ran deep—so deep that he organized a March Madness–like tournament of horseshoes played by the permanent White House staff. (There were brackets and everything!) After leaving the presidency, Bush, like all the men who had held the office before and since, found an outlet for his competitive drive in sports. In addition to being an avid golfer and tennis player, Bush even laid claim to inventing the phrase "You da man!" Yes, seriously.

Barack Obama was the first—but probably not the last—baller president. Obama had a basketball court built on the White House grounds, and invites to his regular pickup games were more precious than getting asked to a state dinner. Obama viewed his competitiveness in pickup as an analog for his competitiveness in politics; once he was in the mix, he wanted to win—and was willing to do whatever it took to bring about that desired result. Obama's rise also dovetailed with the surging popularity of the NBA. Just as Obama was redefining cool in politics, LeBron James, Dwyane Wade, and Kobe Bryant were doing the same on the hardwood.

Then there is, of course, Donald Trump. Like so much else with Trump, the story of his athletic prowess is exaggerated. He was a good baseball player in high school but almost certainly not, as he has often claimed, the best baseball player in the state of New York. He is a good-bordering-on-very-good golfer, but the stories of his many club championships won require a good deal of creative math. He spent years pursuing an NFL team, and if he had managed to buy one—or turn the USFL's New Jersey Generals into one—he might never have had the itch to run for president. Sports and politics appealed to Trump for the same, visceral reasons: Someone won and, more important, someone lost. He liked that—as long as he was on the winning team. Always.

George Orwell once called sports "war without shooting." And there's no question that our modern presidents have understood that sports can be used to unite us and to divide us in equal measure.

Nixon saw bowling as a way to not only court the middle of the country—his "silent majority"—but also cast them against the coastal elites who looked down on bowling as a sport for the middle class.

In the wake of the September 11, 2001, terrorist attacks, there were very real questions about whether sports should continue at all. They did—and, roughly a month later, President George W. Bush strode to the mound at Yankee Stadium to throw out the first pitch in Game 3 of the World Series.

Wearing a bulletproof vest—and with an air of worry palpable in the stadium—Bush threw a perfect strike, a moment that felt like a catharsis, a signal that even though we were down as a country, we weren't out.

And, after four years of the abnormalities and excesses of Donald Trump, it was sports that Joe Biden reached for to make things more, well, normal.

"He's certainly going to look to sports and sports figures to help bring us back into alignment as Americans," Francis Biden, the president's brother, told ESPN.

This book is about the sports our modern presidents played, loved, and spectated—and what those sports can tell us about both who they are and how they chose to govern the country. Sports, like politics, hold a mirror up to us and those we elect to lead us—showing them for who they really are when all the spin, hype, and hyperbole are stripped away.

For our presidents, what so often is revealed in their athletic careers, their fandom, and their leisure pursuits is a raw and unbridled competitiveness and ambition in search of a target.

For George H. W. Bush, raised to always be mannerly and kind to others, sports was where he could let his inner animal out. For his son, George W. Bush, the maniacal running and biking he took up after giving up drinking was a way to funnel his energies and compulsions. For Richard Nixon, his fanatical fandom gave him a way to connect with Joe Q. Public and appear just a little less awkward (and unathletic). Donald Trump viewed sports the way he viewed life—a life-and-death competition where the goal wasn't just to win but to destroy one's opponent.

Competition is sanctioned—and encouraged in sports. It's a safe space where these men felt unafraid to want and want and want—in ways that would have been dismissed as overly forward or arrogant in the context of politics. Sports then was a pressure release valve for many of our nation's leaders, a way for them to sate the ever-burning competitive fires without looking too, well, extra in doing so.

But sports did more than that, too. They showed us the best of what we could be—even if they forced us to face uncomfortable political truths in the process.

Jackie Robinson's integration of baseball led the way for the broader integration of the country. The protests of Tommie Smith and John Carlos at the 1968 Olympics shone a light on inequality in America. Muhammad Ali's refusal to fight in Vietnam forced Americans to come to grips with what we were really doing in Southeast Asia. The U.S. women winning the World Cup in 1999 redefined what "plays like a girl" meant.

LeBron James wearing an "I Can't Breathe" warm-up shirt forced the country to focus on how the police treat young African American men.

"There's a reason that every country has its sports it loves," explained Condoleezza Rice, who served as secretary of state under Bush. "They embody somehow the nation and the national spirit and the national pride, and they rally around these sports figures. At times of national triumph, we rally around them in joy. At times of national tragedy, we rally around them to remember who we are."

Mad Man of the Fairway

Ike Teaches Postwar America How to "Relax"

Dwight Eisenhower loved golf so much that he risked his life playing it—literally.

In 1955, Eisenhower was in Colorado for an extended trip—he arrived in August and was expected to stay until October. (Travel schedules were different for a president back then!)

On a Saturday in September, Ike decided to play at Cherry Hills Golf Club in Denver. The president played eighteen holes in the morning. He was repeatedly interrupted—and angered—through the first round by a game of phone tag with Secretary of State John Foster Dulles. Ike kept a tight lid on his volcanic temper, but he did *not* like to be interrupted while playing golf.

"Finally Dulles and Eisenhower spoke, but when it was all over, Ike was aggravated by the call," wrote historian John Sayle Watterson. "It was inconsequential, he thought."

Annoyed, Eisenhower helped himself to a hamburger topped with onions (delicious!) and then headed out to play another nine holes—this time, he hoped, away from Dulles's calls. But, on the first hole, Dulles called again. "At this point," his doctor wrote, "his anger became so real that the veins stood out on his forehead like whipcords." Eisenhower was so distracted and angry that he cut his third nine holes of the day short—calling it quits on the eighth hole. (Only twenty-six holes of golf!)

Early the next morning, Eisenhower, who was nearing sixty-five and was a chain smoker, started suffering chest pains around 2 a.m.

It was as if the weight of everything—the war, the presidency, America's expectations of him—was crushing him.

———

In the wake of the war, the country and its people were in an expansive mood—looking for a patch of land and life they could call their own. The ubiquity—and increasing affordability—of cars made people more willing to live farther from where they worked. The overcrowding of cities didn't endear major metropolises to its residents.

The suburbs were born. In the 1950s, the suburbs grew by 47 percent—and new housing starts, which had dipped under 100,000 during the war years, surged to more than 1 million annually.

And with this monumental change in American life (and work) came something that most people had never really experienced before: leisure time.

With the war over and America experiencing an economic boom, suddenly people had time to do things other than work. (Hence the baby boom!) And money to spend. But they had little idea what to do with their newfound freedom—financial and otherwise.

Again, as he had during the war, Ike led the way.

As longtime golf writer Ron Sirak noted: "Going into the war [golf] was still primarily a country club game. [Eisenhower] took the game out of the country club and brought it to the people."

And boy did they follow him to the greens. Don Van Natta Jr., author of *First Off the Tee*, a book about presidents and golf, wrote that when Eisenhower assumed office in 1953, an estimated 3.2 million Americans played golf; by 1961, that number had doubled. Yes, doubled.

———

Eisenhower didn't wind up dying on the golf course—or near it (although, if you asked him, dying on a golf course might have been the way he would have liked to go).

In response to his middle-of-the-night chest pains, his personal doctor prescribed a dose of morphine.

It would be twelve more hours before Eisenhower actually went to the hospital. (Medicine was different back then!) The next morning the White House played off Eisenhower's health issue as "digestive upset"; a few hours later they were still insisting it was indigestion. (There is some debate as to whether this was the White House purposely downplaying Ike's condition or whether the White House physician simply misdiagnosed a heart attack as a stomach ailment.)

By early afternoon, Eisenhower's condition hadn't improved. An electrocardiogram was done, which confirmed that the president had indeed suffered a heart attack. He was taken to Fitzsimons Army Hospital, where he began receiving treatment.

(Sidebar: It's worth noting here that there was no Twenty-Fifth Amendment at this point—that wouldn't come until more than a decade later following the assassination of President John F. Kennedy. Which meant that there was no formal plan of succession had Ike been incapacitated or even died. Richard Nixon was the vice president, but there's zero mention of Nixon being around or even alerted that Eisenhower was in a health emergency. Which is all the more striking given that we were in the midst of a cold war with the Soviet Union, a war in which both sides possessed ample caches of nuclear weapons at the ready.)

No longer able to shield the public from Eisenhower's condition, the White House went public with the news of the heart attack. As Sean Braswell wrote in a piece for Ozy News in 2016, the news set off shock waves. "The bull market that had seen stocks triple on Wall Street in the previous seven years went into a tailspin, the Dow Jones plummeting over 6 percent and losing $14 billion in value by the end of what would prove to be the worst single day for markets since the start of World War II."

As it became clear that Eisenhower would live, stocks—and the country—rebounded. He convalesced and recovered in Florida and at a family farm in Pennsylvania. "For five weeks I was not allowed to see a newspaper or listen to the radio," he told a friend of that recuperative period.

A desire to return to the links, not the presidency, fueled Eisenhower's recovery, according to Watterson. "Ike was probably more determined to play golf than he was to serve a second term—he had hoped to serve only four years," Watterson wrote.

During that time, Eisenhower vowed to change his eating habits and to rein in his volatile temper. (He did neither in the long run.) He would return to Augusta in February 1956 (he played twenty-seven holes in two days)—the same month he announced his plans to seek a second term.

In August 1956, Republicans renominated Eisenhower as their party's presidential candidate at the convention in San Francisco. Ike delivered his acceptance speech on Thursday, August 23. On August 24, he made his way to Cypress Point, one of the most prestigious courses in the country, for a round.

"The Golfer who has not played Cypress Point is like the lawyer who has never appeared before the Supreme Court," began an article in *Sports Illustrated* about the president's trip.

Of Eisenhower, *SI* wrote:

When Ike rode his electric caddy off the first tee, he wore a face of exhilarated contentment. He looked like a presidential version of Gordon MacRae astride his horse, singing "Oh What a Beautiful Morning" through the tall corn in the opening scenes of *Oklahoma!* Or like a man who had just re-won the Republican nomination.

He played with Harry Hunt, the president of Cypress; Sam F. B. Morse, a developer; and John McCone, a former undersecretary of the Air Force. The men played a Nassau bet. That means each individual hole is a competition for lowest score. There's also money on the line for lowest score on each nine-hole side and for the entire eighteen holes, too.

The round was such a big deal that *SI* offered a hole-by-hole analysis of Eisenhower's round. "His drive, the best of the foursome, was about 215 yards down the sloping fairway," read the report from the first hole. "He beamed over the compliments from a dozen bystanders. 'Is that the right spot?' he asked, knowing full well it was." Or, this from the sixth: "Here

Ike had an uphill lie on his second and used a brassie. It was a terrific shot but just caught the trees and dropped into a fairway trap. 'I'd better gamble here,' said Ike... [and] plated a five-iron short. Still short of the green, after mis-hitting a wedge, he pitched stony again for a bogey 5."

While Eisenhower and his playing partner—Hunt—lost the match, the reviews of the president's play pegged him at a score in the low 90s. "Ike's very respectable 90 or 91 the first time he saw the course (to say nothing of the fact it was the first full round of golf he played in 3 months) must have left him with a glow of triumph," reported *SI*. "Indeed he enjoyed himself so much that he went out again the next day and the next for 36 more holes."

This is Eisenhower living the life of a privileged—OK, *very* privileged— white man of his day. He was, without question, a symbol of the upward mobility available to some, but only some, in post–World War II America. Remember that *Brown v. Board of Education* wasn't decided until the middle of Ike's first term in office—and the civil rights movement was more than a decade away. It wasn't until 1990 that Eisenhower's beloved Augusta National golf course admitted its first Black member.

Two men helped build the modern world of golf in the United States— Dwight Eisenhower from the White House and Arnold Palmer from the professional golf tour.

"By 1960, every factory and steel mill had a nine hole golf league," said Ron Sirak. "The leagues had two sessions—a morning session for people who worked overnight and an afternoon session... the guys would show up [to the course] in green work pants and work shirt, with the grime of the mills still on them."

While Palmer was dominating the golf tour—he won the Masters in 1958 and then both the Masters and the U.S. Open in 1960—Eisenhower was showing the country what it was like to have a golfing president. Eisenhower's golf obsession began in midlife—he began playing at age thirty-five. (Eisenhower, according to historian John Sayle Watterson, was the first avid golfer in the White House since Warren Harding three decades prior.)

Golf Digest calculated—from an examination of Ike's presidential schedule—that he played golf on one thousand days during his presidency. He had a golf net installed in the White House so he could practice when the weather was bad. He had a putting green installed on the South Lawn. He was regularly photographed swinging a club outside of the White House. Eisenhower had a small tee just outside of the Oval Office; he would hit iron shots in the direction of the White House fountain, where a White House aide would be waiting to retrieve the balls. As historian Watterson noted, Eisenhower even had a mini course built at Camp David.

(Fun fact: It was Eisenhower who coined the name "Camp David"—after his grandson. The presidential retreat in western Maryland had previously been known as Shangri-La, which Eisenhower thought was a little too fancy for him.)

He wasn't just a president who golfed. Eisenhower was a golf obsessive, the kind of guy who in this day and age would be at Golf Galaxy for hours every weekend testing out clubs and talking to the guys who work there about his swing.

Clifford Roberts, a longtime Ike friend and the president of Augusta National, said that the president "was the most enthusiastic golfer I ever knew. He was worse than Arnold Palmer in changing his equipment and style."

He wanted to be good, worked at being good, and, generally speaking, was (pretty) good. "The president shoots a nice game," said golfing legend Ben Hogan, "for a man whose job doesn't give much chance to play or practice." (Oh Ben, if you only knew!)

Eisenhower's biggest weakness—and the source of much of his anger and disappointment on the course—was his short game. "If I could just make this thing work, I'd enjoy the game a whole lot more," Eisenhower once said of his putter.

Roberts diagnosed Ike's short game issues as an issue of temperament. "[Eisenhower] was in too big a hurry...he did not have the natural talent to read the green correctly and he also did not seem to have sensitive fingers in his big-boned hands."

That Eisenhower, the man who led the Allied forces successfully through a complicated and fraught battle with the Axis powers, lacked the patience and the natural ability to read a putting green seems the height of irony.

Eisenhower occasionally took flak for his golf addiction. Joseph and Stewart Alsop, prominent newspaper columnists of the time, referred to Eisenhower as "a nice old gentleman in a golf cart."

Eisenhower was entirely unbothered by the criticism. "Golf had a very calming effect on my grandfather," said Susan Eisenhower, the granddaughter of the president. "People tried to turn his love of golf against him, and he would never budge on how he felt about it. I think what golf did most was to humanize him."

While golf was, primarily, a form of relaxation for Eisenhower, he also used it as a way to foster relationships with other politicians, both domestic and foreign.

"When heads of state visited Washington, they were likely to find themselves at Burning Tree or Chevy Chase [Country Club]," according to Watterson. (At Burning Tree, the mens-only club just outside of Washington, there is an entire room in the clubhouse named in Ike's honor.)

In May 1957, in advance of Japanese prime minister Nobusuke Kishi's visit to the United States, Secretary of State John Foster Dulles invited the prime minister to play golf with Eisenhower.

"President would be glad to arrange a foursome of golf with Kishi afternoon June 20, although President claims his golfing form has become deplorable and he hopes Kishi is not an expert," Dulles wrote to Douglas MacArthur II, the American ambassador to Japan (and the son of the famed general).

MacArthur replied the following day. "This afternoon when I saw Kishi I extended President's invitation for golf game," he wrote. "Kishi was visibly delighted and said he had never dared to hope for such a thing. He accepted with greatest pleasure and asked me to assure President he is not 'an expert.'" Added MacArthur: "I am very grateful to the president and you. I am sure it will be very helpful."

The two dignitaries played on June 19 at Burning Tree. They were joined by Connecticut senator Prescott Bush—the father and grandfather of future presidents—as well as Takizo Matsumoto, a close aide and translator for Kishi. Bush and Kishi teamed up to take on Eisenhower and Matsumoto. (Sources at the time said that the match ended in a tie, a convenient outcome.) Eisenhower gifted Kishi a new set of clubs and new golf bag to commemorate the visit.

A picture of the two men was featured above the fold in the *New York Times* the following day—along with a piece headlined "Eisenhower Takes Kishi Out for Golf."

"The golf match was a little-used technique in the president's personal diplomacy," read the story. "He frequently tries to get on an informal footing with important state visitors at his Gettysburg farm, but he has rarely used the golf course for this purpose."

Even before he became president, Eisenhower had a special relationship with Augusta National, the annual site of the Masters and one of the most exclusive country clubs in the nation. (Ike visited the club 29 times during his eight years as president. He also made 5 visits before he was president and 11 after he had left office—for a grand total of 45.)

"Eisenhower had two ways to relax—to play golf and to paint," said Ron Sirak. "He did both at Augusta."

He became a member in 1948 following a two-week vacation at the course; he told reporters it had been his "best vacation in years."

The appeal of the club for Eisenhower was that he—whether as the hero of World War II or the president of the United States—could be just one of the guys.

"The weird thing about Augusta is that there are all these incredibly powerful people but this is where they let their hair down," explained Sirak. "If I had a list of stuffiest country clubs, this wouldn't be in the top twenty." He added: "Eisenhower was with other people who were very important but they just played golf, drank whiskey, and played cards."

(Sidebar: Eisenhower was an inveterate card player. Historian John Sayle Watterson argued that Ike learned to play poker in his Kansas childhood from a man named Bob Davis, "an odd character...a fisherman, hunter, trapper, guide, cook and poker player." Of Davis, Eisenhower said: "[He] was my hero—a great teacher.")

Davis schooled Eisenhower on the strategy and mechanics of the game. "Playing for matches, [Davis drilled] percentages into my head night after night around the campfire, using for the lessons a greasy pack of nickel cards that must have been a dozen years old."

After injuring his knee during his sophomore year at West Point, Eisenhower turned to poker—and found it to be lucrative. His opponents, Ike recalled, "[knew] nothing about probabilities, it was not remarkable that I should be a regular winner."

Once he graduated and moved to Fort Sam Houston, Eisenhower continued to use his poker winnings to supplement his relatively meager salary. He regularly bought gifts for his eventual bride—then Mamie Doud—from them. That included the engagement ring he purchased for her in 1916.

As Watterson wrote: "The game that Ike played at the card table demonstrated the street smarts that enabled him to survive and inch forward during those interwar and antiwar years when the United States' army barely ranked in the top 20."

Eisenhower kept playing poker through his transfer to Fort Meade, where he served under legendary general George Patton. One of the men he played with lost—and lost badly. So badly, in fact, that he had to pay off his gambling debts with his wife's war bonds. Eisenhower schemed to lose the money back to the unfortunate man. "This was not achieved easily," Eisenhower later reflected. "One of the hardest things known to man is to make a fellow win in poker who plays as if bent on losing every nickel."

During World War II, Eisenhower switched from poker to bridge.

"Friends spoke of his remarkable powers of concentration, nowhere more evident than in bridge," wrote John Sayle Watterson. "In bridge as in his other pursuits, Ike played to win. Clifford Roberts [the president of Augusta National] remarked that Ike considered it almost 'sacrilegious' to play cards with less than total concentration."

So intent was Eisenhower on bridge—and such was its ability to settle his mind—that he was playing it November 7, 1942, as allied forces invaded North Africa, known as "Operation Torch," according to scholar Michael Ledeen, writing in the *Wall Street Journal* in 2015. (One of the men playing with Eisenhower that night—and a frequent bridge partner over the years—was Gen. Alfred Gruenther, who would go on to serve as the NATO commander.)

Ledeen wrote that Eisenhower, Gruenther, and other famous bridge players, including Chinese military leader and revolutionary Deng Xiaoping, were drawn to the game for its similarities to war.

"No board game can replicate the conditions of the battlefield or the maneuvers of geostrategy, for one simple reason: All of the pieces are visible on the table," argues Ledeen. "Card games are better models because vital information is always concealed by the 'fog of war' and the deception of opponents. Most of the time a bridge player sees only one-quarter of the cards, and some of the information he might gather from them is false."

He goes on: "Bridge is largely about communication, and every message a player sends—by bidding or playing a significant card—is broadcast to the player's partner and his opponents. Frequently a player will have to decide whether he would rather tell the truth to his partner (thereby informing his opponents) or deceive the enemy (thus running the risk of seriously fooling his ally across the table)."

Ledeen concludes that "great bridge players are great liars—as are brilliant military leaders and diplomats and politicians."

Eisenhower loved the game. A *Time* magazine profile of Eisenhower's bridge-playing ways, from May 1953, said:

In the White House, Saturday night is usually bridge night. The evening begins about 5 o'clock, in the solarium on the White House roof, is interrupted for a snack or buffet supper, then may continue down in Ike's second-floor study until 10 or 10:30. Guests arriving for a bridge date are likely to find the host waiting for them at the card table, impatiently riffling the decks.

Eisenhower played with a regular group that included Gruenther, Air Secretary Harold Talbott, and Supreme Court Chief Justice Fred Vinson. John Foster Dulles, who would go on to be secretary of state in Eisenhower's administration, "bragged about his mastery of the game and his department long conducted a world-wide bridge tournament in embassies and consulates," according to Ledeen.

A semiregular in the Eisenhower's bridge game was Oswald Jacoby. (When Jacoby died in 1984, the *New York Times* obituary proclaimed him "one of the best contract bridge players of all time.")

Jacoby extolled Eisenhower for his bridge prowess. "The President plays better bridge than golf," said Jacoby. "He tries to break 90 at golf; at bridge you would say he plays in the 70s."

Time described the president's playing style thusly:

Ike maintains a sphinxlike calm when examining his cards on the deal. His manner is similarly detached during the bidding. But his play is marked with barrack-room gusto, particularly when he produces the trump that his opponents have failed to snare, or when he makes his slam or sets his opponents.

Eisenhower's ability to see all angles, plan for all eventualities, and deal with all sorts of personalities in bridge and in life was on display during his most famous hour: the planning and execution of the D-Day attacks.

The task was almost impossibly complex—plan a massive attack under total secrecy with a hugely compressed timeline. (The decision to invade was made at the end of 1943; the invasion was set for May 1944.)

Plus, Eisenhower had to navigate among some of the biggest and most difficult personalities ever to grace the world stage—President Franklin Delano Roosevelt and Prime Minister Winston Churchill—not to mention the myriad military commanders charged with executing the final plans for the landings.

Ultimately, however, after all the meetings, all the strategy sessions, and all the troop movements, the decision—on a very early June morning—came down to Eisenhower himself. There was to be an expected break in a pattern of bad weather that would allow the invasion a window; it was now or never. The bridge player assessed his options carefully and made the call—the invasion would go forward.

Victory was expected. But, always seeing all possible outcomes, Eisenhower planned for what defeat might look like, too.

In a message that was never sent, Eisenhower wrote an in-case-of-failure note that included these words: "Our landings in the Cherbourg-Havre area have failed to gain a satisfactory foothold and I have withdrawn the troops. My decision to attack at this time and place was based upon the best information available. The troops, the air, and the navy did all that bravery and devotion to duty could do. If any blame or fault attaches to the attempt, it is mine alone."

Eisenhower was far from alone in being a bridge obsessive. While the game is seen as the purview of the retiree set these days, it was extremely popular in the 1940s and '50s.

Ledeen noted that in Eisenhower's day "close to half of American families had at least once active bridge player; as of ten years ago [2005], a mere three million played once a week, and their average age was 51." (The *New York Times* ended its bridge column in 2015.)

The game still has its admirers—including regular-guy billionaire Warren Buffett who said this of the game while participating in a 1990 bridge tournament with corporate titans and members of Congress including Sen. Bob Packwood and Congressman (and baseball great) Jim Bunning:

Any young person who doesn't take up bridge is making a real mistake. One bridge game is worth 20 cocktail parties. The reason for this match is to publicize bridge and try to get young people into it. I always say I wouldn't mind going to jail if I had three cellmates who played bridge.

What drew Eisenhower, Buffett, and other luminaries to bridge appears to be the sense of teamwork and community inherent in the game. It is a team game, two people working—without words—together. Going it alone ensures failure. Only by reading the subtle signals sent by the cards your partner chooses to play—and not play—can you hope to win.

The game then embodies the sense of community—and communal strength—that defined America in the immediate postwar period. The idea was that we had beaten back the existential threat of Nazism by working together, so what couldn't we do if we linked arms (and minds)?

It may look odd from this end of the telescope (as we all stare into our phones, perfecting our #brands) but people back then genuinely believed that there was power in numbers and that community was the way to solve most of the problems that ailed us.

While golf became the defining sport in Eisenhower's life, first he played baseball—and then football.

As author and historian Mark Eberle notes, "Baseball was *the* sport" when Eisenhower was growing up in Kansas in the mid-1890s. "Football was just starting."

And so, Eisenhower, like so many other Kansas boys, played baseball. He started off as a pitcher but, according to a story he told his grandson, a cow kicked him in the arm, so he was unable to throw all that hard for all that long.

Center field was where Eisenhower made his name as a ball player in his teen years. "He played with a reckless abandon," Eberle says, recounting a time when young Eisenhower crashed through a wooden outfield fence in pursuit of a ball.

Eisenhower played with his high school team as well as in the summers, with many of the same kids. The teams did their own fund-raising and organized their own schedules; they would "hop on a freight car" sometimes to get to their games.

Eisenhower was the team's best hitter, according to their historical record. But that didn't make him a good hitter by any stretch. He hit .241 for his high school team—the highest in the club, but nothing to draw the interest of any pro scouts.

Speaking of which, it's impossible to talk about Eisenhower and baseball without delving into the (still) ongoing debate as to whether the future president actually played in a semipro baseball game during his younger years.

The controversy began in earnest during Eisenhower's victory tour around the United States following America's victory in World War II.

At a stop in Abilene, Kansas (his hometown), Eisenhower—as he had done several times during the trip—mentioned his time playing baseball.

"I was a center fielder," Eisenhower said. "I went into baseball deliberately to make money, and with no idea of making it a career. I wanted to go to college that fall, and we didn't have money. But I wasn't a very good center fielder, and didn't do too well at it."

The story goes like this: In between high school and college, Eisenhower was looking for a way to make some money—and found it by playing baseball for cash. He did so under the name "Wilson" so as to keep his identity secret—and not jeopardize his amateur status before heading to West Point. (It would also have amounted to a breaking of the honor code at the military academy, which asked its entrants if they had ever played sports for money.)

As historian Michael Beschloss noted in 2014: "The Eisenhower Library houses a 1961 notation by his devoted longtime secretary, Ann Whitman, that 'DDE did play professional baseball one season to make money' and that he made 'one trip under an assumed name.'"

Eberle, for one, casts a skeptical eye on the claim of Eisenhower's pro baseball days. He noted that the Abilene semipro team had eight different center fielders in one eight-week period, and it's possible that Eisenhower could have been one of them.

"I take him at his word that he did play somehow and got some kind of payment," said Eberle, before noting that he could find no evidence of Eisenhower having done so.

"I looked at all the 'Wilsons' and could account for everyone I found evidence of in newspapers," said Eberle.

Once he went to West Point, Eisenhower dedicated himself full-time to football. During his first two years, he played as a halfback and a linebacker.

"At five foot ten and 170 pounds, he used his work ethic, athletic ability and gritty determination to make up for his lack of bulk," wrote historian John Sayle Watterson of the young Ike. He earned the nickname the "Kansas Cyclone" and was proclaimed by no less an authority than the *New York Times* as one of the most promising halfbacks in the East.

A football career was not to be, however. In his sophomore year, Eisenhower tore up his knee, which, at the time, had the effect of ending his playing days. The future president was thrown into a malaise. "Life seemed to have little meaning, a need to excel was gone," he said. He smoked, overate, and generally lived the life of a lush.

The following year, however, the varsity football coach asked Eisenhower to coach the JV squad. And Eisenhower found inspiration there. "Because we used all the formations and signals of the varsity, I was able to send to the [varsity] squad a few performers who made the grade," said Eisenhower.

His coaching career didn't end there. In 1915, stationed at Fort Sam Houston, Ike was offered—and accepted—the head football coaching job at Peacock Military Academy. (He received $150 for his efforts.) The team had a winning record, and the local media gushed over Eisenhower. "Those who have seen this officer operate with a football squad believe him to be one of the best coaches in Texas," said the *San Antonio Express-News*.

The following year, Eisenhower took on another coaching gig—this time running the football program at St. Louis College, a Catholic prep school in San Antonio. (St. Louis College is now St. Mary's University.)

The team was awful, having not won a single game in five years. Eisenhower rapidly turned the squad around—they tied their first game, won five straight and then lost their final game—for a record of 5-1-1.

The team's quarterback was effusive in his praise of not just Eisenhower but his wife, Mamie, and her parents, the Douds.

"We thought more of him than we did of any other coach we ever had," said Jim Sweeney. "We respected him from the time he showed up until he left, and we fought as much for Mamie and the Douds as we did the school. He was very frank and honest and we learned more about honor and discipline from him than we did anywhere else."

That praise is consistent with how Eisenhower, the general, was lauded in later years. "His real strength lies in his human qualities," British field general Bernard Montgomery said of Eisenhower. "He has the power of drawing the hearts of men toward him as a magnet attracts the bit of metal. He merely has to smile at you, and you trust him at once."

Eisenhower's great genius—his ability to get men to trust and follow him—was honed in those days as a football coach. He was learning what it took to motivate men, to get them to understand that the only way to succeed was to work together for some larger goal. The gridiron was the proving ground for the lessons that Eisenhower ultimately used to convince men to run directly into the line of fire for the country.

Transferred to Fort Benning in Maryland in 1924, Eisenhower was recruited to coach the base's football team. And, despite a subpar season, he was selected again to lead the base's team in 1926. "Even 1924's dismal record did not weaken the adhesive on the label I wore," he wrote later in his life. "It still said 'Football Coach.'"

While Eisenhower would never coach football after that, the lessons he learned in doing so—the sum being greater than the parts, the necessity of communication, teamwork—carried over in his leadership on the battlefield and in the White House.

In October 1958, Eisenhower was given a special gold medal from the Football Hall of Fame for his time spent on the sidelines as a coach. In a speech at the event, Eisenhower spoke in elegiac terms about the lessons that football—and competition more broadly—could teach.

"Wherever human liberty is respected, competition is the animator of progress," said Eisenhower. "In football, in business, in politics, in the trades, professions and the arts, the normal urge to excel provides one the most hopeful assurances that our kind of society will continue to advance and prosper."

But Ike wasn't done! He went on:

Morale—the will to win, the fighting heart—are the honored hall-marks of the football coach and player, as they are of the enterprising executive; the successful troop leader; the established artist and the dedicated teacher and scientist...That is the competition we are up against today, and you and I know the contest is likely to be long indeed. Our team is made up of every individual in America. We need to make each one of them the best players we can put on the field.

Later in his life, Eisenhower was more succinct. "I believe that football, perhaps more than any other sport, tends to instill in men the feeling that victory comes through hard—almost slavish—work, team play, self confidence and an enthusiasm that amounts to dedication," he wrote.

———

That knee injury that he suffered at Army as a teenager stayed with him the rest of his life. (These were the days before arthroscopic surgery and the like.) "To this day, I have to be careful of my movements," he wrote in the late '60s.

John Sayle Watterson speculated that Eisenhower's lifelong swing challenges dated back to his college injury. "For a right-handed golfer, the left side—especially the left knee—is critical," he wrote. "The golfer pivots largely on the left leg, which needs to stay anchored while the knee absorbs the thrust."

Watterson went on to quote Eisenhower's son, John, about his father's golf game: Ike had a "powerful swing but a horrendous slice to go with it. He seemed to wind up in the alfalfa an inordinate amount of time, the air punctuated with certain expletives that I had thought were unknown to adults—only to kids."

———

No modern president played more golf than Eisenhower. And none played more rounds at Augusta National, the most exclusive golf club in the country.

Soon after being elected, Eisenhower and his wife went to Augusta to play golf with, among others, Ben Hogan and Arnold Palmer—as well as his erstwhile Republican rival Bob Taft.

Soon after, a cabin—painted white, natch—was built on the Augusta grounds for the president's use. Construction began immediately following the conclusion of the 1953 Masters. A local architect—named Lowrey Stulb—was tasked with designing the three-story, seven-bedroom cottage.

"We had construction crews in Monday morning at eight o'clock after the tournament that year," said Stulb. "We had until October 1. On October 1, they turned keys over right on time."

The cabin, which sits near the tenth hole at Augusta, was specially outfitted to accommodate Eisenhower, with quarters for his Secret Service detail in the basement. Unlike the other nine cabins on the property, a gold presidential seal is affixed over the front porch. (The cabin was renovated in 2018.)

From the dining room of the cabin, you gaze at Ike's Pond where, on a stroll of the grounds with then club president Cliff Roberts, Eisenhower suggested that it would be an ideal spot for fishing. The three-acre pond, which runs through holes eight and nine, was created soon thereafter.

This is, to put a fine point on it, golf heaven. You are on the most exclusive golf club in the world. You are staying in a cabin specially built for you. There is room for Eisenhower to paint. (Ike, who took up painting in his middle age, became a committed artist.) He can play one of the world's best golf courses as much as he wants, which is a lot. There are four rocking chairs sitting outside on the front porch where the president can sit and be, quite literally, the king of all he surveys.

You can understand why Eisenhower would often take extended trips to Augusta, essentially bringing his White House down to Georgia. While he was in residence at the club, he would work from an office above the pro shop. And, as *Golf Monthly* noted, he fell into a regular routine during those trips.

"Eisenhower's stays there followed a regular pattern of work in an office in the morning, and then in the afternoon he would hit some practice balls and then play a round, often in company with Cliff Roberts and the club pro," according to the magazine. "In the evening Ike liked to play bridge."

The most famous story of Eisenhower and Augusta illustrates the limits of presidential power.

On the seventeenth hole, about two hundred yards off the tee on the left side of the fairway, sat a sixty-something-foot loblolly pine tree.

The president didn't like the tree. At all. In fact, he had hit it so many times during rounds at Augusta that he asked the club to have it cut down.

The showdown happened at a 1956 members meeting when—as you will rightly note—Eisenhower also happened to be the president of the United States. Cliff Roberts, the president of Augusta, ruled Eisenhower's request out of order—and told him no.

Yes, you read that right. Augusta told the sitting president of the United States who, not for nothing, was also a hugely popular war hero, that he couldn't have what he wanted on their course. Which tells you absolutely everything you need to know about how Augusta and its members think of themselves and their relationship to power.

The tree, which came to be known as the Eisenhower Tree, stood—in that same pesky spot on the left side of the fairway on number 17—until a brutal ice storm hit Georgia in 2014.

"The loss of the Eisenhower Tree is difficult news to accept," Augusta chairman Billy Payne said at the time. "We obtained opinions from the best arborists available and, unfortunately, were advised that no recovery was possible."

Of the tree, famed golfer Jack Nicklaus said:

When I stood on the 17th tee, my first thought, always, was to stay away from Ike's Tree. Period...I hit it so many times over the years that I don't care to comment on the names I called myself and the names I might have called the tree. Ike's Tree was a kind choice. But looking back, Ike's Tree will be greatly missed.

The tree isn't entirely gone from Augusta, however.

In 2015, Payne announced that two grafts and a seedling from the tree would be replanted on the grounds—although he didn't specify whether the tree would be put in that same place on the seventeenth.

At that same time, Payne also announced that another cross section of the tree would be sent to the Eisenhower presidential museum in Abilene, Kansas.

Eisenhower's golf obsession led him to befriend Arnold Palmer, the charismatic star of the sport that Ike loved so much. The two men came to symbolize the manly virtues—steak eating, cigarette smoking, and, yes, golfing—that defined the '50s for so many. They were the living, breathing embodiments of what America felt like in those days—vanquishers of Nazism, conquerors of the world, with their whole lives in front of them and nothing but endless possibilities.

Their long and close friendship began somewhat inauspiciously. Palmer had won the Masters in the spring of 1958, and the two men's paths crossed at the Laurel Valley Golf Club in Pennsylvania—a club Arnie helped start.

As Palmer recounts in his memoir *A Life Well Played*: "A mutual friend, Ben Fairless, the former chairman of U.S. Steel, introduced us and we shook hands and spoke briefly."

Palmer thought nothing of it. But Eisenhower was galled. Again, here's Palmer:

Some months after that meeting I received a letter from the president on his personal stationery that really floored me. The letter read, in part: "Because of the general confusion the other day, I failed to realize that when Ben Fairless introduced us that you were Arnold Palmer of 1958 Master fame. I hope you will forgive my lack of reaction and accept, even this belatedly, my warm congratulations on your splendid victory."

The two men grew closer and closer as the year went by.

So close were the two that Palmer was invited to address a joint session of Congress on what would have been Eisenhower's one hundredth birthday in 1990.

"He was a man who, to Americans, stood for just about everything we live for," Palmer told Congress. "He was a sportsman, he was a military leader, he was a president and probably just as importantly to all of us Americans he was a private citizen."

Palmer told the story of his thirty-seventh birthday, noting that his wife, realizing "there wasn't a great deal of things she could do for my birthday," decided to invite the president and Mrs. Eisenhower to their home for the weekend.

The Eisenhowers agreed to come. Palmer sent his private plane to pick them up—but only the president got on board. Mamie Eisenhower decided she would rather drive from Washington to Pennsylvania.

"We spent a weekend together," Palmer reminisced. "I had an opportunity to watch a football game with the president. The ladies went and watched a musical. We went into the back bedroom and watched a football game and did men's talk...A birthday like that you remember forever."

For most modern Americans, that era is understood through the lens of Don Draper and *Mad Men*—smoking and drinking in the office, smoking and drinking at long work lunches and dinners, smoking and drinking when you get home at the end of the day. (There was a *lot* of smoking and drinking.)

Both Ike and Palmer were ur-examples of this definition of masculinity. They were tough, single-minded, and certain that what they were doing was exactly the right thing to be doing. They were not second-guessers of themselves. They were not criers.

That they became two of the most famous men of this era, then, isn't surprising. They were emblematic of what it meant to be a man in that moment.

Palmer also recounted the last time he saw Eisenhower—as the president lay in a bed at Walter Reed Hospital in suburban Washington. He had asked that Palmer and his wife, Winnie, come for a visit. They obliged.

"As usual, Eisenhower gave us that same warm reception that we had always received," said Palmer. "When we walked into his hospital room—and he was very ill—his first words were 'By gosh it's great to see you kids.' It's something that today makes chills run up and down my back and make me remember what a great friend I had."

(Eisenhower died of congestive heart failure at that hospital on March 28, 1969.)

Palmer struggled for the right words to describe Eisenhower's import to him and the country. "I guess I can't translate to you the people of America how important he was to all of us private citizens [and] to sports throughout the world," he said at one point.

At another he said he was "saluting Eisenhower on behalf of all the athletes who I think I have some right to represent here for what he has done to the world and to America."

If You're Not First, You're Last

The Legend of John F. Kennedy

On April 5, 1961, John F. Kennedy had the world by the tail. He had just been inaugurated as the thirty-fifth president of the United States, at the tender age of forty-three.

He was in Florida for some R and R. Except that rest and relaxation wasn't the sort of thing that the Kennedy clan went in for.

On that day, JFK played golf with two of his brothers-in-law—Stephen Smith and Peter Lawford—as well as his father—Joe Kennedy Sr.

The lingering memory of that day in the public conscience is a still photograph of the supposedly hale and hearty president finishing his golf swing; it appeared on the front page of the *New York Times* the following day.

But another photo taken that day is far more revealing. In it, Joe Kennedy, clad in a dark shirt and white golf pants, stands laughing with a club in hand while JFK stands next to his dad with a quizzical look on his face—somewhere between bewilderment and bemusement.

Joe Sr. was a gifted golfer with a low handicap and "he would challenge Joe and Jack and beat them every time," according to Kennedy historian Fredrik Logevall.

Joe Sr. wasn't big on coming in second. In anything.

"If we won, Joe [Sr.] got terribly enthusiastic," Jack's sister Eunice recalled. "But then he always kept telling us that coming in second or third doesn't count."

Joe Sr. would often play tennis with his two oldest boys, but that ended when Joe Jr. almost took a set off the old man. Joe Sr. then decided that his tennis-playing days were behind him.

It was a "hypercompetitive" family, said Logevall, a Harvard professor who is writing a two-volume biography of Kennedy. "If they were waiting for a car to arrive, one of them would think up a game that they would play until the car got there," he noted. "Jack had that completely."

When Joe Jr. and JFK would fight, their father wouldn't intervene in hopes it would teach them the competitiveness and desire to win (at all costs) he believed they would need in life.

The winning was the *only* point for Joe Sr.

As Logevall wrote in *JFK: Coming of Age in the American Century, 1917–1956*:

> The point, Joe Senior insisted time and again, was not to play well, to compete for the sake of competing, but to defeat all comers, to secure the top prize. Even good sportsmanship paled in comparison. "We want no losers around here, only winners," he proclaimed.

It was a credo by which Joe Sr. lived his life. By the time his children were teenagers, he had already made a fortune many times over—through any means possible. He traded stocks, sold and bought real estate, sold liquor, and even produced movies. (Rumors that Joe Sr. was a bootlegger during Prohibition—and made oodles of money as a result—appear to be unfounded. Worth noting: Kennedy *did* have close ties to the Bronfman family, founders of Seagrams and long rumored to be part of the illegal booze industry during Prohibition.)

What is undoubtedly true is that he parlayed his wealth into a series of influential positions in government during the second half of his life, including serving as the first chairman of the Securities and Exchange Commission and as the U.S. ambassador to the United Kingdom.

And he used that combination of wealth and political power to grease the skids for his children—most notably his second son, Jack.

But, long before there was a Congressman Kennedy, a Senator Kennedy, or a President Kennedy, the father handed down to the son the relentless drive to win at all costs.

———

Depending on where you choose to look, Jack Kennedy can appear very different. Seen one way he is frail and sickly, in and out of hospitals and infirmaries for much of his youth and teen years.

Seen another, he is a smooth and able athlete—a natural.

"He was beautifully coordinated and one of the best natural athletes I've ever seen," said Lem Billings, a longtime friend. "He could pick up a golf club, having never played golf before, and play pretty decent golf. Same with tennis. So he'd catch a football and do all the things that take coordination."

But, Billings added, "He had very delicate health there. He was lightweight. He played football but for health reasons, he didn't do very well."

———

Kennedy was plagued, from his high school days on, with major health issues.

It wasn't until his early twenties—after a series of hospital stays during his time at Choate and then at Harvard, that Kennedy was diagnosed with Addison's disease, a shrinking of the adrenal glands. Symptoms are wide and serious—up to and including fatigue, dizziness, muscle weakness, weight loss, difficulty standing up, nausea, and sweating. One episode—in 1947—was so serious that Kennedy was administered last rites.

Kennedy, while at Harvard, also suffered a major back injury of somewhat unknown origin—although the most common explanation was that he was surprise-tackled by a friend of the family after a game.

His back was bad enough that he failed the enlistment physicals for the Army and the Navy. It was only through his father's influence—as ambassador to England in the 1940s—that Kennedy was able to serve during World War II.

(Sidebar: In those days, money was what opened the gates for entrance into the military. By the time of the Vietnam War, money was what kept you *out* of the military.)

Kennedy eventually underwent a series of surgeries to lessen the pain in his back—although none did the trick entirely. After one surgery—a spinal fusion—in 1954, Kennedy developed a serious urinary tract infection and nearly died. (He was again administered last rites.)

While in the Senate and the White House, he would, at times, be reduced to using crutches to reduce pressure on his back. When Japanese prime minister Hayato Ikeda came to Washington in 1961, Kennedy used crutches to walk from the presidential limousine to the ramp to board the presidential yacht. (It was named the *Honey Fitz* after his grandfather, the former mayor of Boston.)

"He had back rubs and hot baths, and he would use a brace, but if he didn't use crutches, he had to rely on his willpower," Dr. Thomas Pait, a spinal neurosurgeon, told CNN in 2017. "And he was incredible; he'd walk into a room in pain but start smiling, waving, and walk out the other door, and people would catch him, because he would basically fall down."

That was not the image of Kennedy that the public was served, however. This, from a *Sports Illustrated* profile of the president published in late 1960 shows how the newly elected president was cast:

As the record shows, the President-elect is not only an enthusiastic helmsman but a successful one. Like the other members of his large, vigorous and fiercely competitive family, he is a savage contestant, at 43, whether sailing, swimming, skin-diving, golfing or playing touch football. All the Kennedys have an intense interest in sports, and where-ever the family has lived—from Boston to London, from Palm Beach to Hyannisport—its always rough, usually noisy contests have impressed and awed neighbors. As a minor, if provocative, footnote to history, Jacqueline Kennedy will be the first First

Lady who ever broke an ankle playing football. It happened during a Kennedy clan game of touch football at Hyannisport.

Those touch football games became the stuff of legend—both inside the family and out. Logevall quotes a guest at one of these games:

> Now for the football field. It's "touch" but it's murder. If you don't want to play, don't come. If you do come, play, or you'll be fed in the kitchen and no one will speak to you. Don't let the girls fool you. Even pregnant, they can make you look silly. Above all, don't suggest any plays, even if you played quarterback at school. The Kennedys have the signal-calling department sewed up, and all of them have A-pluses in leadership.... Run madly on every play and make a lot of noise. Don't appear to be having too much fun though. They'll accuse you of not taking the game seriously enough.

It wasn't just in sports where Kennedy's competitive gene came out. Following his 1958 election to the Senate, Kennedy traveled to Alaska with longtime aide Ted Sorenson. Richard Nixon, Kennedy's likely opponent in the 1960 presidential election, had recently visited the Last Frontier. "Jack is determined he is going to visit more places in Alaska and draw bigger crowds," said Logevall. "He wants Sorensen to keep track and compare."

Kennedy began sailing as a young man at the behest of his father, who got the family sailing lessons. (Winning!) Of Joe Jr. and Jack, Joe Senior would say they "were out in sailboats alone here in Hyannis Port when they were so small you couldn't see their heads. It looked from the shore as if the boats were empty."

By the age of fifteen, Jack was an able skipper. That same year, his parents bought him a twenty-six-foot Wianno Senior sailboat dubbed *Victura*. That boat became a favorite of Kennedy's; in the 1960 campaign he and Jackie did a photo shoot for *Sports Illustrated* aboard the *Victura*. "He really wanted to show vigor and good health," said Jim Graham, who wrote a book about Kennedy's love of sailing—titled, appropriately enough, *Victura*.

At Harvard, the Kennedy boys experienced their biggest sailing success. Jack was a freshman and Joe was a junior when they entered the McMillan Cup in 1938—and won it. (The McMillan Cup is the oldest collegiate sailing race in the country.)

"Sailing is where he came out on top," said Logevall.

But it was not sailing that was Kennedy's first and longest love. That honor belonged to football.

"If you said to President Kennedy in the White House 'What would you want to be doing if you weren't doing this,' he would probably say being a football quarterback," said Logevall.

It was a passion that began young. Jack and Joe Jr. were both on their elementary school football team, with Jack at quarterback. At Choate, Kennedy aspired to make the varsity football squad but came up short.

He weighed barely more than a hundred pounds and, even at that young age, struggled. "Football practice is pretty hard and I am the lightest fellow about on the squad. My nose, my leg and other parts of my anatomy have been pushed around so much that it is beginning to be funny," Kennedy said.

His freshman year football coach was even more blunt about his small frame. "The most adept pass catcher was John Kennedy, but his lack of weight was a drawback," he said.

Kennedy's football career would end due to injury—although not one sustained on the field. As historian John Sayle Watterson recounted: "He sustained a serious back injury when a family retainer hurled him to the ground with a flying tackle immediately after the game as an ill-considered practical joke."

Kennedy once told his father—always seeking his approval!—that he would make his high school basketball team and play with Joe Jr. He got cut instead.

The sport that stuck with Kennedy for most of his adult life was neither football nor basketball. It was swimming. And it was swimming that saved not only his life but several of his compatriots during World War II.

Kennedy made the Harvard team as a freshman, displacing the team's backstroke champion. Kennedy swam the 100 meters backstroke and 300 meter medley.

"His physique wasn't anything outstanding," remembered Harold Uhlen, the swimming coach at Harvard during Kennedy's time at the school. "As an undergraduate at Harvard, he was rather frail, as I remember." (Of JFK's younger brother, Robert, Uhlen would say: "[He was] a fairly good swimmer but he was a little heavy in the water...he would sink very easily.")

Even though he performed well as a swimmer, Kennedy's health problems persisted. A story that ran in the *Harvard Crimson* in 1960 told this story of one of Kennedy's health battles:

> During one of these spells, he was in Stillman Infirmary when Uhlen scheduled to hold the time trials for the Yale meet. Jack's roommate, football captain Torby MacDonald, smuggled food into his room, and then smuggled him out of the infirmary in time for the trials. Tragically enough, he failed to qualify.

Kennedy didn't last on the swim team. He stopped swimming at the same time he stopped playing football—after his sophomore year at Harvard.

But, in the summer of 1943, Jack Kennedy, fresh out of Harvard, was captaining a patrol boat in and around the Solomon Islands. One night, while patrolling the Blackett Strait, the boat spotted a Japanese destroyer. Although he attempted to steer away from the enemy ship, it crashed directly into the PT-109—shearing the boat in two.

Two men were never heard from again. The remaining eleven clung to the hulk of the boat that remained above water. Kennedy, as the skipper, was looked to for leadership. He made the decision that they needed to swim for a small island that didn't appear to be occupied by the Japanese.

One of the men was badly burned from an explosion caused by the initial collision. As John Hersey wrote in the definitive piece on the episode in the *New Yorker* in 1944:

Kennedy took McMahon [the engineer] in tow again. He cut loose one end of a long strap on McMahon's Mae West and took the end in his teeth. He swam breaststroke, pulling the helpless McMahon along on his back. It took over five hours to reach the island. Water lapped into Kennedy's mouth through his clenched teeth, and he swallowed a lot...

In spite of his burden, Kennedy beat the other men to the reef that surrounded the island. He left McMahon on the reef and told him to keep low, so as not to be spotted by Japs.

Over the course of the next several days as he searched for friendly faces and rescue, Kennedy embarked on a series of long swims. On one, the current carried him past the island where his men were. "He thought he had never known such deep trouble," wrote Hersey. "But something he did shows that unconsciously he had not given up hope. He dropped his shoes but he held on to his heavy lantern, his symbol of contact with his fellows."

Kennedy floated back to the island and swam in successfully. He and his team were eventually rescued. For his heroism, Kennedy was given the Navy and Marine Corps Medal as well as a Purple Heart for being wounded in action. He remains the only president to have been awarded the Purple Heart.

Because of his status as an ambassador's son, Kennedy became an overnight hero. "Kennedy's Son Is Hero in Pacific As Destroyer Splits His PT Boat," read an Associated Press headline from August 1943.

A *Sports Illustrated* feature on Kennedy shortly after he was elected president in 1960 contained these lines:

Kennedy is a powerful swimmer and was a member of the swimming team at Harvard. If it had not been for his skill as a swimmer and for a hardiness of body and toughness of spirit developed through rough-and-tumble games, he probably would not be alive today.

Kennedy's heroics in the South Pacific effectively launched his political career—with the helping hand (and wallet) of his father helping to smooth the way. Kennedy was elected to the House from Massachusetts in 1946. Six years later he won a U.S. Senate seat. Eight years after that he was elected president.

"JFK's certified heroism proved to be of incalculable value from his first congressional campaign in 1946 to the presidency when a movie, *PT-109*, immortalized—and romanticized—the episode," wrote John Sayle Watterson. "For the rest of his life, Jack Kennedy would be inordinately proud of, and would capitalize on, his war record."

Kennedy kept up swimming in the White House.

A pool had been built during Franklin Delano Roosevelt's time in an office located in a former laundry room in the West Gallery of the White House. FDR suffered from polio and swam regularly as a form of therapy. Roosevelt's wealthy friends built him a pool.

It was a relatively drab affair, however, until the Kennedy clan got their hands on it. In 1961, Kennedy's father, Joe, had a mural of the U.S. Virgin Islands painted on three of the walls in the pool room.

Kennedy became a regular visitor. "After a tough morning in the Oval Office, John F. Kennedy liked to take a dip in the White House pool," wrote Evan Thomas in *Newsweek* in 1997.

But, according to Seymour Hersh, a longtime *New York Times* reporter, Kennedy had other reasons to be so interested in the pool.

"As the Secret Service stood guard outside," Evans continued, "the president routinely skinny-dipped with two of his favorite female assistants, nicknamed Fiddle and Faddle. One day, warned that Jackie was on her way to the pool for an unexpected swim, the president and his fellow frolickers scrambled for cover. 'You could see one big pair of footprints and two smaller pair of wet footprints leading to the Oval Office,' a Secret Service man told Hersh."

This was apparently a pattern with Kennedy. Mimi Alford, who was a nineteen-year-old White House intern in 1962, wrote in a 2012 memoir that soon after she started working in the press shop, she got a call from

Dave Powers, an aide and close friend to the president. He invited her for a swim in the White House pool. She joined two other young women who had received the same invite. Much to her surprise, as they were swimming around the pool, the president of the United States emerged. "Mind if I join you?" Kennedy asked the trio.

Later, Kennedy took Alford on a private tour of the White House that ended with the two of them sleeping together. They had an affair that lasted more than a year.

Kennedy was, by all accounts, the best natural golfer to ever occupy the White House—or at least the man with the best swing to call 1600 Pennsylvania Avenue home. He played varsity golf at Choate—cold comfort after not making the varsity football team—and was on a sort of JV golf team at Harvard as well.

"Looking at his swing, he is definitely the best golfer president," said Luke Kerr-Dineen, the game improvement editor (amazing job!), at Golf .com. Kerr-Dineen noted JFK's "big turn behind the ball" and "head fully over his right foot and trail leg."

When JFK was president, his golf game weakened, according to Kerr-Dineen. In analyzing video from Jack playing during his time in the White House, Kerr-Dineen says that it is "clear that this is a guy who is playing in pain and not having that much fun."

In terms of swing mechanics, his backswing is shorter and "he can't make as big a turn and still has a closed club face, so he winds up hooking balls."

Still Kennedy was almost *too* good a golfer. As Paul Harber wrote in *The Complete Guide to Golf on Cape Cod, Nantucket and Martha's Vineyard*:

Jack Kennedy had kept his golf game almost a secret for a long time, because the sport at that time had been more readily associated with Republicans, an image often underscored by Ike's personal passion for the game. Nonetheless, Jack Kennedy had always possessed the right coordination, but his bad back had made it painful to perform even the simplest of the game's fundamentals: placing the ball on the tee and taking it out of the cup.

Again, the duality of Kennedy—who he was versus who he wanted you to think he was—emerges here. Kennedy was a patrician, a child of privilege—raised on that most of elite games: golf. And he was good at it! Very good! And yet, he went out of his way to hide his ability—even as his White House kept looking for other ways to signpost his health while that health was failing.

His bad back—and generally poor health—notwithstanding, Kennedy was a regular visitor and player at Hyannis Port.

The very fact that the Kennedys made their home in Hyannis Port had to do with golf, according to Paul Harber.

Prior to the early 1960s, when Joe Kennedy moved his clan to Hyannis Port, the family had always summered—that's what people with the wealth of the Kennedys called vacationing—at Hull, a town south of Boston.

But when Joe had tried to join the Cohasset Golf Club in 1923—the club was founded in 1894 and boasts that it is one of the oldest in New England—he had been turned away.

"He was blackballed by the purely Yankee club membership that practiced a widely-applied Brahmin principle succinctly known as NINA: No Irish Need Apply," Harber wrote.

And so, not wanting to be where he wasn't welcome, Joe Kennedy decamped his family to Cape Cod—and the Hyannisport Club in particular. As Harber wrote: "Though Hyannisport was yet another Yankee stronghold, Joe Kennedy had helped many of its members through tough economic times, and here he was able to secure admission."

Admission, yes. Acceptance came slower. "None of the Kennedy family was ever especially loved at this staunch conservative Republican haunt and the club even discharged head professional Walter Hall in 1960, because his friendship with the Kennedys irritated the old members at Hyannisport," wrote Harber.

The man who replaced Hall as head pro at Hyannis Port was a man named Tom Niblet, a legend in Cape Cod golf circles. After years at Hyannis Port, Niblet left to build the Holly Ridge Golf Club in nearby Sandwich.

(Sidebar: Niblet kept his admiration for Kennedy hidden. "If the members at Hyannisport knew about my affection for the man, I probably would have lost my job," he told Harber. "It was exciting just being around the man. John Kennedy was charismatic. Everything about him just energized you. He'd look you in the eye and show interest in what you said.")

During his time at Hyannis Port, Niblet gave lessons to both Rose Kennedy, the mother of the president, as well as his wife, Jackie Kennedy.

Of the Kennedy clan's mother, Niblet wrote—in a 1997 recollection requested by JFK's youngest brother, Teddy—that she was "upbeat and a joy to be around." During the first lesson he gave her the two "spent a lot of time talking about family, hers and mine. She urged me to spend as much time with family as I could. I took her advice and have been thankful for it."

Niblet also recalled the day the president's wife came to the club for lessons. He took a call in the pro shop from someone who identified herself as "Mrs. John Kennedy" and was looking to take lessons. Niblet didn't know if the whole thing was a put-on or whether he really had the First Lady on the line, so he stalled for time and said he had an opening that afternoon.

"As three o'clock rolled around, the Lincoln Continental appeared, and Mrs. Kennedy walked into the pro shop," wrote Harber. "Tom Niblet introduced himself, and she told him he might be in for a difficult time trying to teach her to play golf. 'I didn't think so,' he said." (Niblet later recalled of the day: "I was a nervous wreck before she arrived.") Asked what her goal for the lessons was, Mrs. Kennedy was blunt: She wanted "to beat [her] sisters-in-law."

Niblet wound up giving Jackie Kennedy several lessons—observing that she was well coordinated but not terribly committed to the game. "She might play 5 holes or the inside 9," Niblet told Harber. "Then she would say to me: 'Tom, how come my game doesn't improve?'" Niblet responded, "The answer is simple: Quit water skiing and tennis and horseback riding. Devote some time to the game of golf and you'll improve."

Niblet remembers seeing a military helicopter land at the Kennedy compound and waiting for the phone to ring.

"First he would ask if it was busy up there," said Niblet. "Then I'd say, 'No, it isn't, Mr. President.'"

What happened next? This, according to Harber:

The President of the United States would come up the hill with his golf shoes, pants and shirt in hand; however he never came into the clubhouse. JFK would change his clothes in the bag room, where he kept his clubs and a special White House telephone. In there, Niblet says, the Secret Service would take the President's clubs out of the bag and turn it upside down, just for safety precautions. Then, the Secret Service would get their own golf bags. Instead of golf clubs though, those bags held machine guns just in case.

Kennedy rarely took lessons, but Niblet remembers one time when Kennedy, after walking off the eighteenth green disgustedly, asked him if he had time for a lesson the following day. Niblet agreed.

"When the time arrived though, Kennedy called Niblet and said something else had come up," wrote Harber. "He asked if he could have some time later, and the golf pro said he would keep the afternoon open for the President."

What had "come up"? Again, Harber: "Unbeknownst to Niblet, and to most of the world, the United States was in the midst of an international incident in Laos. 'A few minutes later, I looked out on the golf course,' Niblet says, 'and I saw three huge Marine helicopters land on the edge of the 14th fairway.'"

Out of the choppers emerged the bulk of Kennedy's foreign policy brain trust—including Secretary of State Robert S. McNamara and Joint Chiefs of Staff head Robert Maxwell.

Harber wrote: " 'He had all of these problems,' remarks Niblet with an air of wonderment toward the president, 'and he made the time to call to say he couldn't make a golf lesson.' "

Kennedy didn't ever like to talk about when he played golf or how good he actually was.

He was mindful of the fact that his party had regularly criticized his predecessor for playing golf at every opportunity. One wag suggested that Eisenhower "invented the 36-hole work week." (Ike's predecessor, Harry Truman, hadn't agreed with the Democratic criticism of Eisenhower. "To criticize the President...because he plays a game of golf is unfair and pica-yunish," said Truman. "He has the same right to relax from the heavy burdens of office as any other man.")

Kennedy was well on his way to the 1960 Democratic presidential nomination when golf—almost—got in the way.

Kennedy was playing the legendary Cypress Point course in northern California. Among his foursome that day was Paul Fay, who would go on to become the undersecretary of the Navy in his administration.

On the sixteenth hole, the course's signature hole (and one of the most famous holes in the world), a golfer is required to hit a shot of more than two hundred yards, with a carry over the Pacific Ocean into a peninsula green. For all but the best of golfers, it is a near-impossible shot.

Kennedy on that day in 1960 hit a five iron that flew directly for the flag. Fay was urging the ball to go in even as Kennedy looked more and more queasy. The ball hit the flagstick and wound up six inches from the hole.

"You're yelling for that damn ball to go in and I'm watching a promising political career come to an end," said Kennedy. "If that ball had gone in, in less than an hour the word would be out that another golfer was trying to get in the White House."

———

In 1996, a collection of golf paraphernalia once belonging to JFK went up for auction at Sotheby's. The total haul was a stunning $1.29 million.

The bulk of that—$772,500—went for a single item: A set of MacGregor

Tourney woods and a leather golf bag inscribed "JFK Washington, D.C." The buyer? None other than Arnold Schwarzenegger, the onetime governor of California and, at the time of the sale, the husband of Maria Shriver, a niece of JFK's.

The inflated price raised eyebrows. "For his money, Arnold got the clubs, the bag and at least a dozen 1954 golf balls," film producer David Wolper told the *Los Angeles Times* in 1996. "If you tried to purchase that in Kmart, they would charge you double." (Wolper said he would have bought the clubs himself but, at the time of the auction, "I was out playing golf.")

What Jack Kennedy seemed to intuitively understand was the performative aspect of sports, the way that he could project an image of himself as a healthy all-American boy in the White House even when the reality—as told by his medical records—was something far different.

"He was terrific at projecting an image of a vigorous sportsman," ESPN's Jeff Merron wrote in 2004. "Photos of JFK sailing as President (including one with a young John Kerry) are iconic; they projected to the nation, and the world, a fresh-air, can-do makeup. Truth was, because of his back problems, Kennedy often was in great pain and had a great deal of trouble participating in athletic endeavors."

There's no better illustration of that fact than Kennedy's interest in throwing out first pitches to start baseball seasons. Kennedy was "regarded as a 'great opening President,'" according to Paul F. Boller Jr.'s *Presidential Diversions*.

In 1961, Kennedy was in attendance at the new Washington Senators expansion team's first game against the Chicago White Sox. He threw "what was regarded as the longest and hardest first ball ever tossed by a President," according to Boller. (Those were the days when presidents still threw the ball from the stands. It wasn't until Bill Clinton in 1993 that a president went on the field to throw a first pitch.)

What's decidedly weird—to the modern eye—about the Kennedy first pitch in 1961 is that he isn't throwing it to anyone in particular. Instead, he sort of flings it into a crowd of players—all of who leap and fight for it like bridesmaids trying to catch the bouquet.

The guy who eventually wound up with it was "Jungle Jim" Rivera, a White Sox player. He took it over to get it autographed by the president, who did the deed. Rivera was unhappy with the Kennedy autograph, as it was close to illegible. "Do you think I can go into any tavern in Chicago's South Side and really say the president of the United States signed this baseball for me?" he joked to Kennedy. "I'd be run off." Kennedy re-signed the ball.

Mel Magazine, in 2017, ranked the 1961 toss by JFK as the ninth-best presidential first pitch ever, which isn't bad! (Number one was George W. Bush's toss in the 2001 World Series, which is exactly the right ranking.)

Not content to throw just a single first pitch, however, Kennedy repeated the duty at the start of the Senators' 1962 and 1963 seasons as well. And he threw out the first pitch at the 1962 All-Star Game, which was held in Washington, after briefly glad-handing with St. Louis Cardinals great Stan Musial.

JFK would have been well pleased by this 2020 write-up of his 1963 first pitch in the ultra-glossy *Capitol File* magazine:

John F. Kennedy's back usually ached, and yet on opening day April 8, 1963, he reared back like Sandy Koufax and delivered a strike for the ceremonial first pitch at DC Stadium. He didn't spaghetti arm the toss, and the ball coming from his hand sailed like the dreams of the 43,000 in attendance. What won't be remembered is the home team's travails (the Senators lost, as was habit, 3–1, to the Orioles), but how the president looked. Fifty-seven years is an eternity in fashion, and JFK's gray worsted wool suit (he was a Brooks Brothers man), slim-notched lapel, skinny tie and white dress shirt still look crisp. Timeless, even. Much like the game itself.

It wasn't just baseball where Kennedy was drawn to the pomp and circumstance. Kennedy flipped the coin to start the 1962 Army-Navy game and the 1963 Orange Bowl game between Alabama and Oklahoma. He was scheduled to do the honors at the 1963 Army-Navy Game but was assassinated just weeks before the scheduled December tilt. Fifty years after that 1963 game, the same coin that Kennedy would have used was flipped to start the 2013 Army-Navy game.

Kennedy wasn't above associating himself with winners, either. After the Boston Celtics won their fourth straight NBA championship in 1963, Kennedy invited them to the White House to be honored for the accomplishment. It was the first time a winning basketball team—or any basketball team, really—had made a trip to the seat of national power.

The Celtics were in town to play the Cincinnati Royals on the University of Maryland's campus. The group—led by legendary coach Red Auerbach—was on the standard-issue White House tour when the president heard they were in the building and invited them to visit him personally. (Opportunity knocks!)

Bill Russell, the unquestioned star of those Celtics teams, isn't in any of the pictures the team took with JFK that day. He overslept and missed the tour.

Tom "Satch" Sanders, a member of that 1963 team, described the visit in a 2017 interview with *Bleacher Report*.

"He laughed a lot, he had some stories to tell about when he was a kid admiring the Celtics and he took about 20–30 minutes with us," said Sanders of Kennedy. "That didn't make his staff very happy because that was a lot of time, but he was happy and he was a good conversationalist and we had a lot of laughs."

In 1961, Kennedy traveled to New York City to receive the Gold Medal Award of the National Football Foundation and Hall of Fame for his two years of playing college football at Harvard.

"If I confess to you that I could not even make the varsity squad at Harvard you will immediately understand how well qualified I am to address the National Football Foundation and Hall of Fame," said Kennedy, before adding: "But I come from a family which believes in trying. We have always enjoyed sports of all sorts—football, baseball, tennis, swimming, sailing, even golf. A year ago, for example, we did considerable running."

Also honored that night was Bear Bryant's University of Alabama Crimson Tide as the best college football team of 1961; the Tide finished the season 11-0.

That Alabama team was—like most of the teams in the Southeastern Conference of the day—all white. Bryant was a generally progressive voice on civil rights—he had urged Kentucky to bring in Black players when he coached there—and, as the '60s wore on, battled with segregationist governor George Wallace over his integration efforts within the Alabama football team.

————

Jack Kennedy's last birthday—his forty-sixth—on May 29, 1963, took place aboard the presidential yacht, the *Sequoia*, and typified the excess that had come to define his life, which by that point had begun to spiral out of control—and which most people only learned about much, much later.

The party was strictly a friends-and-family affair—with the president's younger brothers, Robert and Ted, in attendance, as well as some of his closest friends, including then *Newsweek* Washington bureau chief Ben Bradlee and a few celebrities as well—namely actor David Niven.

The menu for the night was pure Camelot: crabmeat ravigote, noodle casserole, asparagus Hollandaise, and roast filet of beef—all washed down with 1955 Dom Perignon.

Guests got on the boat around 8 p.m. and didn't return to the dock until after 1:30 a.m. In between, they got, well, very drunk. According to Bradlee's memoir, Ted Kennedy "mysteriously lost one leg of his trousers some time during the night." Niven told journalist Sally Bedell Smith that the younger Kennedy's pants were "ripped off at the crotch with white underpants on the port side flashing."

Bradlee also recounted that Clement Norton, a friend of the family, committed a major party foul by drunkenly stepping on Jackie Kennedy's gift to her husband—an engraving of a scene from the War of 1812.

The president himself was otherwise occupied, according to Smith. He made a pass at Bradlee's then wife—Antoinette "Tony" Pinchot Bradlee.

"I was running and laughing as he chased me," Tony Bradlee told Smith of Kennedy. "He caught up with me in the ladies room and made a pass. It was a pretty strenuous attack, not as if he pushed me down, but his hands wandered. I said 'That's it, so long.' I was running like mad."

Kennedy was dead less than six months later. It took much, much longer for the image of Camelot that he had worked his whole adult life to build to fade away.

Master of the Senate Softball Team (Sorry I Had to...)

Presidential Power Hitter

Lyndon Johnson just wanted to go to church—and then play a little golf. A nice, relaxing Sunday. For once.

The president and his son-in-law (and future Virginia governor and senator) Chuck Robb were in Williamsburg, Virginia. Church was supposed to be a sedate affair. The president's people had been assured that the ongoing war in Vietnam would not be a part of the sermon.

The pastor apparently hadn't been consulted. He scolded Johnson from the pulpit for his role in the ongoing conflict, recalled Robb.

By the time Johnson and Robb made it to the golf course, the president was fuming. They skipped the first tee because, according to Robb, Johnson didn't want to face the photographers and questions from the members of the media. And, "we stopped after the 17th hole because he knew there would be news media on the 18th."

That day was every day of the Johnson presidency. He could never get away from the job—and the gnawing realities that Vietnam (and how and whether to end the war) pressed on him. There was never any day off for Johnson.

He compounded that unfortunate reality by being a man who had never had any hobbies or interests outside of politics. When the only thing he ever cared about turned sour, he had nowhere else to go.

———————

Johnson was one of our least athletic presidents—big, clumsy, and awkward. He was not only uninterested in sports but actively bad at them—even as a kid. There are no stories of Johnson's youthful heroics on the baseball field or the gridiron. Not a one. "He threw a baseball like a girl," said one classmate.

Sports Illustrated once contemplated doing a feature on the president. They couldn't find much to work with—and scrapped the project.

Johnson himself mocked the idea of time off—or diversions from the duties of being president. "Hobbies!!! What the hell are hobbies! I've got too much work to do to have hobbies," he once said.

Instead, Johnson's youth and young adult life are filled with stories of his keen understanding of how sports could be used to foster and further relationships he wanted and needed to achieve his career goals. Sports was a language lots and lots of people spoke fluently, so Johnson taught it to himself.

The most important relationship of LBJ's political life—with Richard Russell—was thanks to his ability to use sports for his own purposes.

Despite being one of the most powerful men in Washington, Russell was very much a loner, never married, and with few close friends or associates.

"There was another motif as pervasive in Richard Russell's life as power, and it was loneliness," wrote Johnson historian Robert Caro in *Master of the Senate*.

Russell, the Senate majority leader, was a huge baseball fan—"had in his head the day-to-day batting averages, not only of the Washington Senators but of an impressive number of players around the American League," wrote Caro.

And Russell would always attend opening day in Washington with a handful of senators and other baseball-loving members of the administration. "Russell, his aides say, had a wonderful time going to Opening Day with other senators, but, of course, that was a formal occasion, with the invitations made without any participation on his part being necessary," according to Caro.

For the remainder of the season, Russell would attend games alone. Caro wrote:

> It was embarrassing for such a man to be alone. If he was the renowned Richard Brevard Russell, the most powerful man in the Senate, why didn't he have anyone to go with? Would some colleague or staff member or acquaintance see him—and feel sorry for him, or tell people that Dick Russell went to baseball games alone? So Russell went to few baseball games.

Enter Lyndon Johnson, newly arrived senator from Texas. Johnson was looking for ways to get himself close to power—and power in the Senate quite clearly resided with Russell.

After initially hoping to get on the powerful Appropriations Committee in the Senate, Johnson changed course—asking his way onto the Armed Services Committee, which Russell chaired.

"I knew there was only one way to see Russell every day, and that was to get a seat on his committee," said Johnson. "Without that, we'd most likely be passing acquaintances and nothing more. So I put in a request for the Armed Services Committee."

Johnson courted Russell relentlessly, showing up to his office late in the day to simply sit at the foot of the Georgia senator. And he took to inviting Russell to dinner at his home. "He was our visitor many times, but it was much more likely to be on the spur of the moment," Lady Bird Johnson said of Russell. "They'd be working together on something, and they would not be finished with it, and Lyndon would say something about, come on and go home with him, and Lady Bird will give us some—whatever we had. That was the way it usually happened."

All of the hospitality and the kissing up played a role in Russell's increasingly paternalistic view of Johnson. But it was baseball that might well have sealed the deal.

"We both liked baseball," Russell said once when asked about the roots of his relationship with LBJ. "Right after he came to the Senate, for some reason we started going to night baseball games together."

It wasn't "for some reason." It was because Johnson understood where power sat in the Senate. And Russell led the southern bloc of Democrats, the seat of Senate power.

"I do understand power, whatever else may be said about me," Johnson once said. "I know where to look for it, and how to use it."

As Caro wrote of the baseball-going habit of the two powerful men:

Sometimes Lady Bird was invited to accompany them. "They would buy hot dogs . . . and sit and watch and talk about the prowess of this player or that player." And, she noticed, at baseball games Russell was less "aloof . . . he really liked that." If no box seats were available, they would sit in the grandstand above the boxes—two tall men in double-breasted suits and fedoras, hot dogs in hands, sitting close together, talking companionably and laughing together.

John Connally, an aide to Johnson (and later the governor of Texas), was decidedly skeptical of his boss's newfound love of baseball. "I doubt that Lyndon Johnson had been to a baseball game in his life until he heard that Dick Russell enjoyed the sport," Connally told Caro.

Connally would joke with Johnson, recounted Caro. " 'Well I see you've become a baseball fan. Do you know the pitcher from the catcher?' [Johnson] would smile and laugh, and say, 'You know I've always loved baseball.' I said, 'No I've never been aware of that.' But Connally understood: He knew Dick Russell liked baseball games, so he went to games with Russell."

The friendship Johnson used baseball to build with Russell was essential to his future political successes. Russell came to see Johnson as something of a surrogate son, someone to mentor and look out for in future and political endeavors.

Which was exactly what Russell did. He took electing Johnson, like him a son of the South, personally. Without Russell keeping an eye out for

Johnson's presidential prospects there is likely no 1957 Civil Rights Act. And without that act, Johnson might well not be positioned to be Kennedy's obvious vice presidential pick in 1960.

As Doris Kearns Goodwin wrote of Johnson and civil rights: "As a man with presidential dreams, Johnson recognized that it would be almost impossible for him to escape all responsibility for the Senate to act, that failure on this issue at this time would brand him forever as sectional and therefore unpresidential."

Despite growing up in the football-crazy South, Johnson was, from a very young age, most fascinated with where power sat—and why.

"If there was some boys playing ball out in the yard and some men sittin' around whittlin' and talkin', you wouldn't find Lyndon out there with the boys," a childhood acquaintance of the future president told historian Robert Dallek. "No, he'd be right in the middle of those men, listenin' and talkin'. But he wouldn't just talk; he would also argue and pontificate."

What Johnson understood—maybe from all of those conversations with men twice his age—was that sports mattered to people. And Lyndon was a relentless—and earnest—student of people.

As George Reedy, his White House press secretary, once wrote:

He did understand, dimly, that other people had some interests outside of their direct work. But he thought of such interests as weaknesses. I cringed every time he attended a baseball game because he made it so perfectly obvious that he was bored by the whole procedure. He went only when a game was to be attended by a large number of politicians with whom he could transact some business. On such days, I sat at home praying that television cameras would not catch him with his back turned to the field in deep conversation about a tax bill or an upcoming election while a triple play was in progress or when a cleanup hitter had just knocked a home run with the bases loaded.

Chuck Robb confirmed Reedy's impression.

"I'm not sure he got up every morning and looked at the sports section to see who had won in any specific competition," said Robb. "He liked to go to football games but he was a politician at them. He liked to have some personal association with some of the coaches and other athletes from time to time."

As a friend of Johnson's once said: "Sports, entertainment, movies—he couldn't have cared less. His [focus] was so narrow it was almost ludicrous."

On the rare occasions Johnson did play sports, he took on a decidedly bossy mien.

"He had a baseball, and the rest of us didn't have one," recalled Bob Edwards, a childhood acquaintance of Johnson's, to author Robert Caro. "We were all very poor. None of us had a ball but him. Well, Lyndon wanted to pitch. He wasn't worth a darn as a pitcher, but if we didn't let him pitch, he'd take his ball and go home. So, yeah, we let him pitch."

Johnson, in short, wanted to be in charge—even if he wasn't the best. "Whatever they were doing, Lyndon was the head," his aunt told Caro. "He was always the lead horse. Made no difference what come nor what went, he was the head of the ring."

Which is telling. Biographies of Johnson are full of stories about his mediocre (at best) athleticism and his only passing interest in spectator sports. But, those same books are chock-full of stories of the driving ambition that sat at the core of Johnson's being.

"Everything was competition with Lyndon," his cousin Ava told Caro. "He had to win."

Gene Worley, a former member of Congress from Texas who was a frequent golf partner of Johnson's, echoed that sentiment. "Whether it's golf or poker or whatnot, he takes it pretty hard when he loses."

Historian Doris Kearns Goodwin said that Johnson "sometimes reminded me of an exuberant child."

Johnson was the lewdest and crudest of all our American presidents. (Special honorable mention here to Donald Trump and Richard Nixon—both of whom loved to curse and did it frequently in and out of office.)

Hubert Humphrey, Johnson's vice president, chose a sports metaphor to explain how the president approached politics and life.

"He was not delicate," said Humphrey of Johnson. "There was nothing delicate about him. He was not a ballet dancer. He was a downfield blocker and a running back *all the time*." (Fun fact: Johnson's mother had made the young Lyndon take ballet lessons!)

Johnson was vulgar, with men and women.

With men, he would infamously demand that someone—usually an aide—accompany him into the bathroom to continue a conversation—a habit that Kearns Goodwin had described as "a matter of course, bizarre as it was."

Johnson also had a nickname for his penis—"Jumbo"—and, as Caro recounts, he would occasionally swing it around while in the bathrooms on Capitol Hill, remarking: "Have you ever seen anything as big as this?" to anyone within the vicinity. (Johnson also would regularly urinate outdoors, often with other people standing nearby.)

For women, Johnson's behavior was no better. "One hand was shaking your hand; the other hand was some place else, exploring you, examining you," said late *Washington Post* editor Ben Bradlee of Johnson. "He'd be feeling up [*Post* publisher] Katharine Graham and bumping [*Post* writer] Meg Greenfield on the boobs. And at the same time he'd be trying to persuade you of something."

Aside from the way he acted, there was the way he talked.

"It was raining as hard as a cow pissing on a flat rock."

Or: "As straight as an Indian shits."

Or of a potential rival: "It's probably better to have him inside the tent pissing out than outside the tent pissing in."

Or, of someone he believed he controlled: "I've got his pecker in my pocket."

Or, on being in the White House: "The presidency is like being a jackass caught in a hailstorm. You've got to just stand there and take it."

And that's even before we talk about Johnson's near-constant use of the N-word while referring to African Americans. In mostly private conversations during his presidential term, Johnson repeatedly used the words to describe Black Americans as a monolithic bloc.

As historian Robert Dallek noted in *Flawed Giant*, his biography of Johnson, LBJ explained his decision to nominate the well-known Thurgood Marshall to the Supreme Court over a lesser-known Black judge this way: "When I appoint a n——— to the bench, I want everybody to know he's a n———."

Johnson was a man of his time and place, yes. But, he was also a man of extremes. He was more vulgar, cruder, and more willing to use—and speak in—racist ways than many people who held the office before or after him.

———

To the extent that LBJ even liked any sport, it was golf.

LBJ played at times during his presidency and then more actively once he left office.

During his time in office, Johnson, like Kennedy before him, worked to keep his golf outings a secret. He was a member at the uber-exclusive Burning Tree course just outside of Washington but would never let the club know when he was planning to come play. His outings were not listed on the daily schedule that was given to the press. He traveled in an unmarked car to and from the course.

He quit the game during the height of the Vietnam War—for fear of the fodder he would provide his critics; Johnson told aides that if people saw him on the course even as young men were deploying and dying in Vietnam, the public would "eat me alive."

But, unlike in politics, he was never terribly competitive about his golf game.

"Johnson brought to the game of golf none of the intensity and cunning that fueled his rise from the Texas hill country all the way to the White House," wrote Shepherd Campbell and Peter Landau in their book *Presidential Lies*.

Johnson just didn't take the game seriously; he never took a single lesson. "He didn't seem to have much touch or feel for the game," said comedian Bob Hope after finishing a round with LBJ.

Or, as his son-in-law Chuck Robb joked: "I would not call him a threat in the Masters."

Johnson was known for two things on the golf course: a relentless stream of conversation and hitting multiple balls every time a shot didn't reach its desired target.

"He was not different on the golf course and off the golf course," said Robb. "He didn't engage in what some people would regard as regular sports talk. To the extent he had an interaction or [the conversation] had some impact on politics, he would have been a little more interested."

Max Elbin, the pro at Burning Tree, the ultra-exclusive golf club just outside of Washington, said that Johnson "didn't play every week, but he had a hell of a good time. He would josh around, kidding whoever was with him. He'd make comments to the other players—of a personal nature."

(Sidebar: With quotes like that—"comments . . . of a personal nature"—Elbin could have been a politician!)

Johnson's lack of seriousness about the sport led to an utter disregard for keeping score—or trying to play a single ball at a time. Wrote Campbell and Landau:

> He never accepted a poor shot. If he hit a ball he didn't like, he would plop down another ball and hit again—and often again and again and again. As he made his way from tee to green, it could take as many as eight mulligans on each shot until he was satisfied.

He was a devotee of the Hit-Till-You're-Happy school of golf. As the *Atlantic* noted of a round of golf played by Johnson in his postpresidency:

> One day, playing with a few aides and friends, Johnson hit a drive into the rough, retrieved it, and threw the ball back on the fairway. "Are you allowed to do that?" one of the wives whispered to a Secret Service agent. "You are," he replied, "if you play by LBJ rules."

Johnson once joked to a reporter who asked him his golf handicap: "I don't have a handicap. I'm all handicap."

Johnson did have one remarkable moment on the golf course, however.

In February 1968, he traveled to Palm Springs, California, to play golf with former president—and golf addict—Dwight Eisenhower.

The two men played at the Seven Lakes Country Club. (Earlier that month, Ike had made a hole-in-one at the course's thirteenth hole—the only one he made in his life.)

Johnson was struggling with how to end the war in Vietnam—not to mention whether he should run for a second term. He sought the counsel of Eisenhower—the military hero of World War II and the most popular president of modern times. (No one knows what the two men talked about, but a month later Johnson announced he wouldn't run again.)

Eisenhower was the far superior golfer—in general and on that day. Except for one very important hole. As Johnson chief of staff James Jones recounted:

Eisenhower took his golf quite seriously, and Johnson would hit the ball all over the place. And Eisenhower was just steady, right down the middle—150 yards or whatever...and Eisenhower won, as I recall, every hole until the 18th...While the press was all kept away from photographing the previous holes, they were all at the 18th hole.

Johnson teed off on the 18th right down the middle. I don't know how long but it was a long hit. Then he was on in two and parred. Eisenhower lost the hole with just another steady bogey, and Johnson won. Eisenhower was not a particularly gracious loser of the hole—even though he won the match—because the hole Johnson won came in front of the press.

Johnson had long been secretive about golf for fear of being called a hypocrite. (He had been critical of Dwight Eisenhower's slavish devotion to the game; "For eight long years, the South have been used [by Republicans] only as a golf course to tee off from," he once said.)

But he became more transparent about his interest in the game—even though that interest didn't lead to much improvement—as he got toward the end of his term.

As Campbell and Landau write, Johnson once missed a series of short(ish) putts on the White House putting green, with the press looking on.

Writing of Johnson's seemingly newfound interest in the sport, famed *New York Times* columnist James "Scotty" Reston, wrote: "To do it as an escape from agony is the worst miscalculation since the start of the Vietnam War. Golf is not an escape from agony. It is itself an agony."

Despite Reston's advice—or maybe because of it—Johnson did continue to play golf as he aged. He once told the pro at Burning Tree that his sole mission was to be able to play well enough "so that when I get out of this job I can use golf as a winter sport."

—————

Oddly, one of the most quoted lines of Johnson's presidency was about baseball.

"They booed Ted Williams, too, remember?" Johnson said in 1967 amid sagging approval ratings amid ongoing unhappiness about the Vietnam War. "They'll say about me I knocked the ball over the fence—but they don't like the way he stands at the plate."

Williams, it's worth noting, was a lifelong Republican and devoted supporter of Richard Nixon.

—————

Johnson was one of the only presidents to inaugurate a baseball stadium as well. In 1965 the Houston Astrodome opened and Johnson, along with his wife, Lady Bird, were in attendance.

The stadium was massive—a marvel of modern engineering. Nicknamed the "Eighth Wonder of the World," it could hold sixty-six thousand people. The scoreboard—on which Johnson's face appeared that day—was 60 feet high and 300 feet wide. The dome, which was made of Lucite, was 642 feet in total. It was translucent so that Bermuda grass could grow inside. It looked like something from outer space.

"It reminds me of what I imagine my first ride would be like in a flying saucer," said Yankee great Mickey Mantle of playing in the Astrodome.

(Mantle, who was very near the end of his career by 1965, singled and homered in the game.)

Which was the point. Four years earlier, NASA's Manned Spacecraft Center—which is now known as the Lyndon B. Johnson Space Center—had opened. Houston (and Texas more generally) wanted to be seen as on the cutting edge of American technology and innovation. This was the place where the future was happening. (The groundskeepers at the stadium wore space suits. Not kidding.)

The game between the Astros and the New York Yankees was the first baseball game ever to be played indoors. (Connally, LBJ's former aide and now the governor of Texas, threw out the first pitch. Connally, it's worth noting, was shot in the chest, ribs, and arm in the November 1963 assassination of John F. Kennedy in Dallas and almost died.)

Johnson sat with his party in the luxury boxes in right field. (The Astrodome was the first baseball park to have luxury boxes for high-paying customers.) According to reports at the time, Johnson ate fried chicken and chocolate ice cream while watching the game. The White House also requested that nine—yes, nine!—phone lines be ready at the stadium in case Johnson or his advisers needed them.

The Astros wound up winning 2–1 in the twelfth inning. No word on whether Johnson stayed until the bitter end.

But, it was one of only four games that Johnson went to during his five years in office. In 1964, 1965, and 1967, he threw out the first pitch of the season for the Washington Senators. (The team lost all three of those games.)

———

Coming on the heels of Eisenhower and Kennedy, both of whom were uniquely fixated on the relative strengths and weaknesses of America's youth, Johnson wound up inheriting some of that obsession within his own administration.

The Olympics—and how America stood against communist Russia—was a particular pressure point. In advance of the 1964 Summer Olympics in Tokyo, Robert Kennedy, Johnson's attorney general and JFK's little brother, warned the president that "it looks like we're going to do badly."

Kennedy understood that political reality. "I think it would be very helpful politically if you're on top of that," he told Johnson about the U.S.'s performance in the upcoming Olympics.

By that summer—with the Olympics slated to begin in October—Kennedy collected his thoughts into a set of guiding principles for the Johnson administration.

"Part of a nation's prestige in the cold war is won in the Olympic Games," wrote Kennedy. "In this day of international stalemates, nations use the scoreboard of sports as a visible measuring stick to prove their superiority over the 'soft and decadent' democratic way of life."

That reality, in Kennedy's view, made U.S. success in the Olympics paramount. It was "thus in our national interest that we regain our Olympic superiority; that we once again give the world visible proof of our inner strength and vitality," concluded Kennedy. He recommended "encouragement—with action as well as words—by government at all levels."

Kennedy was joined in concern about the coming Olympics—and the possibility of Soviet domination—by Minnesota Democratic senator Hubert Humphrey.

"The Russians are feverishly building toward what they expect to be a major Cold War victory in 1964: a massive triumph in the Tokyo Olympics," said Humphrey. "Once they have crushed us in the coming Olympic battle, the Red propaganda drums will thunder out in a worldwide tattoo, heralding the 'new Soviet men and women' as 'virile, unbeatable conquerors' in sports—or anything else."

The result of these worries and dissatisfaction was a joint effort by the Johnson administration and the U.S. Olympic Committee. A consulting firm—Arthur D. Little Corporation—was hired to study the problems with the American sports system. The effort was headed by Lt. Gen. James Gavin.

Johnson met with Bobby Kennedy and Gavin in June 1964 to discuss the plan. "The improvement of the physical education of our young men and women thereby providing the opportunity for achieving high standards of excellence in amateur sports is a matter of great importance, and I wish you well in this undertaking," wrote Johnson in a subsequent letter to Gavin.

While all of this internal research and debate was going on, the matter of how and whether Americans would be able to watch the Games arose. A proposal made it to Johnson's desk that would utilize NASA's Syncom II satellite to allow a global broadcast of the Olympics—a prospect that the Japanese were decidedly keen on.

Initially, Johnson dismissed the idea. But then Horace Busby, a White House aide, appealed to the president's political sense.

"The Olympic Games will be conducted in October at the peak of the 1964 presidential campaigns," Busby told Johnson. "The telecasts—if technically well done—would be a matter of pride for all Democratic candidates, and would also give the Administration an opportunity to identify with youth, athletics, international cooperation, etc."

Johnson was convinced. "It is heartening that the Olympic Games—a symbol of peaceful competition among nations—can be seen simultaneously by those actually present and by peoples throughout the entire world," the president announced just three days before the Games were set to begin.

The star of those games was eighteen-year-old swimmer Don Schollander, who won four gold medals for the United States—breaking three world records and an Olympic record in the process. That performance tied Schollander with Jesse Owens for the most gold medals won in a single Summer Olympics.

Sharon Stouder, a fifteen-year-old swimmer for the United States, won three golds and a silver—a feat made all the more impressive when you consider that there were only eight women's swimming events in that Olympics.

Sprinter Bob Hayes won the 100-meter dash and ran the anchor leg of the 4 × 100-meter relay for the gold medal–winning U.S. team. Hayes was later drafted by the Dallas Cowboys and is the only person to ever win a gold medal and a Super Bowl championship.

Overall, the United States won 95 medals—edged out by only the Russians with 97. But the United States beat the Russians in overall golds, taking 38 to the Russians' 30.

Johnson cruised to a full term less than a month later.

By the following May, Gavin had completed his report on American sports and shared it with Johnson. Gavin had hoped to make the report public—perhaps in *Sports Illustrated*—but Johnson decided it would remain confidential.

———

Johnson's final year in office—1968—was among the most tumultuous in modern American history. Both Robert Kennedy and Martin Luther King Jr. were assassinated. The war in Vietnam raged on—almost seventeen thousand Americans were killed, the highest death toll of any single year of the war—even as the protests against it grew louder and louder back in America. Violence marred the Democratic National Convention in Chicago.

That chaos and uncertainty were reflected in sports that year as well. The lasting image was of the raised, black-gloved fists of American sprinters Tommie Smith and John Carlos on the medal stand at the Mexico City Olympics, a silent protest of the treatment of Black Americans.

"If I win, I am an American, not a black American," Smith said by way of explanation. "But if I did something bad, then they would say 'a Negro.' We are black and we are proud of being black."

In the wake of King's assassination, most baseball teams moved to cancel their games. The Los Angeles Dodgers, who had integrated baseball thanks to Jackie Robinson, initially resisted. "It angers me that the team which pioneered the advent of the Negro in baseball would take such a stand," said Bill White, the first baseman for the Philadelphia Phillies. (The Dodgers eventually bowed to the pressure and did not play.)

Later that fall, Arthur Ashe became the first Black man to win the U.S. Open men's singles tennis championship. (Ashe emerged as an activist as well, speaking out against the Vietnam War.)

And then there was Muhammad Ali, the former heavyweight boxing champion of the world and the single most famous war dissenter.

Ali had been stripped of his crown for his refusal to fight in Vietnam. "I am not allowed to work in America and I'm not allowed to leave America," he said in early 1968. "I'm just about broke."

Explaining his refusal to fight in Vietnam, Ali famously said:

"Why should they ask me to put on a uniform and go ten thousand miles from home and drop bombs and bullets on brown people in Vietnam while so-called Negro people in Louisville are treated like dogs and denied simple human rights?"

———

For all his lack of coordination in sports, Johnson was, by most accounts, an able and willing dancer.

"He had a good sense of rhythm," said one observer who added that the president did a "smooth foxtrot."

Singer and entertainer Edie Adams, a frequent guest at the Johnson White House, said that the president was a "marvelous" dancer and a "strong lead." She added: "You don't find dancers like that anymore. Usually they're sort of milquetoast fellows but, boy, he knew exactly where he was going."

He danced with Princess Margaret. And Imelda Marcos, the First Lady of the Philippines. And Jackie Kennedy. And entertainer Carol Channing. And lots (and lots) of other prominent women.

His most frequent dance partner was his wife, Lady Bird, who shared his love of dancing. "Dancing is one of my favorite joys," she once said.

In July 1964, Johnson held a state dinner for the president of Costa Rica and his wife. Here's how *Time* wrote about the party:

Lyndon Johnson, it is well known, likes dancing parties. But in Washington these sweltering days, even the two-step is hot work. Thus after a state dinner for visiting Costa Rican President Francisco Orlich and his wife, Marita, President Johnson took his guests out onto the low-lying rooftop adjoining the East Wing, only a few hundred feet from the street, where they danced under Japanese lanterns that swayed in the cooling breeze...

The President himself came on with a stomp of uncertain origin that might have been the presidential version of a step teenagers have dubbed 'the bird.' To the racy tune of the old Edith Piaf favorite "Milord," Lyndon took [his daughter and fellow dance lover] Luci in a modified bear hug and whirled her around while flapping time to the music with his elbows.

Not all the reports of Johnson's dancing suggest the same prowess. In one high-profile incident in 1961, Johnson tried to dance with Helen Chavchavadze, a known mistress of the late John Kennedy. Johnson slipped, fell, and wound up lying on his dance partner "like a lox," according to historian Robert Caro.

Johnson would also, on occasion, make use of the indoor swimming pool at the White House or the outdoor pool he had at his ranch in Texas. His swimming increased following his heart attack in 1955—at age forty-seven—as he would do laps either in the pool in Texas or in the one in the White House.

But, even then Johnson was politicking. He had an extra-long cord installed at the Texas ranch so that he could be on the phone while in the pool. And, as Paul F. Boller Jr. wrote in a book about presidents and their sporting diversions, "he usually had at least one person with him so he could talk politics while moving around in the water."

Bowling Alone

Richard Nixon liked to bowl. Alone.

In 1969, he had a two-lane alley built in the White House basement. And he would often head down there to roll a few frames.

"Sometimes, toward the end of the day, when I feel tired or stuffy, I just go over and bowl," Nixon told the White House press corps about his habit. "I usually bowl about 10 o'clock at night. When I'm here I bowl alone. I bowl seven to 12 games one after another. That gives you a tremendous workout."

Nixon was, by all accounts, a very good bowler. During his presidency he shot a 229—a game that included seven strikes, including four in a row. "I say the president feels happy today about his own athletic achievement," Nixon told several senior staffers, seemingly unaware of speaking in the third person.

Nixon was also keen on making his skill at bowling known to the general public. (Not until Donald Trump took over the White House in 2017 have we had a president as image obsessed as Nixon.) He told Ron Ziegler, the White House press secretary, to sell the press corps on a story on his bowling. The media obliged. And in a photo op, Nixon bowled a strike—without even warming up. ("It was a lucky shot," he acknowledged afterward.)

The image of the president of the United States bowling game after game by himself, however, is a stirring image. And a lonely one. And probably not the one the hyper-aware Nixon would have wanted to project to the war-weary country.

Which was, well, Nixon—both in and out of the White House. He was, by nature, a loner—someone who rarely felt at ease in a crowd. And he was intensely driven, constantly pushing himself beyond the bounds most politicians—or people—would go to win.

As Dwight Chapin, his longtime body man, wrote: "The public Nixon was always rather shy, especially for a politician. He was by nature an introvert, but the private Nixon could relax. He loved sports, for example. Watching sports was a great relaxation for him."

And, at least when it came to bowling, playing the sport was a way for Nixon to unwind from the pressures of the job—competing mostly against himself to improve.

Of bowling's appeal to him, Nixon explained: "Not only are you competing against another bowler, but you're competing against yourself to improve your score." Nixon also once referred to golf as a "waste of time."

(Sidebar: Nixon wasn't entirely antigolf. He played alongside golf fanatic Dwight Eisenhower when the two men were in the White House. "Look here," Ike once told Nixon after the duo had lost a match. "You're young, you're strong, and you can do a lot better than that.")

Nixon picked up the game again as president. A group of Republican donors pitched in to build him a three-hole course at his home in San Clemente—the so-called Western White House—and according to historian John Sayle Watterson, Nixon was shooting in the high 80s and low 90s by the time the 1972 election rolled around.

After resigning the presidency in 1974, Nixon retreated to San Clemente and largely shut himself off from the world. Golf was one of the things that he still enjoyed, and one of the ways he managed to interact with people. "Golf became my lifesaver," said Nixon of the sport.

Work obsessed, Nixon also liked that bowling could be done quickly—all the better to return to work. "In many ways, bowling is better for me than golf because it doesn't take as much time," Nixon once said. "I don't have time to duck out and play golf, but I can duck out and bowl."

But there was another appeal to bowling for Nixon. It spoke to the same sort of sentiments he had long stoked—and that had coalesced in his "Silent Majority" mantra.

Nixon first outlined the idea in a speech in December 1969 as he sought to rally a divided country behind his plan to win the war in Vietnam.

"I know it may not be fashionable to speak of patriotism or national destiny these days, but I feel it is appropriate to do so on this occasion," Nixon said in retort to those who questioned both the U.S.'s continued involvement in the war as well as how American soldiers were conducting themselves in it.

He then turned to the rhetorical high point of the speech, saying, "So tonight, to you, the great silent majority of my fellow Americans, I ask for your support. I pledged in my campaign for the Presidency to end the war in a way that we could win the peace. I have initiated a plan of action which will enable me to keep that pledge. The more support I can have from the American people, the sooner that pledge can be redeemed. For the more divided we are at home, the less likely the enemy is to negotiate at Paris."

The message was simple but profound: Nixon believed that the majority of Americans were on his side—generally and when it came to Vietnam specifically. And while news coverage of the loudest voices might not reflect that, Nixon knew that in their hearts the majority of Americans loved their country and wanted to see it win.

"Let us be united for peace," he urged. "Let us also be united against defeat. Because let us understand—North Vietnam cannot defeat or humiliate the United States. Only Americans can do that."

What, you may (fairly) ask, does all of that have to do with bowling? A surprising amount, actually.

"You know who [are] the lowest class of people in sports—bowlers!" Nixon said. He went on to mock the elites who snubbed their nose at bowling in pursuit of allegedly superior sports, like sailing.

"There are obvious benefits to the President associating himself with bowling, the most obvious being contact with that segment of the population that we consider to be part of the President's constituency," wrote one aide. Another chimed in: "More people bowl than anything else."

While it might seem like an odd claim now, with bowling relegated to the same hours on ESPN as things like the world tag championship and cornhole, during the 1960s bowling—and the (mostly) men who excelled at it—were extremely popular.

As the website Priceonomics has noted: "Harry Smith, the top bowler in 1963, made more money than MLB MVP Sandy Koufax and NFL MVP Y. A. Tittle combined." The website quoted a *Sports Illustrated* profile of Smith that contained these lines:

> Harry does so well that he is able to support a wife and four children in style, tool around the circuit in a maroon Lincoln Continental and indulge a taste for epicurean delicacies. In short, he is the personification of the prosperity that has suddenly overtaken the world of professional bowling.

In 1964, the first million-dollar athlete endorsement deal went to a bowler—Don Carter Jr. The sponsor was a bowling manufacturing company called Ebonite.

Five years later, a quarterback by the name of Joe Namath shaved off his Fu Manchu mustache with a Schick razor for just $10,000.

So, yeah, bowling was a big deal.

It was such a cultural touchstone for Nixon that there was even talk of him attending a professional bowling event—although there was some concern at the staff level that if he went, Nixon would likely have to bowl a few frames. "Wouldn't bother me a bit," said the president.

Relentless self-improvement was the driving force of Nixon's life. He was not a man—athletically, politically, or socially—with many natural gifts.

When Dwight Eisenhower chose Nixon as his vice presidential

running mate in 1952, Ike tried to teach the Californian how to fish for trout. "After hooking a limb the first three times, I caught his shirt on the fourth try," Nixon wrote. "The lesson ended abruptly."

Later, according to historian John Sayle Watterson, Nixon again tried his hand at fishing while on a trip to the Everglades. He went overboard twice. "Fish Catch Nixon," read the caption of a photo of the president clinging to the side of a boat.

But Nixon was the consummate grinder—throwing block after block as an undersized football lineman for tiny Whittier College and then later rolling ball after ball after ball in the White House basement.

"He was willing to pay the price," said Nixon historian Evan Thomas of Nixon's brief football career, adding that on the football field at Whittier his teammates "beat the living shit out of him."

Although Nixon barely played, his time on the bench wasn't wasted. "Dick could analyze and tell you what the tackle was doing and what the guard was doing or where the strengths of the opposition were after viewing it from the bench," recalled one former teammate.

As Nixon later recalled of his brief college playing career: "One reason [coach] didn't put me in was because I didn't know the plays. I knew all the enemy's plays though. I practiced them every week [against the starters]."

(Worth noting: Nixon's reference there to the opposing team as "the enemy." In sports as in politics as in life.)

Nixon was undaunted—and as he aged he would regularly reflect back on his time on the gridiron, particularly in college, as formative. In his 1968 memoir *In the Arena*, Nixon wrote of his college coach Wallace "Chief" Newman: "I learned more about life sitting on the bench with Chief Newman than I did by getting A's in philosophy courses."

For Nixon, football was a metaphor for life—and his life in particular. It wasn't about how many times he got leveled in a practice, it was about how many times he got up. Athleticism wasn't the requirement; resilience was.

"It's good for people to be for somebody, for a team," he would say years after his college playing days were over. "You can learn something about losing as well as winning—I've had some experience with that."

Nixon was also a massive sports fan.

As Chapin wrote of Nixon in his memoir of his years in the White House: "He read the baseball box scores and loved to talk baseball for hours with Julie's husband, David Eisenhower. He knew the players and understood the strategy. Baseball and football were part of his weekend relaxation when he wasn't working."

Much of Nixon's fandom was born of a frustrating lack of athleticism— and a gap between what Nixon was as an athlete and what he dreamed of being. Nixon's life in sports—both as a fan and as a player—had a Walter Mitty quality, according to Evan Thomas, who wrote *Being Nixon: A Man Divided* about the thirty-seventh president.

"He was the everyman who has dreams of being something he's not."

Later in life, presented with a Whittier College football jersey by the team's cocaptains, Nixon joked: "It's the closest I came to ever making the team."

Nixon followed football and baseball religiously. So devoted was Nixon the fan that some in the White House worried that he ran the risk of looking too sports obsessed to the public.

Nixon aide Herb Klein disagreed. "I think it helps many relate to the president," he said. "I think the American public very much wants to look at the president as a strong leader, which it does, but I also think it enjoys a feeling of warmth toward the president such as comes from sharing a mutual hobby such as football or other sports."

And there's no question that for Nixon talking sports was a way to overcome his general awkwardness when it came to dealing with other people.

Of Nixon, famed *New York Times* columnist Scotty Reston once wrote:

Not since Calvin Coolidge have we had a more awkward uncoordinated locker-room character in the White House than Richard Nixon but he buddies up to Ted Williams of the Washington Senators, and never misses an opportunity to demonstrate he is a "real American," following all the batting averages and passing averages in the land. This is not a wholly cynical or political exercise. He is genuinely interested in sports. Games fascinate and divert him from his problems.

Football—and the lessons he learned there—mattered so much to Nixon that he kicked off his 1960 presidential bid on the Whittier Poets field.

————————

For all the ways in which Nixon used sports—and the athletes that played them—for his own political betterment, no one doubted that he was every inch a real fan and, even at times, maniacal in his rooting interests.

One of his first dates with his wife, Pat, was at a University of South Carolina football game. Nixon was a regular at Duke football games, too—he had gone to law school there—and was utterly immersed in the proceedings on the field.

"People would come to watch Nixon watch the game," said Thomas. "He was such a crazy fan. He would just go wild."

Listen to the Nixon tapes—the same ones that doomed his political career—and you can often hear a baseball or football game playing lowly in the background.

"Two factors have always motivated my great interest in sports," he wrote in his memoirs. "First, sports have always provided the necessary relief from the heavy burdens of work and study I have assumed at every stage of my life. Second, I have a highly competitive instinct, and I find it stimulating to follow the great sports event in which one team's or one man's skill and discipline and brains are pitted against one another's in the most exciting kind of combat imaginable."

His own athletic career was decidedly modest, although he wrote that "the happiest memories of those college days involved sports."

Nixon attended tiny Whittier College—located just southeast of Los Angeles. The school was so small that only eleven players were on his freshman team, a reality that allowed "a 150 pound seventeen year old freshman" (in Nixon's own words) to play every game and "wear a team numeral on [his] sweater."

Despite the fact that his playing time declined with each passing year—"The only times I got to play were in the last few minutes of a game that was already safely won or hopelessly lost," Nixon wrote—the experience was a lasting one for him, largely because of the team's coach: Wallace "Chief" Newman.

"Newman was an American Indian, and tremendously proud of his heritage," wrote Nixon about his coach. "He inspired in us the idea that if we worked hard enough and played hard enough, we could beat anyone."

Newman, like Nixon, had a chip on his shoulder. Because of his ethnicity, Newman couldn't get a shot coaching any of the bigger name programs and so wound up on the gridiron at tiny Whittier. Newman taught Nixon to "use that chip on your shoulder, use your anger," according to author Evan Thomas. "The only way you get even is by winning," Thomas said by way of describing Newman's (and Nixon's) philosophy of life.

Nixon put it similarly. "[Newman] had no tolerance for the view that how you play the game counts more than whether you win or lose," he wrote. "He believed in always playing cleanly, but he also believed that there is a great difference between winning and losing. He used to say, 'Show me a good loser, and I'll show you a loser.' He also said: 'When you lose, get mad—mad at yourself, not at your opponent.'"

Nixon was effusive about Newman's impact. "I think that I admired him more and learned more from him than from any man I have ever known aside from my father," he wrote at one point. At another: "There is no way I can adequately describe Chief Newman's influence on me. He drilled into me a competitive spirit and the determination to come back after you have been knocked down or after you lose. He also gave me an understanding that what really matters is not a man's background, his color, his race, or his religion but only his character."

When Nixon won the Republican nomination for president in 1960, he mentioned Newman in his acceptance speech—calling him a "remarkable football coach."

For Nixon, sports—baseball and football in particular—provided him a common language to make small talk with the people who came through the White House on a daily and weekly basis.

"He didn't have a lot of chit chat. He was socially awkward," said Nicholas Evan Sarantakes, who wrote a book entitled *Fan in Chief* about Nixon and sports in the White House. "It was a way for him to reach out to people and make him easy to associate with."

In his fandom—as in the rest of his endeavors—it was difficult to differentiate what Nixon cared about because, well, he cared about it and what he was doing for perceived political gain.

"If it's baseball, if it's college or pro football, it's almost entirely genuine," said Sarantakes. "If you can also get political stuff out of it, fantastic. If it's any other sport, it's political theater."

And despite all his fandom, Nixon *hated* basketball, according to Sarantakes. "He lost 2 teeth in high school in a basketball game [and] he didn't like basketball again until the 1990s."

Nixon's love of baseball is inseparable from his relationship with Ted Williams, the Red Sox great whose first season as manager of the Washington Senators—1969—lined up perfectly with Nixon's first year in office.

The two men's relationship preceded that year, however. Almost a decade earlier—1960—in Williams's last year as an active player, Vice President Nixon and President Dwight Eisenhower attended opening day where the Senators were facing off against the Sox.

As Fred Frommer recounted in his book *You Gotta Have Heart*, a history of the Washington baseball franchise, when Williams came to the plate in the second inning, Nixon told Ike: "This is probably his last season. Let's root for him." To which Ike responded: "That's a good idea."

Williams, who always had a flair for the dramatic, homered in that at bat. (Williams would also end his career with a home run—on the opposite end of the 1960 season.)

Nixon was elated—and took the opportunity to write to Williams about the bomb. "No one could have gotten a bigger charge out of your tape measure homer than we did," he told Williams. "We 'old men' (in our forties, that is) have to stand together."

Williams wound up campaigning for Nixon in the 1960 race despite the fact that John Kennedy hailed from Red Sox country. Even after Nixon's loss, Williams stayed loyal. In 1961, Williams repeatedly rebuffed attempts by Kennedy to come to Cape Cod and visit with him. "Tell 'em I'm a Nixon fan," Williams said, according to Leigh Montville's biography of Williams, *Ted Williams: The Biography of an American Hero.*

The parallels between the lives and careers of Nixon and Williams are uncanny.

"Both Nixon and Williams were of the same generation and grew up in Southern California in the 1920s," wrote Frommer. "Nixon was a Navy lieutenant commander in the Pacific during World War II, and Williams had a distinguished record as a fighter pilot in that war and the Korean War. And they have something else in common: both men left the national stage in a huff in the early 1960s."

Williams left baseball, somewhat bitterly (as he did most things) at the end of the 1960 season. Nixon not only suffered a narrow presidential loss against Kennedy that year but also lost a comeback bid for governor of California in 1962. It was in a postelection news conference following that latter loss where Nixon infamously told reporters: "You don't have Nixon to kick around anymore."

The mid-'60s were also a time of dislocation for the likes of Nixon and Williams. Nixon was, by any measure, a square, and he looked askance at the growing protest movement and the hippie ethos that were, in his view, infecting the decade. Williams was similarly disdainful of the decade's largesse. Williams—famously or infamously, depending on your point of view—had a bumper sticker on his car as the manager of the Senators that read: "If you don't like policemen, the next time you need help call a hippie."

The late '60s brought far more success—for Nixon and Williams. A month after Nixon won the White House over Minnesota senator Hubert Humphrey, Williams was announced as the manager for the Washington Nationals.

Their relationship only bloomed from there. "I know you will bring to the job of managing the same high standards you brought to the art of hitting," Nixon told Williams in a letter sent during the Nats spring training season. "It's good to know we share the same goal: to make Washington a first place city."

Williams returned the favor days later. "I've been on his side ever since I first met him when he was the vice president," the Splendid Splinter told reporters in Florida. "He showed me a genuineness that you rarely see in a politician. What's a politician? A double-talking, bull throwing... I couldn't even begin to tell you."

Nixon was at the ballpark on opening day when the Nationals took on the mighty New York Yankees. (The Nats were an American League ball club back then.)

But two errors marred Nixon's appearance. The box in which he sat bore a presidential seal that read "The Presidnt of the United States." And Nixon managed to drop one of the balls he was set to throw out for the first pitch. True to his nature, Nixon stayed for the entire game—despite the fact that the Yanks took an 8–0 lead and eventually cruised to an 8–4 win.

Nixon was also in attendance later in the season for a thirteenth-inning tilt between the Nationals and the Oakland Athletics, who featured home run hitter Reggie Jackson in the heart of their lineup. Jackson homered twice in the game, including a bomb in the thirteenth that wound up being the game winner.

Nixon was a Nats supporter, but he admired a good dinger, too. "Although I always root for the home team, I have nothing but the highest admiration for your performance on the night I saw you," he wrote in a letter to Jackson.

It also happened that Washington played host to the All-Star Game in that first year that both Nixon and Williams spent in Washington.

Nixon, ever the fan, held a reception at the White House for hundreds—including Hall of Fame players, current all-stars, and sportswriters.

Interesting Nixon fact: While he hated political reporters—just listen to the Nixon tapes!—he was fascinated by and admiring of sports reporters. "I just want you to know that I like the job I have, but if I had to live my life over again, I would have liked to have ended up as a sportswriter," Nixon told the VIPs assembled at the White House that day. "He loved sports reporters," said Sarantakes, who noted that Nixon would regularly call Shirley Povich, the legendary *Washington Post* sports columnist and fellow columnist William Gildea, then only in his early thirties, at home to talk about their pieces. Sports reporters even got to ride on Air Force One—an unheard of honor.

As always, the political show of his rooting was not far from Nixon's mind—or that of his inner circle. In a memo to White House aide Harry Dent, the Republican National Committee urged Nixon to keep up his fandom.

"The interest the president is showing in sports, particularly baseball, is great PR," read the memo. "As you may or may not know, interest in baseball is at an all-time high in the United States and the average fan likes to identify with the President or a public figure who likes the same things he does. The business of calling in the athletes who supported the president, and having in the all-star players, and going to the games is one of the best things image-wise that is being done. I am sure that he does this because he thoroughly enjoys it, but it is also a big plus for us."

Scotty Reston, the legendary *New York Times* political writer and columnist, offered a more psychological take on Nixon's fandom. Wrote Reston:

"Not since Calvin Coolidge have we had a more awkward uncoordinated locker-room character in the White House than Richard Nixon, but he buddies up to Ted Williams of the Washington Senators, and never misses an opportunity to demonstrate he is a 'real American,' following all the batting averages and passing averages in the land. This is not a wholly cynical or political exercise. He is genuinely interested in sports. Games fascinate him and divert him from his problems."

Those problems, as Nixon's term wore on, were many and varied. In retrospect, 1969 might have been the best year in Washington for Nixon and Williams.

The Senators finished the year 86-76, which, according to Frommer, was the first winning season in franchise history and was the best record for any Washington baseball team in almost twenty-five years. Williams was named American League Manager of the Year—news he found out while on an African safari when a *Washington Post* columnist managed to find him. "Manager of the Year? Me? Forget it. Come on. Really!" Williams exclaimed.

Nixon finished the year on a good note, with 67 percent of Americans in a Gallup poll approving of the job he was doing in November 1969— amid his administration's attempts to bring the war in Vietnam to a close. That same month, however, Nixon announced that the North Vietnamese government had rejected his administration's attempts to bring about a peace settlement. His job approval numbers would never go higher.

The 1970s weren't terribly kind to Williams or Nixon. In 1970 the Nationals finished in last place—and Williams's surliness returned.

"During his second year, Ted began to find he couldn't ignite [the players] with his enthusiasm as he did that first year, nor scare them with fines or yelling," wrote Shelby Whitfield, the Senators radio announcer during the 1969 and 1970 seasons.

Williams also feuded with the reporters who covered the team, closing the clubhouse for the first fifteen minutes after every game. Asked about rescinding the media ban during those critical minutes, Williams said: "Neither [Major League Baseball President Bowie] Kuhn, Nixon or Jesus Fucking Christ could change this goddamn ban."

Williams wasn't the only baseball player whom Nixon befriended. A decade before his relationship with Williams began in earnest, Nixon had built a friendship with Jackie Robinson, who, famously, was the first Black player in Major League Baseball.

Robinson, a Black Republican—which was less rare then than now— wrote to Nixon in 1957 praising the then vice president for comments he had made on civil rights. "I know that you realize that in the tasks that lie ahead all freedom-loving Americans will want to share in achieving a society in which no man is penalized or favored solely because of his race, color, religion or national origin," wrote Robinson. Nixon, a wild baseball fan, reciprocated and the two men began a yearslong correspondence.

For Nixon that friendship paid off in 1960 when Robinson, even then a hugely important cultural figure, endorsed his presidential campaign. As the *Chicago Tribune* noted in 2019:

> As a tireless advocate of the "two-party system," Robinson shocked many of his friends when he signed up to campaign full time for Richard Nixon during the 1960 presidential election. The baseball great was disgusted by John Kennedy's open courtship of Southern governors, and also quite taken by Nixon's racially progressive statements.

Things got rocky late in the campaign, however. In October 1960, civil rights leader Martin Luther King Jr. was jailed for his participation in a lunch counter sit-in at Rich's department store in Atlanta.

Robinson pressured Nixon to reach out to King and help secure his release. Nixon demurred. Kennedy, on the other hand, leapt into action—calling King's wife and playing a role in the leader's release.

"I owe a great debt of gratitude to Senator Kennedy and his family for this," said King upon his release. "I don't know the details of it, but naturally, I'm very happy to know of Senator Kennedy's concern."

(Nixon dismissed Kennedy's move, telling Robinson it was "what our good friend Joe Louis called a 'grandstand play.'")

Despite Nixon's unwillingness to act on behalf of King, Robinson stuck with him in 1960. (In his later years, he ascribed that decision to "something to do with stubbornness.") But Robinson's vision of Nixon winning a majority of the Black vote was badly dashed that November; Nixon won only one in three Black voters, a showing that contributed to his narrow loss at the hands of Kennedy.

Four years later, Republicans nominated ultraconservative Barry Goldwater for president. (Robinson had been for moderate New York governor Nelson Rockefeller.) During that campaign, Goldwater had, infamously, said that the GOP was not going to win the Black vote as a "bloc," adding: "We ought to go hunting where the ducks are." That statement, Robinson wrote Nixon, "will be a Republican policy until someone other than Goldwater vigorously denies that the Republican party is not interested in the Negro vote."

Again, Nixon did nothing—perhaps with an eye on 1968 (and the Southern strategy he would run successfully).

While Robinson voted for Lyndon Johnson in 1964, he didn't abandon the Republican Party. "The sooner there is a strong two-party system in New York as well as nationwide, the sooner we get our rights," wrote Robinson to Rockefeller in 1965.

The 1968 campaign run by Nixon was dismissed as "racist" by Robinson. That contest was dominated by Nixon's so-called Southern strategy—an effort to court white Southern voters by playing to their racial animus. Robinson didn't have that much longer to live; he was in failing health during the 1972 campaign but still managed to pen once last letter to President Nixon.

"Because I want so much to be a part of and to love this nation as I once did, I hope you will take another look at where we are going and be the president who leads the nation to accept difficult but necessary action, rather than one who fosters division," wrote Robinson. Nixon never responded. Robinson died October 24, 1972.

———

At a press conference in June 1972, a reporter named Cliff Evans from RKO General Broadcasting asked the president a seemingly innocuous question: to name his favorite baseball players. Nixon immediately named five players: Ted Williams, Jackie Robinson, Lou Gehrig, Mickey Mantle, and Stan Musial.

Evans followed up by asking Nixon "as the nation's number-one baseball fan, would you be willing to name your all-time baseball team?"

The next day, as Washington baseball historian Fred Frommer has documented, Nixon OK'd an effort by the CIA to block the FBI's investigation into the Watergate break-in. It was the formal start of the cover-up that led to Nixon's eventual resignation. "It became known as the 'smoking gun' tape, and it helped lead to his resignation two years later," wrote Frommer.

Nixon took to the challenge with gusto—although it was no easy endeavor. "It was about as hard a task as I have ever undertaken," he later told Evans. "To select a team of nine was just too hard for me to do." (He eventually turned in a three-thousand-word story detailing his picks; it ran on July 2, 1972.)

For the task, the president enlisted the help of his son-in-law, David Eisenhower, who had worked for the Washington Senators in 1970 before moving into the White House.

As Nixon recounted:

It was one of the most enjoyable things I've done because we had a fine afternoon with rain that afternoon at Camp David and we couldn't go outside. So we pored over these numbers and these names and all the fascinating stories of the great men of baseball for two or three hours.

The following day, H. R. Haldeman, Nixon's White House chief of staff, recorded this entry in his audio diary: "The president all cranked up about his baseball all-time great story. Wants [White House press secretary Ron] Ziegler to figure out how to handle it as a Nixon byline. He apparently dictated it yesterday at Camp David and has figured out a super all-time team. One prewar, one postwar, one for the National League, one for the American League."

As Haldeman noted, Nixon—and Eisenhower—wound up going well beyond the initial brief. They split the era into two: one running from 1925—"which was the year when I was twelve years old and first began to read sports pages avidly and follow baseball," Nixon explained—until 1945, and the other running from 1945 to 1970.

And, Nixon didn't just choose his favorite starting nine. No, he formed the team like it would be put together in real life—two catchers, five pitchers, as well as backup infielders and outfielders.

"Working out all the little details of which relief pitcher the American League prewar should be on, and all that sort of stuff," Haldeman said on June 27. "Kind of fascinating and not just a little amusing."

That same day Nixon, with an assist from Haldeman, barraged Ziegler, his press secretary, to tell him who should be the prewar American League relief pitcher.

"The president said to ask you who the relief pitcher was for the American League prewar," Haldeman told Ziegler via phone.

Ziegler had three nominees: "Either Hugh Casey, or Mace Brown, or Doc Crandall. Now I have their games won-and-lost and so forth you may want to look over."

Ziegler relayed the details to Haldeman, who then passed them on to Nixon.

Nixon also picked—like I said, he got *really* into this—a best hitter (Ted Williams), a best pitcher (Sandy Koufax), a best outfielder (Joe DiMaggio), a best base runner (Maury Wills), a best all-around athlete (Jackie Robinson), and a most courageous player (Lou Gehrig).

On Gehrig, Nixon was effusive in an interview with Evans. "Well the most courageous baseball player has got to be Lou Gehrig," he said. "Of course, his courage has been made immortal by the motion picture about him, which brings tears to your eyes even when you see it a second time, and I have seen it twice." (Nixon was presumably referring to the 1942 film *Pride of the Yankees*, a biopic of the Iron Horse and his struggles with ALS; the movie featured many legendary ballplayers—including Babe Ruth and Bill Dickey—playing themselves.)

Nixon recounted that he and Gehrig's wife, Eleanor, had been in regular contact. "His wife writes me from time to time," said Nixon—noting that Eleanor Gehrig had written him "a letter and said that she admired the courage I had demonstrated" in his decision-making on Vietnam.

The president also singled out Red Schoendienst, the great St. Louis Cardinals second baseman (and later manager) for special praise.

He told Evans that Schoendienst had the "best arm of modern times." But, Nixon quickly added, that wasn't why he admired Schoendienst so much. Instead it was the fact that Schoendienst had contracted tuberculosis and managed to recover well enough to continue to play baseball.

"That meant a great deal to me because my older brother died of tuberculosis when I was in my second year of college," said Nixon. "And he had it for five years and that left a mark on my family, on our family. And to see a man get tuberculosis and then come back again and play again in the big leagues, I thought that demonstrated courage at its highest."

(Harold Nixon died in 1933, at age twenty-four, of tuberculosis.)

Why did the lineup project appeal so much to Nixon? "Nixon's mind collected data in the way that later generations would engage in rotisserie baseball," historian Tim Naftali told Frommer. "This was natural to him. Whether it was learning statistics of his favorite ballplayer's, or figuring out who might become secretary of state of some part of the Midwest, that's how his mind worked."

While Nixon relished the effort, it was not all that well received. "When you regard [Nixon] as a sportswriter, you can't help but feeling that he really ought to go back to be President of the United States," wrote *New York Times* columnist Red Smith. "That's a dreadful, difficult line to write." Smith went on: "Above all, he's got to cover the assignment. He was asked to pick his all-time all-star baseball team and he blew it. He picked four teams, with spares."

And Smith wasn't done. He insisted that the list reeked of political calculation by the president. "He has, therefore, saluted young and old, white and black, Latin and Nordic, left-hander and right-hander, Catholic and WASP, Jew and American Indian (Early Wynn). He has chosen fastball pitchers, curveball pitchers, a master of the knuckleball (Hoyt Wilhelm), and even a specialist in a politically unappetizing spitball (Burleigh Grimes)."

Not everyone was a critic. Casey Stengel, the famed Yankee manager who made Nixon's list, said that "it's very nice the President is so well versed in sports with so many things he has to do in his sojourn as president and being international and all he has to take care of so many countries it's an honor he chose me."

(Stengel was a *great* baseball manager; he was, um, less gifted as a wordsmith—although he was very quotable at times.)

Nixon was unbowed by the criticism. In addition to his (very) detailed picks for the all-time baseball teams, Nixon also responded to Evans's question about the most exciting sporting events he had ever seen.

Acknowledging that "I haven't really had time to collect my thoughts," Nixon plunged in any way—naming two moments from baseball games past.

The first was Bill Mazeroski's seventh game-winning home run for the Pittsburgh Pirates in the team's 1960 World Series against the mighty New York Yankees.

"I later talked to the owner of the Pirates about that home run and I asked him what his energy was like," Nixon recounted to Evans. "He said it was so awesome because the Pirates hadn't won—they had not only not won a pennant but they had not won the World Series for perhaps a generation . . . he said the whole stadium—the Pirates stadium—stood up and simply cheered for five minutes after Mazeroski hit that grand slam and won the World Series for them."

(Nixon got that wrong; Mazeroski's game-and-series-winning home run wasn't a grand slam. Mazeroski actually led off the bottom of the ninth inning with the winning homer.)

Nixon's other most memorable moment was Bobby Thomson's 1951 home run—the "Shot Heard 'Round the World"—that delivered the National League pennant to the New York Giants over their hated rivals, the Brooklyn Dodgers.

"When the Giants came into August [they were] twelve games or fourteen games out of first place," remembered Nixon. "They caught the Dodgers at the end of the season and Bobby Thomson clobbered that grand-slammer to beat the Dodgers and put the Giants over the top."

(Again, Nixon's memory failed him here. Thomson hit a three-run home run to beat the Dodgers.)

Nixon didn't see either of those moments in person, though. (He strangely told Evans that he had followed the Mazeroski home run "through the communications medium.") But he was at the October 2, 1963, World Series game between the Yankees and Dodgers when star pitcher Sandy Koufax struck out fifteen batters.

"I remember one thing in particular that day," said Nixon. "As he neared or at 14 [strikeouts], a batter was up and he had two strikes out and he hit a slow roller down the third base line and everyone in the stadium was [hoping the ball was foul]. Because otherwise he would have been out and it would not have been a strikeout. The ball just trickled foul and [Koufax] struck him out on the next pitch."

Nixon was, without question, a genuine fan of baseball—and sports more generally. He loved the stats, the personalities, and the drama of the games. But, he was also a politician at root—and was not above using sports to achieve his political goals.

Nixon body man Dwight Chapin insisted in his memoirs that "unlike most politicians, he attended sporting events, not for political posturing but because he loved the game, whatever game it was...No matter what he did, such as attending a sporting event for the pure pleasure of it, he was endlessly bumping up against a hostile press."

The history of Nixon's use of sports—and even Chapin's own account—however, dispute the idea that Nixon was into sports only for the fun of it.

As Joseph Paul Vasquez wrote in an academic paper published in the *Journal of Global Security Studies*, "Nixon used football during the Vietnam War to align himself with hardline traditionalists amid increasing antiwar protests."

In October 1969, for example, Nixon was at a game between the Miami Dolphins and the Oakland Raiders—the game ended in a 20–20 tie—where he received a standing ovation. That appearance, on October 4, came just ten days before a massive national antiwar rally known as the Moratorium to End the War in Vietnam.

Nixon's trip to the NFL game was the culmination of something he and his administration called "National Unity Week," an overt effort to leverage sports (and Nixon's popularity among fans) to overshadow the coming protest.

Of Unity Week, Tex McCrary, a communications consultant to the president, said: "It could be celebrated with pro-Administration propaganda" at the football games, adding: "Perhaps all games could have a red, white and blue theme or all halftimes begin with 'God Bless America' and end with 'This Land is Your Land.'"

Later that year, Nixon turned up at a college football game between the University of Texas and the University of Arkansas—both of whom were unbeaten. As Vasquez wrote: "Nixon attended the nationally televised game encouraged by aides who thought it would help him solidify his Southern support."

The game was played December 6, 1969, in Fayetteville. Nixon arrived late and spent the first half watching the game—which was touted by ABC as the "Game of the Century"—from the stands. At halftime, Nixon went up to the ABC television booth. (A future president, George H. W. Bush, then a Texas congressman, also attended the game.)

Politics hung heavy over the game as the first draft lottery for the war in Vietnam had been held five days prior. A protest was organized at the game, with a huge peace sign unveiled on a hillside next to the stadium. Nixon saw the protest but ABC never showed it on air.

Nixon played the role of analyst, insisting that despite the fact that Arkansas led at halftime, he expected Texas to pull it out. (Future president Bill Clinton was watching the game on TV and never forgave Nixon for picking against his Razorbacks. He was far from alone; it's estimated that 50 million people tuned in, a staggering number given that only 58 million American households had television sets at that point.)

Texas came from behind to win 15–14, and Nixon made his way to the locker room after the game to present a plaque to Longhorn coach Darrell Royal declaring the team the national champions.

A magazine named the *Partisan Review* once wrote of Nixon: "The trouble...isn't that he watches football but that he makes such an obvious and cheap political gesture of it."

That decision was not without controversy. Penn State's football team also went undefeated in that 1969 season—and many Nittany Lions fans took umbrage with Nixon wading into the college football world.

"It was a terrific idea, except for the fact that we received ninety thousand angry letters and telegrams from Penn State fans because their team had been undefeated for several seasons and had an equally strong argument for the top ranking," wrote Chapin, the Nixon aide. "Penn State Coach Joe Paterno, during a commencement address at Penn State in 1973, said about Nixon: 'I've wondered how President Nixon could know so little about Watergate in 1973 and so much about college football in 1969.'"

Three days after his trip to Arkansas, Nixon traveled to New York City to be honored by the National Football Foundation.

"I simply want to set the record straight with regard to my football qualifications," Nixon said at the start of his speech. "This is a candid, open administration. We believe in telling the truth about football and everything. I can only say that as far as this award is concerned, that it is certainly a small step for the National Football Foundation and a small step for football, but it is a giant leap for a man who never even made the team at Whittier."

Nixon went on to note that he kept portraits of three presidents in the Cabinet Room: Dwight Eisenhower, Woodrow Wilson, and Teddy Roosevelt. And that while all three were very different as men and leaders, they had football in common.

Explained Nixon:

What does this mean, this common interest in football of Presidents, of leaders, of people generally? It means a competitive spirit. It means, also, to me, the ability and the determination to be able to lose and then come back and try again, to sit on the bench and then come back. It means basically the character, the drive, the pride, the teamwork, the feeling of being in a cause bigger than yourself.

As the midterm election year dawned, Nixon's thoughts turned more and more to politics—and the way in which sports could be used to his and Republicans' benefits.

"Nixon spent the second half of 1970 working to manipulate sports for the benefit of himself and his supporters in the midterm election," wrote author Nicholas Evan Sarantakes. "These efforts dominated all his other interests in the athletic world that year."

When Vince Lombardi, the legendary Green Bay Packers coach and an idol of Nixon's, died in September of that year, Nixon interrupted a state dinner in California to address the passing of the legend.

"Vince Lombardi believed in fundamentals," said Nixon. "On the football field this meant blocking and tackling. Off the field it meant his church, his home, his friends, his family. He built his life—as he built his teams—around basic values and that is why his greatness as a coach was more than matched by his greatness as a human being."

The subtext had become text. Football was politics and politics was life. If you loved Lombardi then you loved a certain set of values and issues that represented Republicans—and Nixon in particular.

Nixon's White House was absolutely intent on driving that idea—in every possible venue. In August 1970, Dwight Chapin, Nixon's body man asked two other Nixon aides to put together a list of major college football games in states where the president was slated to visit in his travels for the midterms.

"Most of the states that have target Senate races will not have nationally televised games," reported Bud Wilkinson, one of the aides tasked with the project.

The lone campaign appearance Nixon wound up making in an athletic context was October 18 in Green Bay, Wisconsin. The event was to honor Bart Starr, the legendary Packers QB.

It was a no-brainer for Nixon, who idolized Starr and saw an opportunity to promote the party's prospects in Wisconsin.

As the *Milwaukee Journal-Sentinel* editorial board wrote of the visit:

> As a football fan, President Nixon will be responding genuinely to a nonpolitical lure when he sets foot briefly in Wisconsin Saturday, to appear at the festivities honoring Bart Starr in Green Bay. He will be politicking nevertheless, for it is no coincidence that this trip comes at the height of the nationwide campaigning to elect governors and congressmen.

Nixon, perhaps wary of being seen as overtly political, was careful to walk the line during his remarks. "As some of you may have heard, we're in the midst of another political campaign in this country, but if there's one thing that is nonpolitical, it's being for Bart Starr tonight," he said.

Nixon's office was also highly attuned to the potential blowback caused by associating him too closely with sports. As Sarantakes noted:

Despite Nixon's success with sports, or perhaps because of the Penn State backlash, some members of the White House staff worried about the image he was projecting to the American people. The president's men were afraid that he might end up stereotyped as a man obsessed with sports in general, and football in particular, the way Eisenhower was with golf.

That was not the prevailing view, however. "I think it helps many relate to the president," said Nixon adviser Herb Klein. "I think the American public wants very much to look at the President as a strong leader, which it does, but I think it also enjoys a feeling of warmth toward the President as such comes from sharing a mutual hobby or other sports."

———

One of the most famous—or, more accurately, infamous—stories about Nixon and sports goes like this: During a Washington Redskins playoff game against the San Francisco 49ers on the day after Christmas in 1971, then coach George Allen allowed Nixon to call a play.

It's not at all clear that was what happened, however.

Here's what we *do* know happened. At the end of the first half in that game—played at Candlestick Park in San Francisco—the Redskins had the ball on the 49ers' 8-yard line. The Redskins were leading 10–3 and trying to score another touchdown (or field goal, at least) before the half.

Allen called a play—a reverse to a wide receiver. The 49ers sniffed it out, bringing down the receiver behind the line of scrimmage for a thirteen-yard loss. The subsequent field goal attempt was blocked.

The Redskins never regained the momentum, losing the game 24–20. Afterward, Allen said that the failed reverse was "the game's big, big play... when we came away without any points."

Here's what else we know: Earlier in that season, Nixon had visited the Redskins practice facility—at Allen's behest—as a sort of morale booster following a midseason defeat that left their record at 5-2.

As Jennifer Allen, the daughter of the Redskins coach, wrote in 2002 of the visit:

Nixon spoke with many players, calling them by their first names, and impressing everyone with his knowledge of their individual histories—citing various players' alma maters, where they were born, and where they were rated in the NFL statistically. My father then offered the President a turn at the controls—allowing him to call an offensive play. The President called a reverse. That day, in practice, the play succeeded quite well.

(Nixon and Allen had first met decades earlier—at an NCAA banquet in New York City in 1951. Nixon was a congressman and the guest speaker of the night. Allen was the coach of the Whittier College Poets, Nixon's alma mater. As Jennifer Allen wrote: "They then exchanged a quick discourse on Xs and Os and Arrows, and soon after became apolitical, football loving friends.")

So, we *know* that (1) Nixon and Allen were friends, (2) Nixon had visited the Redskins in the middle of that 1971 season, (3) during that visit he had called a reverse, and, finally, (4) Allen had called a reverse at the end of the first half of the Redskins playoff game against the 49ers.

But did Nixon actually call in the play—either before the game or during it? That's a *much* harder question to answer.

One of the game's announcers immediately seized on the Nixon angle when the play went south. "That must have been a play Richard Nixon called in to George Allen," he said.

In the postgame locker room, one player said that Allen had been giving an "executive order" to run the reverse.

The idea that Nixon had, in fact, called the play into Allen began to solidify in a column by legendary *Washington Post* sports columnist Shirley Povich, written two weeks after the Skins loss.

It was on the eve of the Redskins-49ers game that President Nixon got on a hot line at the White House and confided to Allen one of his hot ideas for beating the 49ers . . .

"George," said the President of the United States. "I'd like to see you use Roy Jefferson on that end-around. It should be a long gainer for you." Quick as a flash, Allen understood that the President was talking about a flanker reverse...According to the explanations offered later in some circles, for Allen it came down to whether or not his name would stay on the White House guest list.

In the mid 1990s, the *Syracuse Post-Standard*'s Sean Kirst did a deep dive into the play—including talking to Billy Kilmer, who was the QB for the Redskins at the time. And Kilmer insisted that Nixon had, in fact, called the play.

"A touchdown might have won it," recalls quarterback Billy Kilmer. "When it came in, (we) thought, 'Damn, they really called it.'"
Kilmer had direct knowledge of Nixon's role in the play. During a private skull session earlier that week, the phone rang and Allen handed it to Kilmer. Nixon was on the other end. He suggested the 49ers might be fooled by a double-reverse, a play Kilmer says didn't exist in the playbook.

But, according to Marv Levy, an assistant on the Redskins staff and later the legendary coach of the Buffalo Bills, the origin of the play was even more convoluted.
Levy told Kirst that it was actually *Allen* who had initially given the play to Nixon—and floated the idea of him suggesting that the Redskins run it—"both for strategic reason and as a gesture of friendship. If it worked Nixon would come off smelling like roses. So it was presented to the team, Levy said, as a presidential request."
Added Levy: "[George] wanted the president to look very sage."
The opposite, of course, wound up occurring. "Afterward, I remember chuckling among ourselves about it," Levy told Kirst. "George gave the play to the president, then it didn't work."
Almost a decade after the initial play call, Allen and Nixon met up in San Clemente, California, which was Nixon's Western White House after he left the presidency amid the scandal of Watergate. (The two men were close friends and saw each other quite often.)

As Jennifer Allen, who was at this particular meeting, recalled:

I remember how the two men greeted one another with an informal handshake and hug. I also remember how I immediately stepped away to allow them their time alone together.

Since that day, I have often wondered why neither my father nor Nixon ever denied or upheld the truth behind "Nixon's Play." Did Nixon really call in the play? And if he did, would my father, known as a do-it-my-way coach, really listen to the advice of an outsider? Maybe neither wanted to take credit for something that failed. Maybe both wanted to protect the other from taking the blame. Or maybe Nixon and my father were simply, like so many others, enamored with the evolution of the story itself.

These were not the questions I considered asking my father or the former President on that late summer day. Just let them be, I thought, as I watched them, the two former leaders, strolling, side-by-side, along the cliffs above the Pacific at sunset.

Both men are long since dead—Nixon in 1994 and Allen in 1990. Which means we may never ultimately find the answer to the "Nixon reverse."

"I'm a Ford, Not a Lincoln"

A Golf Game That Made Bob Hope and Chevy
Chase Famous…

The All American

It was time to get rid of Spiro Agnew. That much was clear.

The former Maryland governor turned vice president had been laboring under a Department of Justice inquiry looking into his income taxes and potential political corruption for months. It was over—and everyone knew it.

Agnew made it official October 10, 1973—striking a deal that did the one thing he really wanted: kept him out of prison.

That problem solved itself—but created a new one for President Richard Nixon: How do you fill a job that is simultaneously utterly quotidian and one heart attack removed from the presidency?

Agnew had prided himself on being indispensable—by being Nixon's Nixon: the guy utterly unafraid of punching whoever needed punching whenever the people above him said to do it.

Given Agnew's spectacular failure, Nixon thought better of finding, well, another Agnew. (To be clear: It's not at all obvious to me that there was *another* Spiro Agnew kicking around out there.)

Instead, he cast his eye in the exact opposite direction. He needed someone likable, easygoing and, above all, steady. Nixon well knew that whoever he picked had to stay in the job—and help steady the slipping ship of state. Plus, he needed someone whom the House and Senate would vote to confirm without much fanfare.

Enter Gerald Ford: Republican congressman, House GOP leader, and, perhaps most important for Nixon, football hero.

Hell, Ford had turned down pro offers from the Green Bay Packers and Chicago Bears to go to law school and prepare for a career in politics. He knew the importance of being on a team—and following orders.

"He learned to listen to teaching and perform his assigned role, that a team is greater than the individual player, and that the best players may not get all the glory," wrote Ford biographer James Cannon.

Ford was, in a word, good. In another word: all-American. Ford was exactly what Nixon needed—and Nixon knew it.

For Ford, the vice presidency made a certain logical sense—the next step forward in a life defined by ever-mounting successes.

It had not always been thus, however.

Born Lesley King in Nebraska, he moved to Michigan, took the last name Ford (his mother remarried) and "caught the energy of the Detroit Lions and the Michigan Wolverines," according to historian Douglas Brinkley, who wrote a biography of Ford for the *American Presidents* series.

Ford's father—from whom his mother divorced when the boy was just sixteen days old—was an alcoholic and would beat his wife. (The impetus for her decision to leave apparently was when Ford's father threatened her with a knife shortly after the future president was born.)

Football provided Ford with a refuge from the turmoil of his background—and he took to it with fervor. "Football became a religion to Ford," said Brinkley. "He worked at being an athlete nonstop. He had wide shoulders and will...That makes you quite effective at being an offensive lineman."

Ford was such a gifted player that he was part of the 1932–1933 Michigan team that won the national championship. He wound up being named the MVP of that team in a vote by his peers, which was an unusual occurrence for an offensive lineman. (The award typically went to players at the so-called skill positions of quarterback, wide receiver, and running back.)

Ford was drawn to all aspects of the sports—up to and including "The Victors," the famed fight song of the University of Michigan football team. "That fight song became his amazing grace," said Brinkley. "Just the sound of that song lifted up his spirits almost as if he was in a religious ceremony."

During his time at Michigan, Ford made one of the most important friendships of his life—with Willis Ward.

Ward, a track and football star in his native Detroit, tried out—and made—the Michigan football team in his sophomore year in 1933. (He and Ford were roommates during their time at the university.) He was only the second Black athlete to do so. (The previous one—George Jewett—played forty-three years prior on a Michigan team that had no head coach.)

In a game the following year—1934—against Georgia Tech, that school's football coach and athletic director insisted his team would not take the field if Ward was allowed to play. (The athletic director—W. A. Alexander—had sent a letter to Michigan AD Fielding Yost the previous year expressing his views that his team wouldn't play Michigan if Ward suited up.)

As the game approached—and a rumor spread through campus that Michigan might accede to Alexander's wishes—students rallied behind Ward. More than 1,500 students signed a petition expressing their belief that Ward should be allowed to play and several hundred said they planned to storm the field and prevent the game from being played if Ward wasn't on the field.

None of that mattered to Yost, who ordered that Ward be sat for the game. Ford protested vehemently and threatened to sit out. He was convinced to play by Ward.

As he wrote in a 1999 op-ed in the *New York Times*, the episode changed him.

Ford wrote that Ward himself opted not to play: "His sacrifice led me to question how educational administrators could capitulate to raw prejudice." He added that his continued support for affirmative action on college campuses was rooted in his experiences with Ward.

"Do we really want to risk turning back the clock to an era when the Willis Wards were isolated and penalized for the color of their skin, their economic standing or national ancestry?" asked Ford.

It's not at all clear, however, whether Ford's version of events is the right one. In 1936, Ward tried to make the Olympic team in track, but suggested he was still bothered by what had happened in his senior year at Michigan.

"[The] Georgia Tech game killed me," he said. "I frankly felt [the Olympics] would not let black athletes compete. Having gone through the Tech experience, it seemed an easy thing for them to say 'Well we just won't run 'em if Hitler insists.' It was like any bad experience—you can't forget it but you don't talk about it. It hurts."

Two decades after the Georgia Tech game, Ward was more sanguine. He wrote about how he exchanged a hug with Yost (the coach and athletic director) after a game against Princeton. "It was the first time he had ever hugged a colored player—when he hugged me," Ward wrote. "He often related that in his 35 years of coaching football that I was the greatest tackle he had ever seen."

Ward, like his roommate Ford, would go on to have an interest in politics. He ran unsuccessfully as a Republican for Congress in 1956 and was a backer of Dwight Eisenhower's presidential campaigns.

"The President's civil rights program, shelved by Democrats in the recent session of Congress, deserves the unstinting support of all conscientious voters," Ward wrote in 1958.

Decades later, the Michigan legislature formally named October 12, 2012, "Willis Ward Day" to commemorate the seventy-eighth anniversary of his historic benching against Georgia Tech as well as "his many accomplishments, steadfast character, and significant contributions to our state."

———

While there were poetic moments for Ford on the gridiron at Michigan, the life of a college athlete in the 1930s was nothing like we think of it today.

Most important, the Big Ten—of which Michigan was and is a part—did not offer scholarships, which meant that student-athletes had to pay their own way through school.

As Ford wrote in a 1974 essay for *Sports Illustrated*:

So the hotshot center from Grand Rapids came to live at Michigan in a third floor 10-by-10 room way in the back of the cheapest rooming house I could find. I shared the rent ($4 a week) with a basketball player from my hometown. We each had a desk and a bed, which pretty much exhausted the floor space, and there was one small window between us.

Ford later wrote of those teams—and the parallels to politics:

If you don't win elections, you don't play, so the importance of winning is more drastic in that field. In athletics and in most other worthwhile pursuits, first place is the manifestation of a desire to excel, and how else can you achieve anything? I certainly do not feel we achieved very much as a Michigan football team in 1934. And I can assure you we had more fun on those championship teams in 1932–33.

Ford's strong senior year—albeit on a team with a poor record—got him an invite to the East-West Shrine game in San Francisco.

(Ford recounted that he got the invite largely thanks to Northwestern coach Dick Hanley. In a game earlier in the year against Hanley's team, Ford had shut down Rip Whalen, Northwestern's star defensive player. Whalen said, "Ford was the best blocking center I ever played against." Said Ford: "I still cherish that remark.")

Ford was one of two centers to make the East team. But the starter—Colgate's George Akerstrom—got hurt in the first two minutes of the game. Ford was called into action—playing offense and defense for the remainder of the game.

When the game concluded, the players were offered two choices: take the train home or take a free trip to Los Angeles to see Hollywood. Ford chose the latter option.

On the train ride from San Francisco to LA, Curly Lambeau, Ford later said, the famed coach of the Green Bay Packers "sat with me the whole way... and he asked me to sign with the Packers. I told him I'd think about it."

Later that summer, Ford played in another all-star game, this one in Chicago. His team played the Chicago Bears and lost 5–0. (Yes, back in those days, the college football all-stars played pro teams in exhibitions.)

Immediately after the game, Ford got his official offer from Lambeau's Packers: $200 a game for fourteen games. The Detroit Lions quickly matched the offer.

Ford was on the horns of a dilemma: play professional football or pursue his interest in the law (and, eventually, politics).

Today that's a no-brainer. Everyone—or damn near everyone—chooses professional sports. But as Ford's contract offers make clear, things were very different back then.

"Pro football did not have the allure it has now and though my interest was piqued I didn't lose any sleep over my decision," Ford wrote in 1974, when he was serving as vice president.

He went back to school. In 1935, Ford was hired to be the assistant football coach and boxing coach at Yale University—where he also pursued a law degree.

"When Ducky Pond, the Yale coach, came to Ann Arbor... to ask me to be on his staff at New Haven, I saw the chance to realize two dreams at once—to stay in football and to pursue a long-nurtured aspiration for law school," Ford would later write.

According to the *Yale Daily News*, Ford made $2,400 in his first years—serving as assistant line coach, junior varsity coach, and scout.

"Of boxing, I knew next to nothing," he later wrote. "No, that's not right. I knew absolutely nothing."

Ford, being Ford, attacked the problem with hard work. While working at his father's paint factory the summer before heading to Yale, he went to the local YMCA three days a week to "get punched around by the

Y's boxing coach." Added Ford: "I didn't get good but I got good enough to fool the Yale freshmen."

Ford's twin dreams—football and law school—were not immediately realized. Academic advisers at Yale were concerned that Ford wouldn't be able to handle his full-time coaching duties and be a law student.

It wasn't until 1938 that Ford was allowed to apply to the law school—and even then he took only two classes.

That same year Ford was promoted to head junior varsity coach in charge of scouting. That position came with a 33 percent salary increase. (That year, Ford's scouting nearly helped Yale beat his alma mater—but Michigan triumphed 15–13.)

Ford's life, like those of so many young men his age, took a decided turn the year after he graduated from Yale in 1941. In the wake of the Japanese attack on Pearl Harbor, Ford joined the U.S. Navy.

After a brief period of service aboard the USS *Monterrey*, a light aircraft carrier, Ford was sent to a Navy Pre-Flight School in California and assigned to the athletic department. He coached the football team, among other duties.

"Gerald Ford's greatest accomplishment of World War II is being an athletic director," said Brinkley. "He comes out of the war as the athlete-coach extraordinaire."

———

Ford actively sought to downplay his athletic prowess because he worried about being cast as a good athlete with a questionable intellect.

He wasn't wrong. Lyndon Johnson, the consummate politician-as-bully, was heard to say that Ford had "played too many games without a helmet."

Ford later wrote that "Lyndon got a lot of mileage out of that quote." But he wasn't above making fun of himself. Speaking at the Gridiron Club dinner one year—a white tie and tails event of the city's elite, Ford said that Johnson was wrong about him not wearing a helmet, pulling out "my old leather bonnet" and plopping it on his head right then and there.

As Shepherd Campbell and Peter Landau wrote in *Presidential Lies*:

You wouldn't have known he was an accomplished athlete—not from the way the President of the United States from 1974 to 1977 was portrayed on television and in the press. Ford was depicted as a bumbling, uncoordinated man who had stumbled his way onto the world stage (as he once did coming off an airplane on an official visit to Europe). Newspapers featured pictures of Ford when he took tumbles on the ski slopes or tried to hit his golf ball out of improbable lies in trees and bushes. And countless articles were published describing how Ford had peppered the galleries with wild shots during golf tournaments.

Responsibility for the caricature—and it was, to be clear, a caricature—lay at the feet (or, more accurately, mouths) of two men: Bob Hope and Chevy Chase.

Hope, who made it a point to play golf with every president, was a regular partner of the president. But he was merciless in his portrayal of Ford's golf game.

"One of my most prized possessions is the Purple Heart I received for all the golf I've played with him," Hope said at one point.

At another: "You can recognize him on the course because his golf cart has a red cross painted on top."

While Hope was an established comedian—and roaster of the high and mighty—Chase was, in the mid-1970s, an up-and-coming comic. That is, until he began to portray Ford on *Saturday Night Live*.

Chase's Ford was—to put it plainly—a bumbling idiot.

In one early sketch—which carried the words "This is not a good impression of Gerald Ford" on-screen—Chase mimicked an Oval Office address by the president.

He sneezed into his tie. He mistook a full glass of water for a telephone receiver. He hung up phones on the wrong receivers. (Telephone humor was all the rage in the '70s.) He "accidentally" banged his head on his desk. He fumbled with charts. And on and on it went. (OK, it was only three minutes long, but it seemed a lot longer.)

In another sketch, Ford bumped into a flag on his way to the podium.

He repeated the phrase "First, may I thank you all for being here" several times. He poured himself a glass of water and then tried to drink from an empty glass. You can imagine where the sketch went from there.

And then there was the 1976 debate sketch. (Dan Aykroyd played Jimmy Carter.) Asked by a debate moderator—played by Jane Curtin—a detailed question on fiscal policy, a confused Chase-as-Ford responded: "It was my understanding that there would be no math."

Memes didn't exist back in 1976 but, well, Ford had become a meme. The best athlete ever to occupy the White House became a bumbling fool in the eyes of the public.

Ford did little to help his own case.

Upon arriving in Austria for a European trip, the president was accompanying his wife, Betty, down the steps of Air Force One on a rainy day when he lost his footing and tumbled down the last few stairs. He regained his footing to shake hands with the Austrian chancellor. "I am sorry I tumbled in," Ford joked.

Later that same day, Ford fell again—emerging from a meeting with Egyptian president Anwar Sadat. "He made what an aide termed a misstep at the top of a steep flight of stairs," reported the *New York Times*. "The aide, Col. Robert Blake of the Air Force, said that Mr. Ford put out his arms and caught himself. Newsmen present said that Mr. Sadat, who was walking with him, grabbed him, preventing a fall."

Ford made more substantive slip-ups as well.

Debating Carter in October 1976, he asserted: "There is no Soviet domination of Eastern Europe and there never will be under a Ford administration," a patently false statement given Soviet control over much of the region.

Max Frankel, a *New York Times* reporter, interrupted. "Did I understand you to say, sir, that the Russians are not using Eastern Europe as their own sphere of influence?"

Ford, seemingly unaware of his mistake, doubled down. "I don't believe that the Romanians consider themselves dominated by the Soviet Union," he said. "I don't believe that the Poles consider themselves dominated by the Soviet Union."

(What Ford apparently meant to say is that America did not formally recognize or accept the Soviet dominion in eastern Europe.)

In a vacuum, that gaffe may not have meant all that much. Ford could have argued that he simply misstated his point and be done with it. But the caricature of him as a bit of a buffoon—fueled by Hope's jokes about his golf game and Chase's impersonation of him—was already out in the ether. The "Soviet domination" gaffe affirmed for many people that Ford was what popular media painted him to be: a dumb jock.

While Ford often downplayed his considerable athletic successes, he wrote eloquently about the importance of sports—and competition—to the American experiment.

In a 1974 essay in *Sports Illustrated* titled "In Defense of the Competitive Urge," Ford saw football—his sport of choice—as uniquely suited to politics, the career he pursued when his playing days were done. Wrote Ford:

> I know it's easy to find similarities in politics. How you can't make it in either field without teamwork and great leadership. How you attract grandstand quarterbacks by the droves. In football you hear them during and after the game. In politics we hear them 30 seconds after our last speech. Or during it. Most grandstand quarterbacks have never played either game, yet are the loudest and most knowledgeable critics. The thick skin developed in football pays off.

Ford was no "grandstand quarterback." He played center—one of the least celebrated but most important positions on the field. The center calls the blocking scheme for the whole offensive line, in addition to hiking the ball to the quarterback. But centers are not, typically, well-known—spending most of their time in the trenches, making holes for and protecting the more glamorous players.

That suited Ford just fine. He had been raised on the idea of the sum being greater than the whole of its parts—and one's work being worth it whether or not you were properly recognized for it.

It was that selflessness—or lack of the need for a spotlight—that made Ford such an unlikely success in politics as well.

He is the only president to have never been elected president nor vice president. He was chosen for those jobs in large part because he was someone who didn't seek them. He was as close to a normal person as you will ever find making it to the upper reaches of politics—someone genuinely committed to seeing the team succeed even if he didn't get the credit for making it happen.

That's not to say that Ford didn't care about recognition. He did. "When you stop winning they not only start booing, they start forgetting," he once wrote.

But Ford was in many ways the anti-Nixon. Whereas Nixon believed he alone was the answer to the nation's problems—and, as a result, relentlessly sought to consolidate power within the White House—Ford was a team player, leaning on his Cabinet and other officials in his administration to a shared victory (or defeat).

For such an accomplished athlete, Ford is remembered most in the popular imagination for a sport he wasn't terribly good at: golf.

Some—maybe much—of Ford's reputation as the duffer-in chief came courtesy of his longtime friend comedian Bob Hope, who had a whole cadre of jokes on the president's golf game.

There was "It's not hard to find Gerry Ford on a golf course—you just follow the wounded."

And: "Whenever I play with him [President Ford], I usually try to make it a foursome—the President, myself, a paramedic and a faith healer."

Ford, as he did with most things, took the ribbing in stride. Mostly—at least when it came to his golf game—because he knew it was true.

"He had real power," recalled historian Richard Norton Smith of Ford's golf prowess. "But his game tended to break down when it came to putting. He never really got good at the finer points of the game."

Amy Alcott, a legendary LPGA player who played several rounds with

Ford after he had left office, agreed with that assessment. "He was not that good a player but he was very engaging," she said.

For Ford, golf was a missed opportunity. As a kid, his parents had urged him to caddy at the local country club to make some money for the family—but the future president refused. "He always felt like he had short-changed himself," said Smith.

Regardless of the reason, it's beyond debate that Ford was, well, a bad golfer. Think of Charles Barkley here. There's no question that the Round Mound of Rebound could ball. Whether on the Sixers or, in his later days, on the Suns, he was a player. But if you watch Sir Charles swing a golf club, I could convince you that he had not an ounce of athleticism in him. It's like all of his basketball ability just somehow drains out when he picks up a club. Ford was like that.

After Ford had left the White House, he joined the board of Citigroup, which was chaired by Sandy Weill. The two men had first met in 1980 when Ford had decided against running again for president and was beginning to entertain the possibility of joining some corporate boards.

Years later, the two men were playing at the famed Pebble Beach course as part of the Bing Crosby National Pro-Am. And as Weill recounted in 2011:

> It was a par 3, and the President, he shanked it on this par 3 and the ball went up in the air and into the woods and we heard a clunk. I was praying it was a tree, but it wasn't a tree, it was a lady's head. And he went over to apologize, and I thought it was a little funny. And he said to me as we walked up to the green with the ball in his pocket, he said, "Sandy, you're not going to think this is so funny. You are my insurance carrier."

Alcott, however, has only fond memories of sharing a foursome with the former president. (She once played with Ford and Bob Hope when she was the returning champion at the Kraft Nabisco tournament at the Mission Hills Country Club in Rancho Mirage, California.)

But it was a chance occurrence off the golf course that stuck with

Alcott most. It was the summer in California, and Alcott happened to be at a grocery store in the Palm Desert area.

"I was walking through the aisles grabbing a few things when all of a sudden there is a man in the bread aisle with a walkie talkie and another guy bending down to look at the different types of bread," she said. "I recognized that it was President Ford and I said 'hello.' He said 'how wonderful to see you' and explained that Betty [Ford] was going to make some tuna fish sandwiches but we're out of bread."

Alcott said she recommended a bread brand and the former president grabbed it. "I asked him about his golf game," she added. "He said 'my golf game is great, much improved.'" She asked him if he knew why he was playing better. "I don't know what I am doing but all I know is I am hitting fewer people," said Ford.

Golf played a central role in the single most consequential moment of Ford's presidency (and life).

On September 8, 1974, he pardoned Nixon. Again, Ford was always the consummate team player, describing Watergate as "a tragedy in which we all have played a part."

It was a decision he had agonized over since coming to the presidency in early August. At a press conference later that month, Ford was overwhelmed with questions about Nixon and was convinced that he needed to find a way to put the former president behind him (and the country) once and for all.

He asked the White House legal counsel to look into the possibility of a presidential pardon. Ford also consulted with his chief of staff, Alexander Haig, as well as his secretary of state, Henry Kissinger, and a select few other advisers.

By September 7, Ford had made up his mind. When he announced the pardon the following day, the reaction was swift—and negative. White House press secretary J. F. terHorst resigned in protest. The public blanched, convinced that the pardon represented some sort of inside deal cut between Ford and Nixon. (There was, in actuality, no such deal.)

"It was a huge disappointment to reporters and the people who trusted Ford," historian Douglas Brinkley told the *New York Times*.

Just a few days later—and with the pardon decision still roiling the nation—Ford traveled to Pinehurst, North Carolina, to dedicate the World Golf Hall of Fame—and to play a round.

Protesters opposed to the Nixon pardon gathered carrying signs like Is Nixon above the Law? and Ford Has a Bad Idea.

Despite the protests, Ford was obviously in a good mood—starting his remarks by poking fun at his own golf game.

"I'd like to tell you the most memorable golfing experience I ever had," he told the crowd. "I was at the Burning Tree course just outside of Washington when Ben Hogan, Arnold Palmer and Byron Nelson came up to me and said they were looking for another great golfer to join them. I said, 'Well, here I am!' . . . and they said, 'Good, you can help us look!' "

Ford then turned to his love of the game. "I enjoy golf," he said. "I enjoy the exercise it provides. I enjoy the competitive challenge. I enjoy the good fellowship before, during and after each game."

And then—in remarks heavy with symbolism with what he had just done in Washington—Ford went on an extended riff about the importance of honor in golf and in life.

"Golf is one of the few games where honor is more important than rules," he said. "Without good sportsmanship, golf could not exist. Without trust, another name for good sportsmanship, governments could not exist either."

And then the symbolism got even more on the nose.

"I have never seen a tournament—regardless of how much money or fame or prestige or emotion was involved—that didn't end with the victor extending his hand to the vanquished," said Ford. "The pat on the back—the arm around the shoulder—the praise for what was done right and the sympathetic nod for what wasn't—are as much a part of golf as life itself. I would hope that understanding and reconciliation are not limited to the 19th hole alone."

Ford ended with a blunt assessment of his current political predicament. "This afternoon, for a few hours, I tried to make a hole in one. Tomorrow morning, I'll be back in Washington trying to get out of one."

The *New York Times* noted that "the president appeared far more relaxed than he had been the last few days." He played nine holes with, among others, Jack Nicklaus, Arnold Palmer, and Byron Nelson; "Mr. Ford slammed the ball 220 yards straight down the fairway on the first hole."

The dirty little secret about Gerald Ford then was that he was a very good athlete. Which should surprise exactly no one—and yet it does.

Consider this: Ford was an avid and gifted skier.

"I used to think of myself as a pretty dashing figure on the ski slopes of the East and in northern Michigan, and could at least count on outstripping my children on the various runs we tried," he wrote in the mid-1970s. "Nowadays, when my family gets together at Vail for our annual Christmas ski reunion, my sons and daughter go zooming by, usually with just the encouragement to make me boil. Such as 'Hurry up, Dad.' They see themselves getting faster and faster as I get slower and slower. They forget all the times I picked them out of the snowbank."

Ford started to ski for the same reason young men do most things—for the girls. (I can personally attest to the truth of this.)

"As a young man, I took up skiing in order to get to know a certain young lady better," he wrote. "She happened to be a devotee, and I an eager beginner. I lost the girl but learned to ski."

(Ford learned to ski in Massachusetts while attending Yale Law School in the late 1930s.)

The Fords rented a house in Vail during the late 1960s and early 1970s. They eventually bought a condo—using $50,000 allocated to the kids' college fund. By the late '70s, they had bought a seven-bedroom, five-bathroom house, which sprawled over 5,900 square feet. (The house was on the market in 2022 for $13 million.)

"Betty and I, our children and our grandchildren are always thrilled to come to Vail to celebrate Christmas and the New Year," Ford said in 2000. "We love it here."

It's not an exaggeration to say that Ford's commitment to Vail helped make the ski town what it now is. In an obituary in the *Denver Post* when Ford died the day after Christmas in 2006, the paper wrote:

> Gerald Ford brought the "winter White House" to Vail and placed the developing ski town on the map by regularly schussing down the slopes. He was considered a friend and regular guy by many here, even while lending his name to innumerable causes in his role as "mountain royalty."

After losing the 1976 presidential race to Jimmy Carter, Ford retreated to Vail to lick his wounds. (Ford won Vail by almost one thousand votes over the Georgia governor.)

The outdoor amphitheater in the town is named after Ford. (It's known locally as the Amp.) As is the town's main park. He helped bring the World Alpine Ski Championships to Vail in 1989 and then again ten years later.

Ford was renowned in the town for buying his own lift tickets and having his name listed in the local yellow pages. He was just Jerry, an average joe who just happened to be the MVP of a major college football team, a House leader, a vice president, and the president of the United States.

"I am a Ford, not a Lincoln," he said when being sworn in as VP. "My addresses will never be as eloquent as Mr. Lincoln's. But I will do my very best to equal his brevity and his plain speaking."

Underdog President Attacked
by Wild Rabbit

Boycott Backlash

O ur story begins in 1979 when James Fallows, a former Carter speech-writer, wrote a long piece on his former boss for the *Atlantic*. (Head-line: "The Passionless Presidency.")

Writing of how Carter spent his weekends, Fallows said:

> He would leave for a weekend at Camp David laden with thick briefing books, would pore over budget tables to check the arithmetic, and, during his first six months in office, would personally review all requests to use the White House tennis court.

Yes, you read that right. The president of the United States would personally approve who could (and who couldn't) use the tennis court at the White House.

Fallows used it as evidence that while Carter came into office with a "rational plan for his time," he soon reverted back to the "detail-man used to running his own warehouse, the perfectionist accustomed to thinking that to do a job right you must do it yourself."

Fallows wasn't the first person to wonder out loud about Carter holding dominion over tennis court time. Witness this exchange between the president and Bill Moyers in the fall of 1978:

Moyers: You were criticized, I know, talking about details, for keeping the log yourself of who could use the White House tennis courts. Are you still doing that?

Carter: No—and never have, by the way.

Moyers: Was that a false report?

Carter: Yes, it was.

(Sidebar: It's not entirely clear what "report" Moyers was referring to.)

Fallows's article landed with a major splash. This was the late '70s and the former-aide-tells-all story line was a relatively rare one. Nowadays, of course, it's a rite of passage. Leave the White House, write a dishy book about its inner workings—with you as the hero—and then cash in.

And it prompted the press to ask Carter directly about the tennis court during a press conference in April 1979.

A reporter asked Carter this: "Fallows says that you signed off personally on the use of the White House tennis courts, but you told Bill Moyers that you didn't. What's the truth about that?"

To which Carter responded, in part, this:

I have never personally monitored who used or did not use the White House tennis court. I have let my secretary, Susan Clough, receive requests from members of the White House staff who wanted to use the tennis court at certain times, so that more than one person would not want to use the same tennis court simultaneously, unless they were either on opposite sides of the net or engaged in a doubles contest.

Which isn't exactly a denial!

And, Fallows didn't back down. In that same 1979 *Atlantic* article, he said that "the in-house tennis enthusiasts, of whom I was perhaps the most shameless, dispatched brief notes through his secretary asking to use the court on Tuesday afternoons while he was at a congressional briefing, or a Saturday morning, while he was away. I always provided spaces where he could check Yes or No; Carter would make his decision and send the note back, initialed J."

According to Matthew Dickinson at Middlebury University, Fallows had it right. Dickinson points to a memo from Carter's official papers that restricted use of the swimming pool and tennis courts to immediate family only—anyone else "can—on occasion—request use from me."

Dickinson also unearthed a February 1977 memo from Fallows to Carter in which the former wrote that "the only perquisite of this job that I care about at all is the tennis court." Fallows went on to note that Hugh Carter, a cousin of the president and a White House aide, had indicated that Carter reserved court use for his immediate family but was open to requests from staff. "I would like to respectfully ask your permission," wrote Fallows.

(Fun White House then-and-now fact: Melania Trump commissioned a renovation of the White House tennis pavilion during her husband's time in office. "History continues to unfold at the @WhiteHouse & I am pleased to announce the completion of the tennis pavilion," she tweeted in December 2020. "Preserving this historic landmark is vital & I want to thank all who helped complete this project." Melania came under considerable criticism for focusing on the rebuilding of the tennis complex while several hundred thousand Americans were dying in 2020 from the coronavirus. "Unveiling a tennis pavilion in the midst of a national humanitarian catastrophe could not be more on brand for Melania Trump than if she had devoted herself to opening the American Museum of Bloodless Soft Core Porn Model Gold Diggers on the National Mall," wrote David Rothkopf, a prominent liberal, on Twitter.)

The Carter court controversy didn't end in the '70s, however. In 1986, Susan Clough, who, you will remember, was Carter's executive assistant, wrote a letter to the editor of the *New York Times* about the matter. (The *Times* had contacted Fallows earlier that year to reconfirm his tennis court reporting.)

There was no defined policy per se, and when the inquiries began early in the Administration, many were addressed to the President, since the tennis court was on the grounds of the White House, and the White House was where the Carters lived. The majority of tennis court requests were handled without any involvement of the President or the First Lady.

Mr. Fallows's requests were usually sent as a part of his cover notes transmitting speech drafts to the President. By the time the incoming drafts were seen by President Carter, my office would have already responded to the request. However, occasionally my empathetic side would prevail, particularly if it was evident that a given staffer or supporter was feeling somewhat estranged from the President. The incoming correspondence or note of phone call would then be submitted with an index card clipped on top, briefly recommending some sort of action to be taken. President Carter was thus saved the time of reading through the incoming paper(s) unless he was inclined to do so, while at the same time he could be aware that one of his advisers or friends had tried to contact him.

That explanation seems to suggest that Carter did, at least on occasion, OK the use of the court though, right?

The point is this: The media latched on to the tennis court story as yet another example of a man who was (a) simply in way over his head or (b) a grim micromanager who couldn't see the big picture. Whether the story was apocryphal or not became a side point. The message it conveyed rang true with many Americans: Carter didn't get it.

––––––––––

Carter first caught the tennis bug back in Archery, Georgia—the tiny town where he grew up.

Tennis courts weren't a common site in Archery. But Carter's childhood home had one.

"There was a dirt tennis court next to our house, unknown on any other farm in our area, which Daddy laid out as soon as we moved there and kept clean and relatively smooth with a piece of angle iron nailed to a pine log that a mule could drag over it every week or so," wrote Carter in the memoir of his childhood, *An Hour Before Daylight.*

The court wasn't just for show, either. Men from the neighboring community of Plains would gather at the Carter family farm to play. "Unless there was a big group, they usually played singles, with the player who first lost a set dropping out if others were waiting," wrote Carter of the matches. "The winner stayed on the court as long as they wished. Usually that was my Daddy."

Carter's father had "good control of the ball and a wicked slice that was effective on the dirt courts around Plains," according to his son, who rated his father "an outstanding tennis player."

It wasn't long before the young Carter was being taught to play by his dad. "Daddy was impatient for me to grow up, and began giving me tennis lessons as soon as I was old enough to hold a racket," Carter recounted. "Although I eventually became the top player in high school, I could never beat him—and he certainly never gave me a point."

Again, Carter—as a kid and throughout his adult life—was drawn to a solo sport where *solitude* is the watchword. In tennis it's just you out there. Can you outsmart and outwit the opponent? Can you outlast him? No team is coming to save you. It's all on you—and you alone. Either figure it out yourself—or lose.

———

Aside from tennis, Carter, like so many boys growing up in the South in the 1930s and 1940s, spent much of his youth outside—hunting and fishing.

For Carter, fishing was his primary interest. He and his father would fish around their hometown of Plains—and in other spots throughout southern Georgia.

"Many of the most highly publicized events of my presidency are not nearly as memorable or significant in my life as fishing with my daddy… when I was a boy," Carter would write of his youth. "Certainly, none of them was as enjoyable."

(Fun presidential trash panda fact: According to Carter, he was a sought-after companion during hunting trips in his youth because he could climb trees better than most. Why was he climbing trees? To shake raccoons out of them, of course.)

In the early 1970s, Carter took up fly fishing.

"Carter worked hard at it," wrote Paul Boller in *Presidential Diversions*. "He steeped himself in information about fishes, fishing rounds, and fishing techniques, held a conference of fly-fishermen at Camp David...went fishing with expert anglers and experimented with wet and dry flies of his own making while casting lines."

Much of Carter's fishing took place at or near Camp David. As he recounted in his 1988 book *An Outdoor Journal*:

We'd go out to Camp David, the press following or meeting us there by the hundreds sometimes. We'd get out of the helicopter. The press would go back to their hotels and motels in Maryland. We would change clothes, get back on the same helicopter, fly about the same distance northward into southern Pennsylvania, land in a pasture away from the highways and spend two or three days fly-fishing on Spruce Creek.

Carter would often fish with his wife, Rosalynn, who grew to be an able fisherman in her own right. They purposely downplayed these trips and, as a result, much of the public was ignorant about the fact that the president was an accomplished outdoorsman. Given Carter's issues with appearing weak and meek, it might have done his image some good for the public to know that he was an able hunter and fisherman.

The first major piece that Carter wrote after leaving the presidency—in early 1982—wasn't about politics or his presidency. It was about fishing.

It was a lengthy recollection—seven pages!—of a trip he took to Spruce Creek the previous summer. And it ran in *Fly Fisherman* magazine. (Yes, that is a real magazine from back then!)

Titled "Spruce Creek Diary," the essay was a paean to the outdoor life and was chock-full of nerdy details understood only by the most devout anglers.

"I couldn't wait until after our early supper, though, so I floated a small yellow-bodied Adams far under the overhanging limbs and soon netted a nice streambred brown trout," Carter wrote at one point. (And, no, I have no idea what any of that means.)

At another: "As dusk approached, we were in a heavily wooded area, waist-deep in the cold water, casting Green Drake patterns upstream into the riffles and along the overgrown banks." (Riffles are where water in a stream is more shallow; and, yes, I had to look that up.)

At one point, Carter seems to grow reflective about his 1980 defeat at the hands of Ronald Reagan.

"In addition to our discussions about fly-fishing strategy and tactics, my fishing companions commiserated with me over my loss in moving from the White House back home to Plains—but not in reference to the elections," he wrote.

The loss Carter was referring to was two prized fishing rods that some-how didn't make it in the move from DC to Georgia. "These rods, not the election campaign, seemed to be the more serious loss to all of us as we discussed important matters by the tumbling waters of the Pennsylvania creek."

That image of Carter—solitary, defeated, and yet not embittered—is fitting.

He's often cast as the unlikeliest of presidents, a peanut farmer from Georgia who, thanks to the lingering effects of Watergate on the body politic, wound up in the highest office in the land. People wanted some-one they could trust after years of Nixon. And Carter was the most honest man in American politics at the time (and maybe still).

But, that's a misread of Carter. He's not an unlikely president, just an unassuming one. Carter, more than anyone who has held the modern pres-idency, was someone whose life was not entirely defined—either then or now—by that fact. The presidency was a stage of his life, not the entirety of it. And so, while losing the presidency was a difficult blow, it wasn't, for Carter, the life-altering moment that it is for so many politicians.

In fact, Carter went on to accomplish more as an ex-president than any other man who has left the office since. "He used the White House as a stepping stone for greater achievement, meaning they are connected—the presidency and the post-presidency," said historian Douglas Brinkley. "Jimmy Carter is being seen as one of the great humanitarian and state persons of the 20th and 21st century."

Baseball was ever-present in Carter's young life—although he was not a standout. As he wrote in his memoir of his youth:

> I could hold my own in all the childhood games with my regular playmates, but the baseball team in Archery was out of my league. There were ten boys on a team, including a "backstop," whose position was behind the catcher to handle wild pitches...I was sometimes permitted to play backstop, perhaps because I always had a bat and ball and did well with the glove. I really wasted my time at the plate, too afraid of being struck by the hard-flung and often wild pitches to hit the ball.

That didn't stop Carter from playing. As he wrote of his childhood: "All of us loved to play baseball, including farm boys like me who couldn't go out for the school team because springtime farm work interfered with regular practice."

He tells of games that would last weeks in which "we'd have three batters, a catcher, a backstop, pitcher and then the rest of the team, sometimes with several infielders and outfielders. Whenever one of the batters made an out, he would go into the last field position, and everyone moved up a notch."

Carter's biggest athletic success in high school was—despite his diminutive size—basketball. ("I liked baseball more, but Daddy didn't want to spare me from work during the spring planting and growing," Carter said.)

Of basketball, Carter wrote: "This was really the most important sport as far as interscholastic competition was concerned, because games were played at night and parents with day jobs could attend."

There was another advantage to playing basketball. Because there would always be a girls' game before the boys played, the teams would share a bus to away games. "Long trips in the dark gave us a chance to pair off on the back seats and do some enthusiastic petting," he admits.

Carter earned the nickname "Pee-Wee"—he was five foot six in high school—but wrote that he was the "quickest" on the team. "We depended a lot on fast breaks whenever our team got the ball on the opponents' end of the court," explained Carter.

(He sprouted three inches in his freshman year of college—and was named to the intramural all-star team.)

But Carter's was a baseball-loving family. He describes his father and uncle as "fascinated" by the sport.

The elder Carter played pitcher and catcher for a local American Legion team "and enjoyed the sport for the rest of his life as a committed spectator."

Carter would travel with his family to nearby Americus, Georgia, to see his father's team play. "It was serious baseball with the teams wearing uniforms and spiked shoes," he remembered. "Once when Daddy was catching, he blocked the plate as an opposing player slid in with spikes high; he had to spend several weeks on crutches with the resulting injury."

The Carters also went to their fair share of pro baseball games—"Class D" teams that were "an integral part of the immense web of farm systems that existed in those days to feed superior players step by step into the major leagues."

When Carter was ten years old, the St. Louis Cardinals came to Americus to play a game. His father suggested that young Jimmy go out on the field and get the autographs of stars Frankie Frisch and Pepper Martin. Carter approached the two men with a pencil in one hand and a paper bag that had once housed roasted peanuts in the other.

"Frisch, who was acting as player-manager, signed the bag, but Martin looked down, spat some tobacco juice that almost hit me and said 'Get your ass off the field, boy!' For years, I kept the peanut bag—with just one autograph—safe in our store."

In his memoir, Carter recounts how even during the lean years caused by the Great Depression, his mother and father as well as his uncle Buddy and his wife would save up money to go see out-of-town ball games.

"They planned the trips for after crops were laid by and when they wouldn't miss our Baptist church revival, and so they could see the maximum number of games, with at least one doubleheader," wrote Carter.

Carter's parents were part of baseball history during one of these trips. In 1947, they were in the stands when Jackie Robinson broke the color barrier by playing a game for the Brooklyn Dodgers.

Carter said that his mother "always considered it to be one of God's special blessings" that they were at the historic game and that for the rest of her life she loved the Dodgers—even after they moved to Los Angeles in 1958.

"She watched or listened to every Dodger game she could, and after our family became famous she would call Dodgers manager Tommy Lasorda on the telephone to complain about managerial decisions he had made," remembered Carter. "When Mama died, we found a complete Dodger uniform in her closet, even including cleats, with a letter signed by the entire team."

Carter, like many Americans, took up jogging in the late 1970s. (Ron Burgundy was one; "I believe it's 'jogging' or 'yogging.' It might be a soft *j*, I'm not sure, but apparently you just run for an extended period of time! It's supposed to be wild," he said.)

He had run cross-country in high school (and pole vaulted). And as a plebe at the Naval Academy he had competed on the cross-country team.

Carter started running again in the late 1970s. "I start looking forward to it almost from the moment I get up," Carter told the *New York Times* at that time. "If I don't run, I don't feel exactly right."

Carter was, despite his unassuming nature, quite competitive. (He had his father, Earl, to thank for that.) He didn't want to just run. He wanted to win—or at least have the chance at victory. So he started entering running competitions near Camp David; Carter finished his first four 10K races without incident. But he wanted to break fifty minutes—his best time.

In September 1979, Carter decided to enter the Catoctin Mountain (Maryland) Park Run. As *Sports Illustrated* recounted: "As the President's party approached, the runners and spectators, most of them relatives of the competitors, burst into cheers. Mrs. Carter peeled off into the crowd, while Carter removed his blue warmup jacket, pinned on his No. 39, pulled up his black (yes, black) socks and donned a yellow headband that drew his eyebrows upward and gave him an anxious and vulnerable look."

The race started without incident for Carter, who was pacing to finish around the forty-six-minute mark. (He ran alongside White House physician William Lukash.) Carter had run the decidedly hilly course several times before.

"The course should be an advantage for him," one running aficionado told *SI* before the race. "He'll have no trouble finishing. It's just a question of how fast he'll do it."

It was not to be, however. About a third of the way through the race, Carter and his group—which included *Washington Post* columnist Coleman McCarthy—came to a steep incline.

Here's how *Sports Illustrated* described what came next:

> Approaching the crest, the President began to stagger. McCarthy, now running on Carter's right, wrote in the *Post* the next day, "His face was ashen. His mouth hung open, and his eyes had an unfocused look."

Lukash and a Secret Service agent who had been running directly behind Carter grabbed the president before he collapsed. Carter was soon shuffled into a private car and whisked away.

Though some feared a heart attack, the eventual diagnosis was far more benign: heat exhaustion. Carter managed to rally—appearing at the awards picnic to hand out trophies and even joke about his near collapse.

"They had to drag me off," he said. "I didn't want to stop. The main thing for those of us who are senior citizens and joggers is to keep on."

And Carter took time to extol the virtues of running. "It's a great thing, running," he said. "We have added a new dimension to our lives and I hope that in the future all of you will become evangelists, as I am, to get more and more Americans to run."

The problem for Carter was that the story—and the photos of his struggles—became huge national news.

"Carter, Exhausted and Pale, Drops Out of 6-Mile Race," read the headline in the *New York Times*. (And, yes, it was on the front page—accompanied by a picture of Carter with his yellow headband on.)

The lede of the story was even worse for the president: "President Carter, wobbling, moaning and pale with exhaustion, dropped out of a 6.2-mile foot race today near his weekend retreat at Camp David, Md. The President, an avid jogger who will be 55 years old on Oct. 1, apparently suffered no lasting ill effects after abandoning the run near the two-thirds mark."

Wobbling and moaning is not a good look for any president but especially one who, like Carter, found himself battling poor poll numbers roughly one year away from his reelection race.

In September 1979, Carter's approval rating in Gallup polling sat at a meager 30 percent. Inflation was at 13.3 percent for the year, the highest since the mid-1940s.

His failure to complete the road race—and the resultant press coverage—played into the notion that Carter was struggling.

"The picture stuck irrevocably in people's minds, shaping their overall perception of his leadership in a far more forceful way than any of the positive actions he was taking," wrote historian Peter Bourne.

It didn't help that a month prior—in August 1979—the Banzai Bunny incident occurred.

What is the Banzai Bunny incident, you ask?

Well, Carter was vacationing in Georgia in the last days of the summer when he decided to take a boat out on a pond to fish. A group of hounds chased a wild rabbit into the water near where Carter was fishing. "Wild rabbits...all of them know how to swim," Carter told the *Washington Post* in 2005.

The president batted away the killer bunny with his oar. It was not—or at least should not have been—a very big deal. But then White House press secretary Jody Powell told the media about the face-off—and all hell broke loose.

"There was nothing to it," Carter told the *Post*. "When Jody told it, it became a very humorous and still-lasting story. Lots of people that had tame bunny rabbits threw them in swimming pools and said their rabbits could swim, too."

It didn't help that a photo of the incident got out—and one in which Carter looked decidedly wary of, well, a rabbit.

Political cartoonists had a heyday with the episode—drawing a massive menacing rabbit towering over the president in a tiny boat.

A musician named Tom Paxton wrote a song about the bunny incident titled "I Don't Want a Bunny-Wunny." It included these lines:

> *Along swum a rabbit and he tried to climb in.*
> *And what did Jimmy say?*
> *"I don't want a bunny wunny in my widdle wow boat."*

So, yeah. As WNYC put it in a story on the bunny imbroglio:

Carter, who'd grown up in the country, calmly used his paddle to splash water at the critter and scare it away. But a photo of the encounter that the White House unwisely released to the press made the president look somewhat comical and small. How was a guy who let a rabbit get the drop on him supposed to guard the U.S. from attack by the Soviet Union?

The reporting of the bunny incident dove-tailed—in a disastrously bad way—with the seizure of the American embassy in Iran by the Ayatollah Ruhollah Khomeini. On November 4, 1979, a group of Iranians—numbering in the thousands—stormed the embassy in Tehran, taking more than fifty personnel hostage. (The United States had long supported the recently deposed shah Reza Pahlavi as a way to keep Iranian oil flowing to America.)

After a brief polling bump for Carter, his numbers began to crater (again) as it became clear that the hostages weren't coming home anytime soon. After a failed rescue mission—which led to the deaths of eight American military members after their aircrafts collided into each other during a retreat—Carter was increasingly portrayed as feckless and weak, an image that his struggles in the running race and his rabbit confrontation had helped fuel.

(Sidebar: The hostages were eventually released on January 20, 1981— roughly thirty minutes after Carter's presidency had ended. The credit for the release went to incoming president Ronald Reagan, who had crushed Carter at the ballot box the previous fall—even though Carter and his administration had done the vast majority of the heavy lifting to see the hostages home safely.)

———

Star swimmer Rowdy Gaines was in a hotel room in Austin, Texas, when he heard the news: Jimmy Carter had just announced that the United States would boycott the 1980 Summer Olympics to be held in Moscow, Russia.

"I remember every single detail," Gaines said of Carter's announcement some four decades later, "and I don't remember what I ate for breakfast yesterday."

Gaines, a junior at Auburn at the time, was widely regarded as a leading contender to win multiple medals in the pool during the 1980 Games. He disagreed with Carter's decision, insisting that it played into the Soviets' hands.

"The old cliché of mixing politics and sports is so true," Gaines said later. "The [Soviets] used it to their advantage by winning more medals and the propaganda helped them tremendously and it ruined so many people's athletic careers. The best thing we could do then was to go over there and kick their ass."

The seeds of the boycott were planted in late 1979 when Russia had invaded Afghanistan, murdered its ruler, and put in a puppet government loyal to them.

Carter, in an appearance on *Meet the Press* on January 20, unveiled the planned boycott.

"Unless the Soviets withdraw their troops within a month from Afghanistan," Carter said, he would call for "the Olympic games [to] be moved from Moscow to an alternative site, or multiple sites, or postponed or canceled."

Three days later, on January 23, Carter doubled down on the promise in his State of the Union speech.

"While this invasion continues, we and the other nations of the world cannot conduct business as usual with the Soviet Union," he said. "I have notified the Olympic Committee that with Soviet invading forces in Afghanistan, neither the American people nor I will support sending an Olympic team to Moscow."

That was only the start of the process, of course. Carter, despite being president, couldn't unilaterally declare the country was out of the Olympics. That decision fell to the U.S. Olympic Committee.

Carter began a two-pronged strategy: He would lobby the eighteen members of USOC while also putting pressure on American allies—Great Britain, France, Germany, and the like—to join the United States in boycotting the games.

"I don't want the onus for the failure of the Olympics to fall exclusively on the United States," Carter told his foreign policy advisers. "It must be seen as a legitimate worldwide political reaction to what the Russians are doing in Afghanistan."

One of Carter's key men in that effort was Muhammad Ali, who was dispatched to Africa to try to convince those nations of the necessity of the boycott. Criticized as nothing more than a yes man for Carter, Ali, during the course of what was supposed to be an African tour to drum up support for the boycott, announced that he now opposed such a boycott.

"I'm not here to take America's whipping," said Ali. "I'm not here to take punishment for America. I'm not here to push nothing on nobody."

He added: "There are two bad white men in the world, the Russian white men and the American white man. They are the two baddest men in the history of the world and if these two white men start fighting, all of us little black folks are going to be caught in the middle."

Wrote legendary *Washington Post* columnist Shirley Povich: "The whole fiasco was not all Ali's fault. Much of the blunder can be traced to the White House."

The struggles with Ali presaged the broader problems Carter would run into on the world stage. Although a strong majority of Americans—upward of 55 percent—supported the boycott, Carter simply couldn't convince top U.S. allies to join him in walking away from the Olympics.

The belief was that such a boycott would not hurt the Soviets in any meaningful way and would, in, fact, bolster the nation. "The only way to compete against Moscow is to stuff it down their throats in their own backyard," said multitime gold medal winner Al Oerter, echoing Rowdy Gaines's view.

Lord Kilannin, the head of the International Olympic Committee, summed up the views of the world community nicely. "Whatever the rights and wrongs of the Afghanistan affair, the judgment of one man, already scrambling for his political life in the American presidential election campaign...had turned the Olympic arena into what was to be its own battleground," he would write.

Right around that time, the 1980 Winter Olympics opened in Lake Placid, New York. And, out of nowhere, came the U.S. hockey team.

Coached by Herb Brooks, the team, which was filled with young players with next to no experience, weren't seen as medal contenders. Or anything close to it.

But, they went 5-0 in the group stage—including a 7–3 shellacking of well-regarded Czechoslovakia. Still, hopes were low—especially when the Americans drew the Russians, who had won five of the last six hockey gold medals, in the first medal round game.

The Soviets scored first, but less than five minutes later the Americans knotted it at 1–1. Again, the Soviets pushed ahead, but with no time remaining on the clock in the first period, the American team got their second goal to tie the game heading into the first intermission.

Inexplicably, the Soviet coach took out his legendary goalkeeper—Vladislav Tretiak—at the start of the second period. But the Soviets were the only team that managed to score, leading after two periods 3–2.

The Americans scored on a power play halfway through the third period to tie the score at 3–3. Minutes later Mike Eruzione scored the fourth goal to put Team USA on top with ten minutes remaining.

As the final seconds ticked down, Al Michaels delivered one of the most famous calls in all of sports: "Eleven seconds, you've got ten seconds, the countdown going on right now! Morrow, up to Silk. Five seconds left in the game. Do you believe in miracles? YES!"

The "Miracle on Ice" was born.

As the *New York Times* wrote:

From New York to Los Angeles, at sports arenas, in theaters, and in barrooms, family rooms and other watering and television watching spots, hockey fans and Americans who had never before seen a hockey game cheered wildly, hugged one another and groped for superlatives.

Dave Zirin took a more cynical view of the U.S. victory over the Soviets in his book *A People's History of Sports in the United States*, writing:

It was a propaganda tonic, a counterweight to the "shame of losing Vietnam," the USSR's invasion of Afghanistan, the energy crisis, and the fact that as the Olympics opened, fifty-two Americans were held hostage by student radicals in Iran.

Suddenly, Oerter's notion—needing to whip Russia's ass to show them where power in the world really stood—was being played out in real time. And Carter's boycott plan looked worse and worse.

"The Olympic situation seems to be disintegrating," a White House aide told Zbigniew Brzezinski, a top adviser to Carter. "If we are not careful, our magnificent hockey win may fuel domestic sentiment against the boycott."

Attempts to offer an alternative to the Moscow Olympics went nowhere. And Carter never personally appealed to the European powers, instead allowing emissaries to do his bidding. That, according to historian John Sayle Watterson, meant that "the Europeans never took the boycott as seriously as they might have."

As winter turned to spring, it became clear that Carter's hope of turning the world against the Soviets had failed—and failed miserably. While the U.S. Olympic Committee begrudgingly agreed to go along with Carter's boycott, a number of major European powers—France, Spain, Italy, and Great Britain chief among them—announced in March 1980 that their teams would be going to the Olympics. (All told, eighty countries were present at the Moscow Olympics.)

The United States was left generally isolated, although West Germany, Canada, and Israel did stand with America in boycotting the games.

For Carter, it was another blow in a long-running series of losses for him and his administration. Carter had hoped to lead a unified world coalition against the march of communism but instead had demonstrated the relative weakness of his hand in world affairs. On the domestic front, Carter received little to none of the rally-round-the-flag effect he and his advisers had undoubtedly hoped to achieve.

Carter would later acknowledge the folly of a partial boycott, noting that the ultimate impact was "politically damaging" for him.

Jimmy Carter wasn't the sportiest president—by a long shot. But the four years he was in office saw a blending of sports and entertainment that, while de rigueur these days, was unimaginable back then.

No longer were teams just teams. They were the stuff of pop culture legend. There was the Steel Curtain defense of the Pittsburgh Steelers led by "Mean" Joe Greene and L.C. Greenwood. In baseball, there was the Big Red Machine in Cincinnati with larger-than-life figures like Pete Rose and Joe Morgan. Reggie Jackson was transforming into "Mr. October" in the Bronx as he bombed three home runs on three consecutive pitches off three different Dodger pitchers in Game 6 of the 1977 World Series.

Suddenly our sports heroes were no longer confined to just sports anymore. They had become cultural figures. And sports leapt its rails to become a Hollywood fascination.

The four years Carter spent as president might have produced the most classic sports movies of any four years in modern history. Consider the films that came out between 1976 and 1979:

- *The Bad News Bears* (1976): Morris Buttermaker likes to smoke, drink (Budweisers), and make money. Which makes him an unlikely coach of a Little League baseball team. (He is, it's worth noting, a washed-up minor leaguer.) But this is the worst baseball team imaginable—until, that is, Buttermaker (played by the incomparable Walter Matthau) recruits a hard-throwing girl (Tatum O'Neal) and things start to change. (Admit it—you never saw that coming!) She recruits punk kid—and baseball savant—Kelly Leak to the squad, and suddenly the Bears aren't bad news anymore.
- *Rocky* (1976): A rewatch of this Sylvester Stallone showpiece—I did this recently with my kids—reveals two things: (1) There is precious little fighting in the movie; and (2) The fight scene at the end between unheralded challenger Rocky and the charismatic champion Apollo Creed is still freaking awesome. Is this the best of the *Rocky* movies? It is not. That's *Rocky 3*. But it's still damn good.
- *The Bingo Long Traveling All-Stars & Motor Kings* (1976): ~~Lando Calrissian~~ Billy Dee Williams is Bingo Long, a star pitcher in the Negro Leagues in the 1930s who recruits some of his friends (and the best players in the league) to join his own barnstorming baseball team. That doesn't sit well with the Negro League owners who set up a winner-take-all game—if Bingo's side wins, they get back into the League. I won't spoil it for you but, um, this is the movies, so you can probably figure out how things end. Also, did I mention young ~~Darth Vader~~ James Earl Jones and young Richard Pryor are in this movie?
- *Pumping Iron* (1977): Without this movie, we might not have had two things that have become essential in our modern culture: sports documentaries and Arnold Schwarzenegger. This documentary— on the sport of bodybuilding and the culture growing up around it—made the Austrian muscle man a star in the United States and

weight lifting a popular pursuit. Also, Lou Ferrigno, aka the original Incredible Hulk, is in it!

- **Semi-Tough (1977):** If I had to pick one movie to show an alien who wanted to know what the 1970s were like, this would be the one. It's about football, I guess. Burt Reynolds plays a running back and Kris Kristofferson plays a wide receiver. And they both looooove the ladies—wink wink, nudge nudge. Oh, and also, those two guys live with the daughter of the owner of the team. You can't imagine the crazy antics those three get up to! "It's all about passes, but not the kind you throw. It's all about scoring, but not on the field" is a real line from the trailer to this, um, film.

- **Slap Shot (1977):** There aren't that many great movies about ice hockey. (A quick list: *Miracle, Mighty Ducks,* and, well, not that much else.) But *Slap Shot* definitely qualifies as one of the greats— and not just because Paul Newman stars in it. The plot is relatively thin: A minor-league hockey team in a down-on-its-luck town realizes that on-ice violence sells to its fans—so it produces a team that gives its fans what it wants, including three brothers (the Hansons) who typify the new, er, aggressive attitude the team has adopted. (Fun fact: Director George Roy Hill and Newman teamed up in *Slap Shot* as well as *Butch Cassidy and the Sundance Kid* and *The Sting.*)

- **Heaven Can Wait (1978):** Warren Beatty is a quarterback for the Los Angeles Rams who is killed in a car crash. But—plot twist!— it turns out he was not supposed to die in that crash and so he is placed in the body of a multimillionaire. He then buys the Rams and leads them to the Super Bowl as their quarterback. But then he is shot and killed and another QB comes in, who is then killed by a vicious hit. Except that Beatty is allowed to occupy his body and lead the Rams to the Super Bowl. Does it make any sense? No. But do the Rams win the Super Bowl? You bet they do!

- **North Dallas Forty (1979):** The movie, based on a novel by former Dallas Cowboys wide receiver Pete Gent, is widely seen as one of the first critical looks at the NFL ever. The main character, played by Nick Nolte, is an aging wide receiver who is barely scraping by—thanks to a heavy reliance on painkillers. It paints Nolte—and football—in a decidedly unappealing light, a violent game played by violent men who barely contain their rage (and their other passions) in other areas of their lives.

- *Breaking Away* (1979): A kid from Indiana obsessed with Italian cycling does *not* seem to be the basis of a terrific sports movie. And yet! I daresay *Breaking Away* is the best movie about cycling ever made. And it ends with that most wholesome of things—the lead character with his feet taped to the pedals as he wins a race called the "Little 500." Who could ask for anything more?

- *The Fish That Saved Pittsburgh* (1979): The cast of this movie alone makes it a classic: Julius Erving, Kareem Abdul-Jabbar, Meadowlark Lemon, Norm Nixon, Connie Hawkings, Cedric "Cornbread" Maxwell...I mean...Also, disco is prominently featured throughout this movie, which is about a team of basketball players with the Zodiac sign Pisces. (Fish—get it?) The soundtrack has music by the Four Tops, the Spinners and, wait for it, Loretta Lynn.

- HONORABLE MENTION: *Caddyshack*: It came out while Carter was still president—July 1978—and is, without question, the funniest sports movie ever made. "Former greenskeeper and now about to become the Masters champ..."

Win One for the Gipper

Winning Time for Reagan

Ronald Reagan was not, in any standard sense, a sports fan. He wasn't scheduling his free time around who was playing when—and rarely watched live sports on TV.

The one notable exception to that lack of interest was Notre Dame football, according to Jim Kuhn, who was Reagan's body man for a time in the White House. Why? Because Reagan had famously played George Gipp in the 1940 classic *Knute Rockne, All American*.

The plot of the movie goes something like this: Knute Rockne is a famous football star for Notre Dame. After he finishes his playing career, he starts to coach for the school. Along comes a freshman running back named George Gipp who leads the Fighting Irish to even greater football heights. But, after the final game of the season, Gipp is struck down by illness. As he is dying, he turns to Rockne and tells him that his last wish is for the coach to tell the team to "win one for the Gipper."

"Having the chance to test for the part and getting the part of George Gipp had such a major effect on Reagan," recalled Kuhn. "That was the movie that launched Reagan's acting career." (Reagan had worked behind the scenes to get the movie made, leaning on Hal Wallace, an executive at Warner Bros.)

Of Gipp, Reagan once said: "He has remained very much a part of my life, indeed playing him was the role that moved me into the star category. Curiously enough, at political rallies during my last campaign, there would always be signs out in the crowd referring to me as 'the Gipper.' And believe me, I liked that very much."

To watch Reagan play Gipp is to watch Reagan become Reagan. The young Gipp is cocksure, confident in his abilities and his natural talent. But he is also reserved—keeping almost everyone, with the notable exception of Rockne and his wife, at arm's length.

That is Reagan to a tee. He was friendly to everyone, a natural people person. But, he never let anyone—outside of his wife, Nancy—get too close. Lots of people knew of Reagan. Almost no one actually *knew* him. He had lots of acquaintances but almost no real friends.

"Although he loves people, he often seems remote and he doesn't let anybody get too close," wrote Nancy Reagan of her husband. "There's a wall around him."

Historian H. W. Brands, who has written a biography of Reagan, said that he possessed the "ability to appear likable," adding, "He was likable in a wholesale sense. He had almost no close friends."

Gipp in the movie is effectively a cipher. He's really on-screen for only fifteen minutes or so—going from cocky kid who wows Rockne and takes the college football world by storm to his deathbed in a flash. There is no internal world of George Gipp. He is purely a two-dimensional football star struck down with an unexplained, deadly illness that involved coughing and a sore throat. (Feels like maybe doctors could have helped there?!) He's basically a cardboard cutout.

Reagan was like that, too—a political Everyman on whom people projected whatever they wanted. Reagan could be whatever you hoped and dreamed of him. He was a shapeshifter. He was what you wanted him to be. He was playing the role of your ideal American president. His interior life—if he had one—was forever a mystery.

Reagan's general lack of fandom dovetailed with his concern that by going to a game—of any sort—in person, he would be a distraction and wouldn't add anything. And that sense was even more acute following John Hinckley's assassination attempt on Reagan in 1981.

"After Hinckley, he felt that anywhere he went he was a security threat to other people," said Kuhn. "He didn't want to put everyone through the inconvenience of going through magnetometers."

So, Reagan, that most patriotic of presidents, never attended an Army-Navy football game during his eight years in office.

Every once in a while, Reagan's inner circle would try to convince him to change his nonattendance policy, hoping to get a bit of a political pop from being seen out and about.

Kuhn recounted that in January 1988 the Washington Redskins were hosting the Minnesota Vikings in the NFC championship game.

"We cooked up this idea... what would it take to get Reagan to do a drop-by at that game," said Kuhn. One afternoon while Reagan was in the gym at the White House, Kuhn put the idea to the president. "I wouldn't take 'no,'" he remembered. But the more insistent Kuhn got, the louder Reagan clanged the dumbbells he was lifting together to block out the entreaties. (Reagan didn't go to the game; the Redskins won 17–10 and went on to cruise to a Super Bowl victory two weeks later.)

While Reagan was an indifferent sports fan, he was a dedicated exerciser.

"They had a room upstairs in the [White House] living quarters devoted to weights and the latest workout technology," said Kuhn. "The first thing he did when he got upstairs was get into his workout clothes and start lifting weights." Added Kuhn: "He wanted to stay in shape. He was very regimented about it."

While Reagan was not much of a baseball player—or fan—he understood the power the game held over the American public. (Remember: This was the early 1980s, and the dominance of football as the country's favorite sport was still emerging.)

"If he had a role in some major sporting activity, some ceremony, some game and he could do something to demonstrate his athletic prowess, he liked doing that," said Kuhn. "He liked being with the teams, throwing a football or throwing a baseball. He knew it humanized him more when people saw him doing something like that more than being in the Oval Office."

Reagan liked being around athletes, recalled Mark Weinberg, a former aide to Reagan. "He loved having winning teams at the White House," said Weinberg. "Those were fun events for him."

Early in his first term—March 1981—Reagan invited a number of all-time great baseball players to the White House to be honored. Commissioner Bowie Kuhn announced that it was the largest gathering of Hall of Famers in a single place at a single time.

"The nostalgia is bubbling within me, and I may have to be dragged out of here because of all the stories that are coming up in my mind," Reagan told the players. "Baseball—I had to finally confess over here, no, I didn't play when I was young. I went down the football path. But I did play in a way, as Bob Lemon well knows, I was old Grover Cleveland Alexander, and I've been very proud of that. It was a wonderful experience." (Reagan portrayed Alexander in a 1952 movie called *The Winning Team*.)

At that same gathering, Reagan was given an Oakland A's jacket—courtesy of manager Billy Martin, who was not able to make it to the event. "Hey, look, Ma, I made the team," Reagan joked. He was also given a painting of Grover Cleveland Alexander; "This is just wonderful," Reagan said of the gift. "I never had more fun or enjoyed anything more in my life than when we were making that picture."

Joe DiMaggio, who attended the event, told historian Bill Mares, "I think the president enjoyed the visit even more than we did."

While winning sports teams had, on occasion, stopped by the White House to celebrate in the past, it was Reagan who formalized the trip—welcoming team after team and reveling in their victories.

Reagan understood that being associated with winning was good for him—even if he knew little and cared even less about the sport in question. Whether or not he pored over box scores every morning was beside the point. And that point was this: Americans liked sports. And they especially liked winning sports teams. So standing next to the World

Series winner or the Super Bowl champs or the Stanley Cup holders was a very good thing for a politician whose job was dependent on staying in the good graces of the public.

And so, Reagan invited championship teams to the White House at every opportunity. Which, given his decided lack of knowledge of and interest in sports, led to some awkward and hilarious moments.

In 1985, Reagan brought in the Kansas City Royals—fresh off of their World Series win over the St. Louis Cardinals.

On the night that the Royals beat the Cards in Game 7, the White House had—as they often did—set up a phone line so that Reagan could call into the winning locker room. As Kuhn remembers, the players had zero interest in hearing from Reagan in the immediate afterglow of their victory, and the whole thing was a "mess." Reagan made an error of his own, referring to star Royals closer Dan Quisenberry as "Jim."

When the Royals came to the White House later that month, Kuhn briefed Reagan on the faux pas—and made sure that Quisenberry was the first Royal the president would meet so he could fix his slipup.

When Quisenberry greeted Reagan, the president said, "I know I called you Jim." To which Quisenberry, known for his one-liners, responded, "That's OK, Don." Reagan loved it and was bent over laughing, according to Kuhn.

Reagan had no better luck throwing out first pitches. In 1986, he opened the baseball season at Memorial Stadium where the Baltimore Orioles were playing the Cleveland Indians.

Reagan had been working on his throw with Jim Kuhn outside the White House before heading down to the game. But, knowing his athletic limitations, Reagan ventured only about halfway down the third base line to make his throw.

He wound up uncorking a heater that flew far over catcher Rick Dempsey's head and wound up bouncing all the way to the first base line. Dempsey's assessment? "Good hard fastball, sailing high."

"You could hear the crowd laughing at Reagan," recounted Kuhn. "He's pissed. He told one of the Orioles guys—run down there and tell Dempsey to get him the ball he's going to throw it again. I gave the ball to Reagan. I said, 'This time you know what to do, don't you?' He burned that one in there."

Here's how the UPI wire covered the story: "Reagan Pitches, Misses on Day 1." The wire service also noted that Reagan watched the first few innings of the game from the dugout, technically a violation of the rules of baseball because nonplayers are not allowed in the dugout.

Two years later, Reagan's toss hadn't improved much. This time he was at Wrigley Field, a sort of homecoming for Reagan after his years broadcasting Cubs games.

The Cubs were playing the Pittsburgh Pirates in the final series of the season. Reagan, after surviving an assassination attempt early in his term, had to put on a bulletproof vest in the tunnel under the stadium. When he emerged into the Cubs dugout, he was surrounded by players.

Dressed in a blue velvet Cubs jacket over his shirt and tie, Reagan took the mound. Or, more accurately, the dirt where the mound began. The pitch he uncorked was described, charitably, by the WGN announce team as "high and inside."

Kuhn was more blunt. "The first pitch he threw flew out of his hand at a right angle," he said. "He almost killed a Chicago policeman."

Reagan signed the ball for then-rookie Cubs catcher Damon Berryhill as well as the ball girl who had accompanied him to the mound. But then something strange happened. The president reached into the pocket of his Cubs jacket and pulled out another ball. He made clear to Berryhill he wanted to throw another. And with the Cubs catcher perched just off the third base line, Reagan threw again—and this time it looked more like he knew what he was doing. "It was a macho man showing off his athletic prowess," said Kuhn.

It was also a man deeply aware of his image. Consider it: Reagan had gone to the pitcher's mound that day with an extra ball in his pocket—just in case the first throw didn't go as well as he wanted it to. The first throw was a rehearsal for Reagan. The second was him perfecting the performance. And he had absolutely no qualms about asking the Cubs catcher—and everyone else—in the ballpark to wait on him as he got the throw down to his satisfaction. Reagan knew that if he left it at that first throw, the newscasts and newspapers would be filled with his crappy toss. And he couldn't have that. So he ensured that he would have a do-over.

Weinberg notes that Reagan was ever aware of the message being sent in these photo ops. "It wasn't lost on him or his handlers that bringing a winning team to the White House and having them give him a jersey were not bad visuals," said Weinberg.

Shortly after securing a second term, Reagan hosted the Los Angeles Lakers, who had just won the NBA championship.

"Today we'll say, 'Hail to the Lakers,'" said Reagan. "You're no longer simply Los Angeles's heroes. Today, you belong to the whole country."

The president met privately before the ceremony with team owner Jerry Buss, head coach Pat Riley, and perennial all-star Kareem Abdul-Jabbar. "One thing that Reagan kept talking about was that Kareem ducked his head down coming into the Oval Office...even though he didn't have to," remembered Kuhn. "Reagan talked about that for weeks afterward."

In 1987, Reagan welcomed the Super Bowl champion New York Giants to the White House. He compared their physical play to that of teams from the 1950s: "No one who saw your performance during those close games in the middle of the season and your overpowering victories in the playoffs and the Super Bowl can doubt [that]," said Reagan.

After the official ceremony, the players gathered outside as Reagan and his wife prepared to head to Camp David, the presidential retreat. Reagan emerged with a Gatorade bucket, an homage to Giants linebacker Harry Carson's habit of dumping Gatorade on head coach Bill Parcells after big wins. Reagan dumped the bucket on Carson—only this time it was filled with the president's favorite food: popcorn. Carson returned the favor, dumping popcorn on Reagan.

While Reagan is remembered far more for his horsemanship than any excellence on the athletic fields, his first love was actually football.

Of why he picked the sport, he once wrote: "I never cared for baseball because I was ball-shy at batting. When I stood at the plate, the ball appeared out of nowhere about two feet in front of me. I was always the last chosen for a side in any game. Then I discovered football: no little invisible ball—just another guy to grab or knock down, and it didn't matter if his face was blurred." (Reagan's eyesight was decidedly poor.)

"When I entered Dixon High School in 1924, I was thirteen and worshiped football more than anything else in the world," he wrote in his memoirs. "I wanted desperately to play for the school team. The fact that my brother was already a star on the team only intensified my resolve." (Neil Reagan was three years older than his brother—and a gifted athlete.)

Reagan's problem? He was tiny. He barely broke five feet tall and weighed just over one hundred pounds as a ninth grader. He was so undersized that the school didn't have a pair of football pants that were small enough to fit him. The coach wound up wrangling him "an antique pair of football pants with thigh pads made out of bamboo," wrote Reagan. "I'd never seen anything like those pants before but they fit."

Reagan made it through tryouts but didn't make the team his freshman year. In the summer before his sophomore year, he "decided [he] had to do something fast to build up [his] muscles for the next season" and so he took a job—at thirty-five cents an hour—helping to build houses around Dixon, Illinois.

Reagan caught a break the fall of his sophomore year. The conference his high school was in decided to create a whole new division composed of players who weighed 135 pounds or less. Reagan very much fit the bill. Not only did he make the new team but he was elected captain and played both tackle and guard.

Wrote Reagan of his attraction to the offensive line:

I loved playing on the line. For me, it was probably a marriage made in heaven. It's as fundamental as anything in life—a collision between two bodies, one determined to advance, the other determined to resist; one man against another man, blocking, tackling, breaking through the line.

By his junior year, Reagan had sprouted; he was now nearly six feet tall and weighed a solid if unspectacular 160 pounds. But, despite his newfound size, he found himself relegated to the bench for the first half of the season.

"Then on Saturday morning, the coach, who decided he was unhappy with the playing of one of our first-string guards, convened our regular practice meeting in the locker room and, reading off the starting team, said—I'll never forget it—'*Right Guard, Reagan,*'" wrote the president. "Once I got in, I never let the other guy get his position back. The first-string job was mine for the rest of the season and during my senior year, when I'd grown even bigger, I was a starter from the beginning."

Reagan had caught the football bug. As he wrote: "I'd like to be able to recall that my burning desire to go to college was planted first and foremost in a drive to get an education. But, at seventeen, I think I was probably more motivated by love for a pretty girl and a love of football. Going to college offered me the chance to play football for four more years."

Why did football appeal so strongly to Reagan? He once explained, in blunt terms: "It is the last thing left in civilization where two men can literally fling themselves bodily at one another in combat and not be at war. It's kind of a good, clean hatred. I know of no other game that gave me the same feeling that football did."

Reagan chose Eureka College—a tiny Christian school about ninety minutes due south of Dixon—for two main reasons. First, his high school girlfriend—Margaret Cleaver—had decided to follow her two older sisters to the school. Second, a star fullback on Reagan's high school team— Garland Waggoner—had gone to Eureka and starred on their football squad.

The coach was Ralph "Mac" McKinzie, who had won twelve letters during his own time at Eureka, captaining three sports in the process. But perhaps McKinzie's greatest accomplishment was that he was named head coach of the football team while still a student at Eureka!

As in high school, Reagan's football life got off to an inauspicious start. "I soon reached the conclusion that Mac McKinzie didn't like me," wrote Reagan. "He was not only unimpressed by my high school exploits, he kept me on the bench most of the season and I spent much of my freshman year sulking about it."

His lack of success on the gridiron that year left Reagan with more time for another pastime: politics. He got deeply involved in student-led protests against Eureka's president, Bert Wilson, for a decision to lay off faculty and make a series of other cuts to deal with smaller donations to the school's endowment in the wake of the Great Depression.

Reagan was chosen to make the case for an all-campus strike. "Giving that speech—my first—was as exciting as any I ever gave," he wrote. "For the first time in my life, I felt my words reach out and grab an audience, and it was exhilarating."

A strike was approved. A week later, Wilson resigned.

Reagan didn't initially return to Eureka for his sophomore year. But during a visit to campus he ran into McKinzie, who asked why he wasn't back at school.

"When I told him I was broke and couldn't afford another year at Eureka, he promptly went to bat for me," wrote Reagan of McKinzie in his memoir. "Within an hour or two, the college had renewed my Needy Student Scholarship covering half of my tuition and agreed to defer the balance of the tuition until I graduated."

McKinzie's advocacy for Reagan didn't translate to the football field. "He could look at me and make me feel inadequate," Reagan would write of his coach. He began the season as fifth string, but, he wrote, "I resolved to block and tackle as hard as I could during practice to catch his eye."

Halfway through the season, in a practice, McKinzie assigned Reagan the task of blocking one of the assistant coaches on a run play. McKinzie told Reagan to do his worst to the coach, who was one of his former teammates.

"Never before or since did I throw such a block," recounted Reagan. "When I hit our ex officio coach he ascended as if he'd been hurled by a shot putter and seemed to dangle in mid-air for several moments before plummeting to the ground."

The following week, Reagan was inserted into the starting lineup. For the rest of his college career, he rarely came out of a game.

"I owe Mac a lot," he wrote later. "He didn't dislike me after all; he just saw some things in an eighteen-year-old kid that needed some correcting."

If football was the sport that Reagan excelled in, it was swimming—lifeguarding in particular—where he began to find his sense of self.

At fourteen, Reagan applied to be a lifeguard at Lowell Park on the Rock River—colloquially known as the "Hudson of the Midwest."

For the next seven years, Reagan returned to the lifeguard stand. He was paid $17 per week—plus all the food he could eat from the concession stand.

For Reagan, it was a dream job: perched above the people, tasked with rescuing someone at a moment's notice.

"He relished his responsibility of saving lives (and had plenty of opportunity to exercise it; the stretch of Rock River that he oversaw was treacherous)," wrote Paul Lettow in a biography of Reagan. "Initially frustrated that few of those he saved thanked him for it, Reagan began to mark a notch in a log for each person he rescued. While reconciling himself to public ingratitude—'I got to recognize that people hate to be saved'—he felt an increasing sense of accomplishment as the notches, eventually seventy-seven in all, spread over the log."

Yes, Reagan claimed to have saved seventy-seven lives over his seven years as a lifeguard. That's eleven lives every single year! (Warning: Be careful swimming in the Rock River.)

As John Sayle Watterson notes in his *The Games Presidents Play*, there were rumors kicking around Dixon that Reagan's life-saving numbers had been artificially inflated by "damsels in only modest distress" who wanted to get up close and personal with the handsome lifeguard.

Reagan, looking back, saw lifeguarding as an introduction to his first professional career, acting. "I was the only one up there on the guard stand," he said. "It was like a stage. Everyone had to look at me."

Reagan biographer Lou Cannon said that being a lifeguard was a "job perfectly suited to [Reagan's] personality," adding: "Lifeguards are solitary objects of adoration who intervene in moments of crisis and perform heroic acts without becoming involved in the lives of those they rescue."

But acting was still a little ways off for Reagan. After graduating from tiny Eureka College, Reagan's job prospects were middling, due in large part to the Depression gripping the country. (His father worked as an unpaid volunteer for Franklin Roosevelt's presidential campaign.)

The young Reagan had a vague idea that he would like to try his hand at sports announcing, and he made his way to Chicago in search of a job in the field.

"When I went to Chicago, I met rejection everywhere I went," wrote Reagan in his memoir, *An American Life*. "When I suggested I wanted to become a radio announcer (I never mentioned my real goal of becoming a *sports* announcer), I was practically laughed out the door, usually without even an interview."

Reagan made his way to Des Moines, Iowa—hoping a smaller market might be more willing to give a chance to a radio novice. He found work in nearby Davenport, working for WOC.

Reagan's interview for that job consisted of him reenacting the fourth quarter of a Eureka College football game against Western Illinois that he had, in fact, played in. While Reagan had missed a block—from his position as guard—in that game, when he announced the game—from memory—"I didn't miss that man in the secondary—I delivered an earth-shattering block" that led to the game-winning score. "Having announced the touchdown, I just grabbed the mic with both hands and said 'That's all.'"

The re-creation of an actual event with a bit of embellishment to make him look a bit more heroic is a constant theme of Reagan's life. He was, at heart, a storyteller. And the story he was telling was about himself and what his own journey meant about America and its innate goodness. Fudging a few details along the way—a missed block made, for instance—was OK because it was in service of that larger narrative tapestry that Reagan was weaving.

A few months later, a full-time job opened up at WHO in Des Moines, and Reagan leapt at the chance. His primary job was to broadcast Chicago Cubs games. But this was the 1930s—long before announcers traveled to games to watch them and then tell listeners what they were seeing.

The job Reagan had was much more difficult. A telegraph operator would translate the plays from Morse code (!) and then hand them on a slip of paper to Reagan. It was up to him to embellish the action, painting a scene for those listening in.

In one famous/infamous episode—on June 7, 1934—the Cubs were playing the St. Louis Cardinals. The game was tied 0–0 in the ninth inning. Dizzy Dean was on the mound for the Cards and a Cub named Billy Jurges was up to bat.

Then, suddenly, the telegraph line went dead. Reagan was flying blind, literally. Recalled the president years later:

There were several other stations broadcasting that game and I knew I'd lose my audience if I told them we'd lost our telegraph connection so I took a chance. I had Jurges hit another foul. Then I had him foul one that only missed being a home run by a foot. I had him foul one back in the stands and took up some time describing the two lads who got in a fight over the ball. I kept on having him hit foul balls until I was setting a record for a ball player hitting successive foul balls and I was getting more than a little scared. Just then my operator started typing. When he passed me the paper I started to giggle—it said: "Jurges popped out on the first ball pitched."

That episode is illustrative of the skill set that served Reagan so well in his future careers of acting and politics. He was quick on his feet. His gig as a radio announcer ultimately got him his first chance at Hollywood stardom. In 1937, Reagan convinced his WHO bosses to send him to California to cover the Cubs spring training. (For twenty years—from 1921 to 1941, the Cubs trained on Catalina Island. The island—as well as the baseball team—were owned by William Wrigley Jr.)

While he was in California, Reagan did a screen test for Warner Bros. (He missed a Cubs game for it!) Reagan came back to Iowa for the start of the season, but just days after he returned the studio offered him a job: seven years with a one-year option—paying $200 per week. He immediately accepted and moved to Los Angeles.

While Reagan became famous for his role as George Gipp, that wasn't the only sports figure he played during his time in Hollywood.

As I noted, Reagan had played famed pitcher Grover Cleveland Alexander in *The Winning Team*, which came out in 1952.

Reagan, starring opposite Doris Day, who played Alexander's wife, "portrayed Alexander's struggles with epilepsy, alcoholism, and his triumphant return to pitching, leading to a victory in the 1926 World Series," according to the Reagan Library. Later while he was president, Reagan was given his old costume from the movie as a present.

The studio wouldn't let Reagan mention that Alexander had been epileptic. "I've always regretted that the studio insisted we not use the word, although we did try to get the idea across," he later said.

(Writing in the *Washington Post* in 1987, then Speaker of the House Tip O'Neill related how he had taken a desk once belonging to President Grover Cleveland and had it put in his office. When he told Reagan, the president responded: "That's very interesting. You know, I once played Grover Cleveland in the movies." "No, Mr. President," O'Neill said. "You're thinking of Grover Cleveland Alexander, the ball player.")

The movie made an estimated $1.7 million at the domestic box office—a modest success for the studio. (The biggest grossing movie of 1952 brought in $36 million.)

While Reagan wasn't responsible for the Olympics being awarded to Los Angeles in 1984, he understood the power of the games—and sought to take advantage of the eyes of the world on not just his home country but his adopted home state.

What, exactly, Reagan could and should do at the Olympics proved to be a bit of a logistical nightmare, according to Kuhn. "We thought 'we can't screw this up,'" said Kuhn, noting that he and several other Reagan aides grappled for weeks to find the best way to get Reagan in the Olympic spotlight without him being a distraction from the proceedings.

They eventually settled on a private event with the U.S. Olympic team. The problem was that the event was scheduled for hours before the opening ceremonies were set to begin. So, after the event, Reagan, First Lady Nancy Reagan, and a handful of aides—which included Kuhn—cooled their jets in a private room at the University of South California for three hours—just waiting for the opening ceremonies to begin. "We had plenty to do and Nancy loved to be on the phone," recalled Kuhn about the wait.

Reagan reemerged to open the games, with a seventeen-word "speech."

Said the president: "Celebrating the Twenty-third Olympiad of the modern era, I declare open the Olympic Games of Los Angeles." He then went on to give a brief interview with ABC's Peter Jennings, telling the anchor that the Russians, who boycotted the Los Angeles games, were "losers."

At the event earlier in the day with the athletes, Reagan had nodded to his own theatrical past as a way to motivate the six hundred American Olympians. "Go for it!" Reagan told them. "For yourselves, for your families, for your country. And, you can forgive me if I'm a little presumptuous, do it for the Gipper."

Without the Soviets and the Eastern bloc countries participating, the Olympics turned into a gold medal cavalcade for the United States. The U.S. won 83 gold medals—more than four times as many as the next country (Romania). All told, the U.S. won 174 medals, drastically outpacing West Germany, which finished second in the medal race with 59.

That domination—even with the absence of the Soviet Union (or maybe because of it) helped fuel the Reagan message of America's increasing dominance on the world stage, its emergence as the one, true superpower.

While Reagan never actively played any sport beyond his experience on the football team at Eureka, he did keep a very active lifestyle—largely thanks to his lifelong fascination with horseback riding.

"That's been my sport for many years now and I would hate to ever have to give it up," Reagan once wrote. "It's a great, healthy exercise, in addition to being a lot of fun."

(Reagan, a notoriously nervous flier, once said, "The highest I want to go is on the saddle of a horse.")

He defended riding against people who suggested it wasn't much of a real exercise regimen. "A lot of people don't realize what good exercise horseback riding is," he said. "You don't just get on a horse and sit there as if you are in a deck chair. When that horse takes its first step, every muscle in your body reacts and moves with it. And the faster the horse moves, the more your muscles react."

Reagan started riding as a teenager when he was working as a lifeguard on the Rock River. He served in the Cavalry corps during World War II, although he spent time overseas due to his poor eyesight. (In a 1983 letter to a Texas schoolgirl, Reagan wrote: "I have been nearsighted all my life and when I was young I felt as you do about wearing glasses but I wore them.")

"He was one of the best horsemen that you could ever see," recalled former aide Jim Kuhn. "He rode in the English style. People I know who rode English when they saw pictures of him riding with his heels down, they said this guy had great form."

Reagan continued to ride when he became a movie star. In *Stallion Road*, Reagan did all the riding and jumps himself. The plot of *Stallion Road*, you ask? "A veterinarian and rancher [Reagan] and a novelist compete for the affections of a horse breeder during an outbreak of anthrax," according to IMDB—where it gets 5.9 out of a possible 10 stars. The screenplay was written by William Faulkner, who said of the film: "If you're a horse you'll like the picture."

Four years later, Reagan used his equine skills again—in a picture called *The Last Outpost*. (Plot: "Despite their fighting on opposite sides during the Civil War, brothers Vance and Jeb Britton have to set their differences aside in order to survive an Indian attack.")

Reagan's commitment to horseback riding kicked up a notch when he and his second wife, Nancy, bought Rancho del Cielo, a 688-acre property outside of Santa Barbara, as Reagan was finishing up his second term as governor of California in 1974.

When Reagan was elected president in 1980, the ranch effectively functioned as his western White House. Reagan spent oodles of time there—too much for some of his aides, who referred to it as "Rancho del Lazio." (Reagan also fancied riding a horse in Washington; he wanted to ride one at his inauguration until the Secret Service shut down the idea.)

It's very hard to separate how much of this was Reagan doing what he enjoyed and how much of it was Reagan playing the part of dedicated westerner—on horseback at his ranch, far from those stuffed shirts back in Washington. The important thing to know is that for Reagan there was no separation—playing the part *was* him. George Gipp was Reagan. He was always always always playing a role—football star, westerner, president. Acting was his default way of interacting with the world.

Regardless, Reagan wouldn't hear criticism of the time he spent at the ranch—or how he spent it. In response to a suggestion from Mike Deaver, a longtime top aide, that Reagan limit his trips to the ranch amid media criticism, Reagan blanched.

"You can tell me a lot of things," he told Deaver, "but you're not going to tell me when to go to the ranch. I'm seventy years old and I figure that ranch is going to add some years onto my life, and I'm going to enjoy it."

By the summer of 1987, Reagan had spent 290 days of his presidency at his California ranch and 374 total days in California, according to presidential biographer Lou Cannon. (One example: In August 1987, Reagan took a twenty-five-day California vacation; the *Los Angeles Times* estimated the cost to taxpayers at more than $600,000.)

Reagan kept seven horses on the ranch property during his presidency. His favorite—and preferred mount—was El Alamein, an Arabian. It was a gift from Mexican president José López Portillo prior to Reagan's first inauguration in 1980.

The president's penchant for horseback riding required the Secret Service to adjust—they had to find people who could ride and keep up with Reagan during his many trips to the California ranch.

Enter agent John Barletta, who was a regular companion of the president when he wanted to ride. He learned to ride young; his father was a member of the mounted police force in Boston. Barletta joined the personal protective unit of the Secret Service in the final days of Jimmy Carter's time in office—having little idea that his horse skills would be needed.

"President Reagan did the most dangerous thing you can do," recalled Barletta. "He rode horses. When he first got elected, he would go back to his beloved ranch and his beloved horses. The problem was, by no fault of their own, the agents couldn't keep up with him. They were falling off left and right. One agent finally fell off and broke his arm, and the president jumped off his horse and helped him. That's when they said, 'We're supposed to be protecting him. He's not supposed to be taking care of us.'"

The call came to Washington in search of members of the Secret Service who could ride well. On his first trip out on horseback with the president, Reagan tested Barletta. (Reagan's Secret Service code name was the appropriately-Western "Rawhide.")

"He said, 'John, I'd like to trot,'" remembered Barletta. "I said, 'Mr. President, you can do anything you want.' He was testing me. When he saw that I could do it, the president turns to me and says, 'John, I'd like to canter.' We got going at a fast clip for a while, and he raises his hand and says, 'Whoa.' I have no idea what he's doing, and I run right by him. His horse was going nutty because I went by him. He rides up to me and says, 'Now John, when the commander of the cavalry tells his men to whoa, you stop.' I said, 'It'll never happen again, Mr. President.' We both got a good laugh and headed on our way."

(Sidebar: Barletta rode a gray Arabian, a horse that looked very similar to Reagan's El Alamein. The reason? So that people from afar—especially those who wanted to do Reagan harm—couldn't tell the difference between the two men when they were on horseback.)

Reagan rode every single day he was at the ranch—usually by himself (although, inevitably, with Secret Service lurking nearby) or with Nancy. The solitary nature of the pursuit appealed to Reagan who was, at heart, a loner.

What's clear is that, for Ronald Reagan, being on the back of a horse was his happy place—away from the worries and rigors of the office he held for eight years.

"There's nothing better for the inside of a man than the outside of a horse," he was fond of saying.

In 1987, responding to a letter from an old friend as to whether he still jumped his horses on the ranch, Reagan wrote, "We still ride but since we only get to the ranch a few times a year and my longtime favorite 'Little Man' has gone to horse heaven, I've decided it wouldn't be fair to the job I have. I used to feel that way when I was doing movies. While I was making one I wouldn't jump. It is a sport where accidents can happen to the best of riders and while I miss it I have to feel it wouldn't be right to have to cancel a summit meeting or such while bones mended."

Reagan would also, occasionally, use his horseback skills to help out the country's diplomatic efforts.

In a 1982 trip to the United Kingdom, Reagan traveled to Windsor Castle where he rode alongside fellow equine buff Queen Elizabeth II.

Robert Hardman, a biographer of the royals, pointed out that "President Reagan had singled out one event above all others as the most important element of the entire presidential grand tour of Europe: the prospect of riding with the Queen in Windsor Home Park... Over the next few weeks, numerous confidential memos flew to and fro across the Atlantic about the president's ideal horse, saddle and riding style, along with ideas for dinner guests at the Queen's banquet."

Some British historians credit the riding trip with Reagan's ultimate support of the British defense of the Falkland Islands from Argentinian aggression.

———

Reagan, like almost every twentieth-century president before him, golfed. But he was no Dwight Eisenhower or even Bill Clinton or Barack Obama. Reagan, for example, was the first post–World War II president to never play a round at Burning Tree, the ultra-elite golf club located just outside of Washington.

His golf game waxed and waned, and he generally kept it under wraps, for fear it would clash with his image as a horse-riding, brush-clearing westerner.

"You youngsters probably don't remember but when I was young, golf was a sissy, rich man's game," Reagan recalled in 1970.

In the 1940s as his movie career was surging, Reagan joined Hillcrest Country Club in Los Angeles, which boasted the likes of George Burns and Jack Benny as its members. Reagan's first wife, Jane Wyman, enjoyed the game, which made it easier for Reagan to get out on the links.

"As an actor for Warner Brothers, I was always occupied making one picture or another, and golf was a relaxing way to spend a weekend afternoon."

In the 1950s, when Reagan traveled the country as a spokesman for

General Electric, he played even more—with his handicap dipping as low as 12.

Once Reagan got into politics—he was first elected governor of California in 1966 with a landslide victory over Pat Brown—he played less and less golf. (Reagan's second marriage, to Nancy Davis in 1952, also curtailed his golf game; she wasn't a golfer and he didn't like to be away from her for the long stretches that golf demanded.)

Reagan had one set golf date every year; he, along with Secretary of State George Shultz, would play every year on New Year's Eve at Sunnylands, the sprawling estate of publishing magnate Walter Annenberg.

Reagan was also involved in one of the most infamous incidents in the history of Augusta National, maybe the most revered golf course in the entire country.

In October 1983, Reagan traveled to the golf mecca for two days of playing—alongside Shultz, Treasury Secretary Donald Regan, and New Jersey senator Nicholas Brady. (Shultz, a golfing fanatic, was a member at Augusta.)

When that group reached the sixteenth hole, word came that a man had crashed through the gates of the private course and was holding hostages in the pro shop.

He was a forty-five-year-old Georgia man named Charlie Harris. Harris grew up near the club and had worked concessions during the annual Masters tournament at Augusta. He was out of work and not happy about it. And so he decided to demand a conversation with the president.

"I never had any idea of shooting the president," Harris said years later. "If I'd wanted to kill him, I'd have driven up to him and done it. I just wanted to talk to him. I was protesting our government giving our jobs to foreign people."

As time wore on, Harris let each of the six hostages go. By that time, Reagan had been put in the presidential limousine for his safety—although he did try to call Harris. "This is the president of the United States," he said. "This is Ronald Reagan. I understood you want to talk to me…If you are hearing me, won't you tell me what you want?" But the call never went through.

By 4:20 in the afternoon, two hours after Harris crashed the gates and long after Reagan was gone from the course, Harris surrendered. "With Reagan gone, I put my gun down and figured I might as well take my punishment," he told *Golf Digest* years later.

Twenty-four hours after the episode, a suicide bomber drove a truck filled with explosives into a Marines barrack in Beirut, killing 241. Which is why almost no one remembers the Augusta incident.

That same year, Reagan held an event in the Rose Garden honoring the Washington Capitals and the 1984 U.S. Olympic team. A small rink was even constructed. (The two teams were playing each other in an exhibition.)

"What's the penalty for delaying the game?" Reagan joked as he took the podium after a solid five minutes of hand shaking with the various athletes arrayed behind him.

"Athletic rivalry is the best spirit of competition," Reagan said before telling the players that he "follow[ed] their progress" and that "last year you were great."

Reagan's lack of fandom is revealed, however, even in his short speech. He mentions that he was at the Capital Center—where the exhibition was to be played—the previous week and there was a rodeo in town. Except that Reagan pronounced it "ro-day-o"—as in the fancy street in Beverly Hills, California.

As Reagan wrapped up his remarks, he exhorted the group to "play ball," which was, well, weird. What followed was a classic bit of stagecraft by the old actor.

After Capital captain Rod Langway said to Reagan that "we hear you were a pretty good athlete in your day," he showed Reagan how to shoot a few pucks at the goalie. Reagan stepped up to try his hand. The first puck he shot went in. He immediately headed back to the microphones and declared, "You will never see me hit another puck again" to much laughter from the crowd.

Reagan then grabbed another puck, put it down, and hit it at the press pool—again to considerable laughter. "It wouldn't have hurt them," he joked.

Horseshoes and Handshakes...

A Pitcher Named Poppy

A Good Sport: GHWB...

You Da Man

George H. W. Bush's mother, Dorothy, was a gifted tennis player. And a very competitive person.

So competitive, in fact, that she dreamed up a mythical ranking committee as a way to measure her kids (and herself) against each other. She would say, "Let's see how that fares with the ranking committee" whenever there was a dispute among her children, according to CBS Sports' Jim Nantz, a close friend of the family.

The committee existed as a way for the matriarch of the Bush family to install two fundamental values in her brood: that competition was a good thing and that there was a way to behave and a way not to behave with your competitors.

Dorothy was a "tennis maven," in the words of John H. Sununu, who served as chief of staff to the president (and spent time as the governor of New Hampshire).

There was a tennis court at Walker's Point, the Bush's summer compound in Kennebunkport, Maine, and it was in near-constant use as the president was growing up.

"His mother was a tremendous influence on him and the sports character was formed on the tennis court," said Sununu. "She loved tennis and she inculcated tennis into all of her children. She thought it had char-acter-building aspects to it—calling your and your opponent's shots in and out stimulated a sense of fairness and honesty."

Doro Bush Koch, the daughter of the forty-first president and the sis-ter of the forty-third president, said that her father and grandmother were very close. "She had a huge influence on him. Dad adored her," said Koch. "Even Dad's siblings would say that his mother and he had a very special relationship."

She was a person of "deep faith" who "believed in all the Christian tenets," said Koch. "You don't think too much about yourself. You work hard. Discipline was a part of it. Dad embodied all of those wonderful things."

Bush's mom also had a pet saying—about sports and life: "Don't brag and always bend your knees when you volley." Her son would regu-larly mention that quote during his years in the White House, recalled Sununu. "In there was a lot of the formula that he paid attention to," he said.

As Bush Sr. wrote of his mother in a letter to his own granddaughter in 1996:

She was a great athlete—the best of all her friends... Her best sport was tennis. At age 17, she was the runner up in the National Girl's singles tournament being held at the Merion Cricket Club in Phila-delphia. But she never bragged about that... She taught us all about sportsmanship—some by bawling us out when we were bad sports, and some by example. She never complained or found excuses when she lost.

Jean Becker, George H. W. Bush's longtime chief of staff after he left the White House, said that the president would regularly tell a story about coming home after a soccer game touting the fact that he had scored two goals. "His mother chastised him," Becker said. "She asked, 'George, how did the *team* do?'"

That sense of the purposeful sublimation of self to team predated even Bush's mom. As Koch wrote in her book *My Father, My President*:

[The] family philosophy was spelled out in a letter that Dad came across a few years ago… The letter was written by my great-grandfather George Herbert Walker as he was steaming out of New York Harbor past the Statue of Liberty on a ship to France.

The letter, addressed to his four youngest children, included these lines:

Be good losers and winners too, play fair, and if in doubt, give the other fellow the benefit of it, and you will also grow to be good sportsmen, than which there is nothing finer. Give me a man who is one, and I will show you a man of high character and principles.

For Bush, the son of a senator and raised in wealth, sports taught him humility—and to always remember that how you carried yourself during a competition was just as important as the outcome of the game or match.

"He was one of the most gracious people I have ever met," said Sean Coffey, who served as the president's body man. "He was raised by his mother to be self-effacing and practice humility."

That self-effacing nature made Bush a gifted public servant—always quick to share credit and defer attention to others—but complicated his four years as president.

A man disinclined to take credit is not a man made for the modern presidency, which rewards those who willingly hog the spotlight and grab kudos perhaps best meant for others. Bush was trained—from a very young age—not to toot his own horn. Which made him a lovely person to work for—to a person those who worked in his White House revere him—but not, maybe, the perfect fit as president.

What's striking is how different the public perception of Bush during his presidency was from this image of the hypercompetitive—and hypersuccessful—athlete.

An October 1987 *Newsweek* cover story carried the headline "Fighting the 'Wimp' Factor" and included these lines:

> Bush suffers from a potentially crippling handicap—a perception that he isn't strong enough or tough enough for the challenges of the Oval Office. That he is, in a single mean word, a wimp.

The cover image—of Bush clad in a yellow rain jacket behind the wheel of his favorite boat—didn't do the president any favors either.

That perception dogged Bush throughout the campaign. "Fairly or unfairly, voters have a deep-rooted perception of him as a guy who takes direction, who's not a leader," Peter Hart, a Democratic pollster, said of Bush.

Bush took the notion deeply personally. Of the *Newsweek* cover, he wrote in his personal diary: "The cheapest shot I've seen in my political life."

The image haunted him. A son of privilege—his father had been a senator, after all—he didn't share the sort of up-from-your-bootstraps backstory that the public loved. Bush's patrician background—and the perceived aloofness that went with it—was made worse by Reagan's common touch—and the distance he and his wife kept from the Bushes when they shared the White House.

Bush compounded that negative perception during a famous/infamous incident at the National Grocers convention in Florida in 1992.

Bush was being shown a new electronic scanner. According to the pool report, Bush had a "look of wonder" on his face during the presentation.

The media pounced.

According to an account of the incident in the *New York Times* headlined, "Bush Enters the Supermarket, Amazed":

> The look of wonder flickered across his face again as he saw the item and price registered on the cash register screen... Some grocery stores began using electronic scanners as early as 1976, and the devices have been in general use in American supermarkets for a decade.

The message was clear: With the economy headed into a recession—it would become official later that year—the president was deeply out of touch with how normal people lived. He didn't even know what a grocery scanner was!

The reality was far more kind to the president. The scanner Bush was being shown was, in fact, new. It was able to weigh items and to read ripped and torn barcodes. His wonder was at least somewhat justified.

The scanner incident was indicative of a broader theme of the Bush presidency: He—and it—looked far better in the light of history than in the moment.

As Evan Thomas, who edited the "Wimp" story for *Newsweek* back in the late '80s, wrote in 2018:

> The elder Bush, it's true, could sound tinny as a politician. He lacked the common touch of his son, who was more of a true Texan than his East Coast transplant father. Bush could seem vaguely uncomfortable asking for votes. He had trouble with the pronoun "I," dropping it as the subject of a sentence. "Not going to do it!" he might say. He had perhaps too successfully internalized the sermon of his High WASP mother, Dorothy Walker Bush, to never boast— to beware of what she called "the Great I Am."
>
> But Bush's humility was at once genuine and born of a deep and secure sense of self and place. He had been raised (as a matter of patrician duty) to humble himself in great causes, in service to God and country. His physical bravery was unquestionable. In World War II, he was commissioned as the youngest aviator in the U.S. Navy, a mere 19 years old. He flew into battle with dauntless courage. Shot down by the Japanese, he was rescued by an American submarine.

Also, in 2018, the *USA Today* editorial board wrote of Bush that he "personified a time when Democrats and Republicans could work together and when careful international diplomacy was not scorned as a sign of weakness."

That reexamination comes after Bush was roundly derided by Republicans—and mocked by Democrats—as he joined the ignominious list of presidents who had lost a bid for a second term.

In C-SPAN's 2021 survey of presidential historians, Bush ranked twenty-first, just behind the man who beat him (Bill Clinton ranks nineteenth) and eight spots ahead of his son, George W. Bush.

Like his presidency, Bush's athleticism was the understated type. You might not know it to look at him, but with the exception of Gerry Ford for football, Bush was the most athletic president to ever sit in the Oval Office.

———————

Bush never sniffed playing professional ball. (The market for a light-hitting corner infielder was—and is—pretty sparse.)

But that doesn't mean he never played with major leaguers. He did—and he stood out.

The scene: Denver, 1984. The Old Timers game at Mile High Field. And a very persistent Warren Spahn.

Bush happened to be in Denver in his official capacity as vice president. And he found himself staying in the same hotel as some of the legends of the game—including Spahn, Whitey Ford, Juan Marichal, Billy Martin, and Moose Skowron.

Someone got word to Bush that he was sharing a hotel with these eminences of America's pastime. So, Bush, a baseball nut, popped into a room where a bunch of them were gathered for a quick picture.

"Warren Spahn says to the Vice President, 'You ought to come to the game,'" recalled Sean Coffey, Bush's body man at the time. It was the first in a series of escalations from Warren Spahn.

The Secret Service initially balked, pointing out that they hadn't swept the stadium as part of their typical safety protocol. But they eventually relented—swayed by the fact that no one except for a few living baseball legends knew Bush would even be there.

Bush showed up at the stadium the next day and Spahn had a jersey waiting for him. (It was a uniform from the Denver Bears, the local minor league team.) Spahn cajoled Bush to put it on and then invited him to come to the dugout with the team. Bush hesitated—he wasn't sure if the Secret Service had cleared him to go out onto the field like that—but he leapt at the opportunity once he was cleared to do so.

As Bush appeared in the dugout, the public address announcer informed the crowd that he was at the game. "To say he was given a chilly reception was an understatement," said Coffey. "The fans didn't come to the game to see politics. There were more boos than anything else."

In the fourth inning, Spahn turned to the veep and said, "You've got to bat." And suddenly the second most powerful politician in America was in the batter's box facing down Milt Pappas. Bush lined a hard single to left center field—and the crowd began to warm to him. He was erased on a force-out at second but got another good round of applause from the fans as he made his way back to the dugout.

(Sidebar: There was considerable speculation after the game that Pappas had grooved a pitch to Bush, allowing him a bit of glory. Both men denied it.)

Bush, understandably, thought his night was over—and had to be pleased with himself. Enter Spahn who, as the vice president approached the dugout, told him to grab a glove and play first base in the next inning.

The first batter up was Orlando Cepeda, the famed San Francisco Giants slugger. Cepeda hit a rocket down the first base line that looked headed for a double. Bush, who was in his midsixties at this point, leapt to his left, knocked the ball down, and delivered an on-the-mark, underhand flip to the pitcher covering first for the out.

The fans erupted in applause. "It was stunning," remembered Coffey. "He had the crowd in the palm of his hand."

The vice president went to bed after the game. Coffey did not. He went out drinking with the likes of Skowron, Martin, and Don Larsen, still the only man to pitch a perfect game in the World Series.

Early the next morning, as Coffey was in the shower nursing a hangover, Bush knocked on the door with a mission: deliver a bunch of golf shirts with the vice presidential seal on them to the various players he had met (and shared a field with) the night before.

"It was six thirty in the morning," Coffey said. "I was banging on the doors of these hungover retired ball players. Not a single one answered the door...I wound up shoving part of the shirt under each door."

Why did George Herbert Walker Bush love sports so much?

"He was the most competitive person I ever met in my life," said Jean Becker, Bush's longtime chief of staff in his post–White House days. "It didn't matter whether it was golf or tennis or horseshoes. In his later years, he would challenge the grandkids to who would be the first to fall asleep."

Becker told me about an annual Christmas party the Bushes held while he was in the White House as president and vice president. Usually, she said, the gifts would be various things that First Lady Barbara Bush had been given over the previous year. Rather than just dole out the gifts, Bush would "make up some bizarre guessing game and whoever got the answer first would pick the first present," said Becker.

Any conversation about George H. W. Bush's competitive spirit naturally leads back to his mother, Dorothy. She was a nationally ranked player and might have been the best athlete in the clan. Her uncle, Joseph Wear, won a bronze medal in doubles tennis at the 1904 Olympics in St. Louis.

In sports, however, Bush could let it all—or most of it—hang out. "Sports was a way for him to unleash his inner macho," said Coffey. "It was a place where competitiveness and beating out others was sanctioned, it was OK."

Bush's mom could be tough on him. As Bush once told *Forbes* about his mother: "I once complained to her after a poor tennis match that I was off my game. And she said, 'You don't have a game. Get out there and practice.'"

Whether by chance or by personality, Bush was always most drawn to team sports—baseball most of all. "He was very big on team and teamwork," said Becker. "I remember him wondering how people who didn't play sports learned the concept of team. 'How did you learn the true meaning of teamwork,' he would ask."

His mother came up in another round of golf—this one with former LPGA great Amy Alcott at the Hillcrest Country Club in Los Angeles. (Los Angeles mayor Dick Riordan joined them for the round.)

Alcott remembers that as they were walking up to the third hole, the subject turned to moms. "I knew how close he was to his mom," she said. "I started telling him about my mom; he was fascinated about the closeness of our relationships with our mothers. He started to get a tear in his eye."

(Bush had seen Alcott win the U.S. Women's Open in Nashville in 1980. She was one of his favorite golfers and he wanted to play with her. The previous day—while she was playing golf with, wait for it, Kenny G—she had been passed a message that there was a phone call for her and that she would probably want to take it. "It was one of his security guys asking if I wanted to play golf the next day," Alcott remembers.)

Alcott's assessment of Bush? "He was an average golfer but a very good putter. And he was someone who liked to see other people do well."

In 1991, John Sununu came to Bush with a proposal: It was the fifty-year anniversary of Red Sox great Ted Williams hitting .406 (still the last player to hit over .400 for a full season) and New York Yankee legend Joe DiMaggio's fifty-six-game hitting streak. (Bush was a diehard Red Sox fan; Sununu rooted for the Yankees.)

The plan they cooked up was this: Bush would award Williams and DiMaggio a presidential medal at the White House. Then he, Sununu, and the two baseball legends would hop in a plane and jet to Toronto—where the president was slated to throw out the first pitch at the All-Star Game.

"We did it so we would have them in the plane for two hours and talk baseball," remembered Sununu.

Bush, like Richard Nixon before him, befriended Williams. The two men, who might have appeared opposites from afar, had much in common—most notably that each had served as a fighter pilot during World War II. (Williams also served in the Korean War.)

Amazingly, the two men were enlisted at the same place and same time in 1942. As Anne Keene wrote in the *Dallas Morning News* in 2018, "Fate would have it that Bush and Williams were selected from a pool of applicants by the Naval Aviation Cadet Selection Board in Boston. Their names were both misspelled on the memo to the chief of naval personnel as: WILLIANS, Theodore Samuel, and BUSH, George Herbert Nalker. The subject of the memo with slightly blurred lettering read, 'Enlistment papers, transmittal, of.'"

(Williams, already a star baseball player at age twenty-three, was at the top of the list of enlistees. Bush, then just eighteen and a relative unknown, was fifteenth on the list of twenty-one.)

Williams and Bush stayed close over the years as Bush's political star rose. Williams, still a celebrity in New England long after his playing days were over, campaigned for Bush in the 1988 New Hampshire primary where Bush, then the vice president, beat back a challenge from Kansas senator Bob Dole.

———

Baseball's appeal to Bush was, according to Sununu, a function of the times in which they both grew up. (Bush was born in 1924; Sununu was fifteen years his junior.)

"There was a magic attraction in the 1940s and 1950s to young men in baseball," said Sununu. "Radio was just beginning to carry games" and you would often have to jiggle the dial four or five times to get any game to be audible. The thrill of that hunt—and the voice coming through the radio telling you of balls and strikes and outs on a field that you could only imagine in your head—sucked in Bush, Sununu, and lots of boys of their generations.

"It created an allegiance to a team and an allegiance to a sport," said Sununu. "That's how he fell in love with baseball."

Bush began playing baseball more competitively at Phillips Academy in Andover—now a co-ed school known as Phillips Andover. "Boys schools are such that if you have any physical capability, you try out for the team," said Sununu of Bush. And Bush had ability. He was the captain of Andover's 1942 team, and the school paper described him as a "very dependable hitter and a really slick fielder."

Whenever Bush would come back to the school in later years, he would always make a point to stop by the baseball diamond. "I think perhaps visiting our baseball diamond brought back fond memories from his youth out there on the field with his best friends, in that uniform, representing the school he loves so much," said Kevin Graber, the high school's baseball coach, in 2019.

Bush went on to be a two-year captain of the Yale baseball team. And, the team was good. In back-to-back seasons the Elis made it to the national world series and lost—effectively enshrining themselves as the second best team each year.

In that role, Bush had a somewhat-chance encounter with the legendary Babe Ruth.

On June 5, 1948, Ruth came to Yale to officially present his memoir—*The Babe Ruth Story*—to the school's library. In an on-field ceremony Ruth handed the book to Yale's baseball captain—none other than George Bush. A photo exists of the meeting, a snap made all the more powerful by the fact that Ruth died just over two months later.

More than fifty years later, the Topps trading card company issued a card to commemorate Bush's time on the Yale team—printing one hundred of them and delivering them to the White House.

"The only thing that bothered him," remembered Sununu, "is that they put his batting average on there."

Bush gave Sununu, a fellow baseball fan, a handful of the cards. Sununu sent them to be formally graded. Which was when he—and Bush—learned that they weren't the only ones who had the card.

Some had been apparently smuggled out of the Topps manufacturing plant even before they had been given to the president. But the card grader—Professional Sports Authenticator—found that there were discrepancies between the two versions of the card!

"We realized the difference when a former White House official submitted his cards for certification," said Joe Orlando, the president of PSA, in 2013. (The White House official was Sununu.) "We now know the White House–issued cards have an almost laminated, reflective look to the front, while the other George Bush cards look and feel just like the regular Topps cards produced for their 1990 baseball card set."

Added Orlando: "It has long been said that only one hundred cards were made for this project. While there has been some dispute over the years as to exactly how many were manufactured, as a result of this study we are now certain that more than one hundred were produced. One version actually made it to the White House and the other one did not."

———

There's one baseball story that sounds too good to be true—probably because it is. And it goes like this: Bush invented the now-ubiquitous term "You da man!"

The story—or stories, since there are two—goes like this:

Story 1 (as told by Texas representative Roger Williams in 2018): Bush was at a Colt .45s game in 1961 in Houston. Rusty Staub was one of the stars of that team. Staub reportedly wanted to meet Bush. (Which, in and of itself, is sort of weird, considering that Bush, at the time, was an oil executive. He wouldn't win his first office—a House seat in the Houston area—until five years later.)

Anyway, Staub came toward Bush, and, as the future president later recollected, "I don't know why I said it and don't know what it meant, but when he came closer to me I said, 'You da man.'"

Later, Bush told the story to Houston Astros owner Drayton McLane. (In December 1964, the Colt .45s became the Astros.) McLane reportedly responded, "Well, if you haven't gotten any credit for it, we are playing the Dodgers tomorrow night, will put on the diamond vision your picture, and we will put, 'You da man.'" As Williams recounted: "The next night they did and he got the credit for 'You da man.'"

Story 2 (as told by *New York Times* columnist Maureen Dowd): "One of the only things that 41 ever boasted about was when he began hilariously claiming, after he got out of office, that he had coined the phrase 'You da man!' in the '60s."

Dwight Eisenhower

John F. Kennedy

Lyndon Johnson

Richard Nixon

Gerald Ford

Jimmy Carter

Ronald Reagan

George H. W. Bush

Bill Clinton

George W. Bush

Donald Trump

Joe Biden

Doro Bush Koch, the daughter of the late president, wrote in her own memoir about the Staub legend. "He maintains he was inspired to shout it to Houston Astros' Rusty Staub as he rounded third base following a home run, and it slowly caught on from there," Koch wrote.

So, which was it? Did Bush invent "You da man" after Staub had hit a home run? Or when Staub approached Bush to introduce himself?

Probably neither.

All the way back in the second half of the nineteenth century, Otto von Bismarck was quoted as referring to British prime minister Benjamin Disraeli this way: "The Old Jew, he is the man." Yes, really.

The *Urban Dictionary*—yup we went from Bismarck to the *Urban Dictionary* that quickly!!—entry is dated 2007 and defines "you da man" as "Usually, it shows admiration from the person who says it towards the person to whom the sentence is intended." It offers no etymology of the phrase, however.

In 1999, Jesse Sheidlower, a former editor in chief of the *Oxford English Dictionary*, wrote this of the origins of the phrase: "The affirmation 'You the man!' appears to have gotten popular in the mainstream only since the early 1990s. The expression originated among black speakers, and the use of the verb-less 'You the man' instead of 'you're the man,' and the pronunciation 'You da man,' are both intended to reflect a common Black English usage."

By the late 1990s, the phrase had sunk far enough into the culture to make it into that era-defining film *Armageddon*.

In case you either (a) never saw that classic (shame on you!) or (b) forgot it, the plot went like this: A group of deep-sea miners are secretly recruited by the federal government to take a spaceship, land it on a massive meteor on a collision course for earth, drill into it, and plant nuclear bombs to explode it into smaller, less Armageddon-causing pieces. Yes, that was really the plot. (After Harry Stamper aka Bruce Willis blows up the meteor—and himself—and saves Earth, Michael Clarke Duncan's character says in wonderment, "You're the man, Harry.")

Nowhere, other than in Bush's memory, is the phrase credited to the former president. Of course, there isn't anywhere that claims Bush *didn't* invent the term. Most language experts trace its origins to the early 1990s when people started shouting it to golfers after they had hit good tee shots.

The sport that Bush leaned on most to serve his political ends wasn't tennis or baseball, however. It was horseshoes.

"He used horseshoes to create a variety of relationships," said Sununu, Bush's chief of staff in the White House.

The proximity of the horseshoe pit to the Oval Office was no accident then. (It was directly outside the office, next to the swimming pool.) They were all-weather clay—at the request of the president. (Sand was the usual base for a horseshoe pit.)

"It was horseshoe diplomacy," recalls Brian Yablonski, the twenty-something staffer charged with the management of both the horseshoe pit and the twice-yearly—once in the fall and once in the spring—tournaments featuring the White House permanent staff that Bush held. "Big decisions were made on the horseshoe pitch. Relationships were built and friendships were forged."

Sununu remembered that the first time Russian president Mikhail Gorbachev came to the White House, the two men walked by the horseshoe pit. Gorbachev grabbed one of the shoes and threw a ringer on his first toss. The White House Protocol Office got the shoe, framed it, and presented it to Gorbachev that night with a small plaque.

Bush, for what it's worth, also played horseshoes with Queen Elizabeth in 1991. (She gave him four silver horseshoes with "EIIR" engraved on them.) He played with Russian president Boris Yeltsin. And the prime ministers of Australia, Canada, and Japan. And singer John Denver.

Bush was competitive in everything he did—including throwing horseshoes. He was a member of the National Horseshoe Pitchers Association and averaged—yes, averaged!—twenty-five ringers a game.

And he took it all very seriously—especially the twice-yearly tournaments which Yablonski was put in charge of.

"I was a twenty-one-year-old staffer so they weren't going to hand me the State of the Union address to edit," Yablonski said. "The horseshoe thing was because I was the low guy on the totem pole."

But the access that Yablonski got to the president was something decidedly unusual for a staffer of his greenness.

"Before big matches, he would have me go to 7-Eleven and get bags of ice and we would lay them on top of the clay," explained Yablonski. The ice would keep the clay from melting and turning gummy. "That was his idea. That's how in the weeds he would get."

Yablonski recalled that many a time he would be sitting at his desk— right outside the chief of staff's office—and his phone would light up and he would be told, "The president needs to see you in the horseshoe pit."

Bush loved pomp and circumstance with his sports—including horseshoes. He would introduce Yablonski as the "White House Horseshoe Commissioner." And Yablonski's title wasn't merely ceremonial. "My job was to come out and I had calipers to measure whose shoe was closer," he said. "The president wanted a fair and independent judge."

When Yablonski left the White House, Bush had his measuring calipers mounted on a wood block with a glass case over it as a keepsake for the young staffer.

The two big tournaments held at the White House were the busy season of the horseshoeing year for the president. The tournaments had names—because of course they did. There was the Fall Classic in, well, the fall, and the Sweet 16 tournament to coincide with the NCAA basketball March Madness in the spring.

And the teams were not made up of Bush's cabinet or members of Congress or even foreign dignitaries. Instead, they were teams of the permanent staff at the White House.

So, the executive chefs had a team. And the White House electricians. And the butlers. And the groundskeepers. And the White House military office. And, yes, the president and his son Marvin.

"These were career civil servants in the White House who never got any glory," said Yablonski. "The president elevated them intentionally into part of the family."

(Yablonski, due to his role as the horseshoe commissioner was one of the non–career staff who had a spot in the tournaments. He often played with Tim McBride, Bush's personal aide. At one point, Yablonski ran into First Lady Barbara Bush in the Oval Office. Mrs. Bush asked about his team with McBride. "I said we had just beat the White House chefs and Mrs. Bush responded, 'That doesn't say much; the chefs aren't all that good.'")

There were brackets. And scouting—by the president.

"Gorbachev was doing his state visit in the middle of our Sweet 16 invitational tournament," recalled Yablonski. "We were sitting in a room and he was getting ready to go meet Gorbachev in the Rose Garden. The president started asking me for a scouting report on the White House military aides because he had heard they had a good horseshoe thrower."

(The electricians wound up beating the president and Marvin in their next match; the president, like many athletes, got caught looking ahead at his opponents.)

Legends grew in the horseshoe circles of the White House. The "Housemen"—who were charged with the upkeep of 1600 Pennsylvania Avenue—were always the team to beat. They had a guy named Ron "the Mouth" Jones who was "about as big as an NFL lineman," according to Yablonski.

The president would work to get in Jones's head before he pitched the shoe. "You do know you are pitching against the leader of the free world right now," Bush would tell Jones. Added Yablonski: "The president was not above using his office to intimidate. There was a lot of good-natured smack talk."

For the finals every year, Bush would invite the families to the White House so they could watch. There would be awards given.

"It was competitive but there was a thoughtfulness to it," said Yablonski. "He wanted everyone to feel like their role was important. It was a great staff morale booster."

———————

While the horseshoe tournament was for the behind-the-scenes staff at the White House, Bush did have a few very famous friends in sports, too.

Nantz, the voice of CBS Sports, first met Bush at the lowest point of the president's political career.

Nantz had played golf at the University of Houston—he was teammates with PGA legend Freddie Couples—before launching his broadcasting career, and a friend from the team had grown close to Bush during his time in the White House. Bush peppered the friend with questions about Nantz, and so a golf outing was proposed.

It came to pass in early 1993, soon after Bush had lost his bid for a second term to Bill Clinton. The two men met at the Memorial Park public course in the heart of Houston. The motorcade pulled up, Bush hopped out and made his way to the clubhouse.

"Four greens fees, two carts for us, and two carts for the [Secret Service] agents," Bush told the club pro, according to Nantz. "They instantly said, 'Mr. President, you're our guest, you're not paying.'"

But Bush insisted. "If I'm not paying, I'm not playing," Bush said. "If you do comp us, I will never come back here again. I am going to think that you think I expect to be comped again. I don't want you thinking I think that I can come out here for free."

The pro acquiesced. The president paid. (Nantz remembers the total cost: $262.)

On the first tee, the foursome agreed to play for a dollar on the front nine, a dollar on the back nine, and a dollar for the entire eighteen. The president and Nantz were partnered together and coming up to the sixteenth hole, they had secured the victory. Bush pulled Nantz aside and said seriously, "These guys want to press us? Should we let them?" (Pressing would mean that the final three holes would be worth three dollars.)

Nantz admitted to being slightly confused. "Sometimes when people are talking about gambling, 'one dollar' could mean a thousand dollars," he said. But he quickly realized that Bush was asking him about just three dollars—three hundred pennies. "Now I understood the spirit of the man," said Nantz. "I said 'Let's live dangerously...let's do it.'"

Nantz was a regular golf buddy of Bush—and even played social coordinator when the forty-first president and the man who beat him wanted to get together.

Bush and Clinton had joined forces in early 2005 to help raise money for relief efforts in the wake of the massive tsunami that hit southeast Asia at the end of 2004.

The two men had grown friendly during that experience—this was at a time before the idea of politicians from opposing parties being friendly was anathema—and wanted to get together socially.

But they needed an "intermediary" (in Nantz's words) to set things up. Nantz agreed and the two former presidents said they would defer to his schedule since he was busier than they were. (Nantz took the original call from Bush asking for a favor at the Final Four in St. Louis.)

A date was set—June 28 and 29. A location was picked: Bush's Walker's Point compound in Kennebunkport, Maine.

The only thing that remained was how to get Clinton in and out of Maine without attracting lots of attention. (Neither former president was terribly keen on drawing a press horde for a social visit.)

It was decided that the two presidents—plus Nantz—would rendezvous at a point up the Maine coast from Walker's Point. (Clinton had a book signing in Maine by way of explaining his presence in the state.)

How? By boat—of course. A boat piloted by none other than the forty-first president of the United States. It was a foggy day and "he was operating off of instruments," Nantz recalled. "He cut back the engine and we glided into a port. It was right out of a spy novel."

Clinton, wearing orange, was easy to spot—in spite of the fog. Bush hopped off the boat and the two men embraced.

Rather than go back via the boat—Bush explained to Clinton that it had been a choppy ride up—they decided to hop into a Suburban and make the drive back to Walker's Point. "It was just two former presidents coming down I-95," Nantz said. "Clinton was on the window side behind the driver, I was sitting in the middle, and Bush was on the other side." They ran into traffic—95 traffic spares no man, not even an ex-president—and all Nantz could think was "If all of these cars only knew that there happened to be two presidents of the United States in the car next to them."

That night the group—which included Barbara Bush as well as the president's daughter Doro Bush Koch—had dinner in a private room at a place called Striper's. (It's still there!) Mrs. Bush leaned over to Nantz and asked him to make a toast to commemorate the historic coming together of two former presidents.

Nantz remembers what he said word for word. "One of the most amazing things that can ever be said about the greatness of our country is that two former political rivals can come together out of love and respect and friendship just to enjoy one another's company."

The following year, the two presidents—and Nantz—got together again, again at Walker's Point. They were looking for someone to add to their foursome, and Nantz suggested New England Patriots QB Tom Brady who was, after all, in the area.

"I thought the phone call had dropped," said Nantz, describing the silence on the other end from Bush. "He said, 'You really think Tom would play golf up here with us?' He was so innocent about his own stature. I said, 'I like our chances.'"

Nantz called Brady, and Brady agreed to make the trip. He did so by helicopter, which landed on an ample green lawn right outside of Bush's office at Walker's Point. They played—they switched partners every six holes—and, as Nantz recalls, he and the star QB beat the two former presidents with ease.

───────────

Nantz wasn't Bush's only famous friend in the sports world. He was also extremely close to bodybuilder-turned-politician Arnold Schwarzenegger.

Schwarzenegger first met George Bush in the early 1980s. The legendary bodybuilder had been invited to the White House by Ronald Reagan, who, a Hollywood star himself before becoming a politician, liked to be around other celebrities.

"He was vice president. He was always very nice and came over to our table and talked to us at great length," recalled Schwarzenegger in a 2018 interview with CNN's Jake Tapper. "He was a very sincere man and just a wonderful human being."

When Bush was running for president in his own right in 1988, he reached out to Schwarzenegger in the final days of the campaign; Bush wanted to lean on Schwarzenegger's star power for a rally in Columbus, Ohio.

That appearance came as a result of a relationship between Schwarzenegger and Jim Lorimer, who was, at the time, vice president for government relations for Nationwide Insurance. (Nationwide is based in Columbus.)

Lorimer recounted in 2018 that he called Bush's office as the campaign's final weekend neared and said, "I can guarantee 10,000 people for a fundraiser if you will come here—and would you like to have The Terminator or Conan to introduce Vice President Bush?"

Bush was so happy with the reception in Columbus that he asked Schwarzenegger to introduce him in New Jersey and Chicago—among other locales—on the final swing of the campaign. "He called me 'Conan the Republican,'" remembered Schwarzenegger decades later.

When Bush became president, he named Schwarzenegger the chairman of the President's Council of Physical Fitness and Sports—a high-profile role in the fitness-obsessed White House of the forty-first president.

"He sent me to all 50 states to create fitness rallies and summits," said Schwarzenegger. "He wanted to create more physical education classes all over the U.S. He wanted everyone to stay fit."

As part of that effort, Bush and Schwarzenegger would lead "Great American Workouts" on the White House grounds.

"The body is a terrible thing to waste," Schwarzenegger said at one such event in 1991. The event was also attended by athletic luminaries like basketball coach Pat Riley, golf pro Lee Trevino, Olympic track star Edwin Moses, and gymnast Mary Lou Retton. Macaulay Culkin—of *Home Alone* fame—was even there!

For his part, Bush lifted some weights, shot hoops, and went on a Stair-Master and a treadmill. "For many of us, fitness is already a part of our daily routine," Bush said. "But too many still look at exercise as optional.

And one in four adults don't exercise—one in four don't exercise at all. For the sake of our nation's health, that simply has to change."

The Bush-Schwarzenegger friendship wasn't just for show, either. The two men genuinely liked and respected one another. After Bush passed in 2018, Schwarzenegger called him "a mentor and a father figure at the same time."

During Bush's four years in the White House, Schwarzenegger was a regular visitor to Camp David, the official presidential retreat located in western Maryland. "I was up there literally every month," said Schwarzenegger at one point.

Because this was Bush, his downtime was filled with sports—and lots of them.

"It was exhausting," Schwarzenegger said of his trips to Camp David to visit the president. "We were doing sports from morning to night. We were doing skeet and trap shooting, horseshoe throwing, working out with weights and Wallyball, which is volleyball against the wall with Marines. And bowling. By the time I went to bed I was exhausted."

One of Schwarzenegger's trips to Camp David became the stuff of presidential legend. It was January 1991 and it had snowed. Bush insisted on taking Schwarzenegger out to learn how to toboggan.

Schwarzenegger was a newbie to the whole thing—since European sleds are steered by the feet while a toboggan is steered by a cord tied to the front of the sled.

The outing is captured forever in a famous photo where Schwarzenegger is sitting in the front of the toboggan attempting to steer while the president of the United States sits behind him with a giant smile on his face. (Bush later sent a copy of the photo to Schwarzenegger with the caption "Arnold—Turn, damnit, Turn.")

What the photo didn't capture is the incident involving the two men and then First Lady Barbara Bush. "We crashed into Barbara Bush, who broke her leg after that," Schwarzenegger said in 2018.

Which is interesting! Because in contemporaneous accounts of that day in 1991 it was reported that Barbara Bush had broken her leg entirely on her own—in a sledding accident down an icy hill.

Anna Perez, the First Lady's secretary, said that the president had yelled, "Bail out, bail out" at his wife but she hadn't done so. "She doesn't know why she didn't bail out," added Perez. "She just held on and the next thing she knew, there was the tree."

Did the White House cover up the fact that the world's strongest man and an overzealous president had broken the First Lady's leg?

It appears as though that was the case! In his memoir, *Total Recall: My Unbelievably True Life Story*, Schwarzenegger wrote of the incident: "The president and I came down the hill too fast and crashed into Barbara, and she ended up in the hospital with a broken leg. I still have the photo President Bush sent me afterward."

Schwarzenegger credits his time as the face of fitness in the country— and, specifically, his relationship with Bush—with turning him on to the possibility of a career in politics.

"It was a really great learning experience," Schwarzenegger told Tapper in 2018 of his role as head of the fitness council. "As I was traveling from state to state, [Bush] would never differentiate in talking about a Democratic or Republican governor...I learned from him the good sides of politics. You can cross the aisle; you can talk to the other side and respect the other side even if you disagree."

When Schwarzenegger announced his candidacy for governor of California in 2003, Bush endorsed him. After Schwarzenegger won, Bush invited him to be the keynote speaker at the 2004 Republican National Convention, where George W. Bush was set to be nominated for a second term.

Touting the gains made in the first term, Schwarzenegger said: "We are back because of the perseverance, character, and leadership of the forty-third president of the United States, George W. Bush!"

He told Tapper later that even though the elder Bush was seated far from where he was speaking, he could see that "he was so proud of me."

The men's friendship remained strong over the ensuing decades. Schwarzenegger would go to Houston to visit with the former president— often having lunch with Bush and Barbara.

"He taught me so much, but most of all, he taught me the power of serving a cause greater than yourself," Schwarzenegger said in a statement when Bush died in 2018. "I count myself lucky for many reasons; but for the opportunity to call George Bush a mentor, I can't help but think I'm the luckiest man in America."

Schwarzenegger was on hand in August 1992 when Bush hosted the U.S. Olympic team at the White House following their star turn in the Barcelona Olympics; the team won 108 medals, the most since 1904 in a nonboycotted Olympics.

Bush said that he and his wife were entranced by the games, joking that the First Lady had asked him to rearrange a few chairs and he shot back, "What's the degree of difficulty?"

In his speech to the Olympians, Bush was clear about his belief in the power and necessity of sports in American life.

"Sports are not abstract," he said at one point. "Fitness is not abstract. These things mean something. Sports are flesh and blood. Americans see you, and they can relate to you."

At another moment, Bush noted:

"You showed how competition lifts the human spirit and that now that spirit really lifts the American character. When I was a kid I read about the game being well worth the candle burned long into the night. Now I'm told your nights in Barcelona were long, but I'm betting that candle is going to still last longer."

And at still another Bush reflected on the unifying—and barrier-breaking—nature of sports: "You all must have sensed it there in the village in meeting East and West Germans, black and white South Africans, North and South Koreans. One by one these old divisions gave way. The world watched as countries that didn't even exist in the last Olympics took their place on the field and the medal stand too."

Worth noting: The most famous members of the 1992 U.S. Olympic team—the so-called Dream Team of NBA players that included the likes of Michael Jordan, Larry Bird, and Charles Barkley—were not at the White House ceremony. But that didn't stop Bush from making reference to them; he praised Barkley, the notably outgoing Round Mound of Rebound, for "overcoming his shyness" in helping the USA win the gold medal in hoops.

The tradition of successful sports teams visiting the White House—particularly the Super Bowl champs—was really invented in the modern era by Bush's predecessor in office: Ronald Reagan.

But it was Bush who broadened the practice, inviting the 1991 Stanley Cup Champion Pittsburgh Penguins to the White House—the first full NHL team to appear there following a championship. (Reagan, natch, had welcomed a smattering of New York Islanders players to the White House following their 1982–1983 championship.)

The visit, which happened just a month after the Penguins won the Cup, came together at the last minute—thanks to the advocacy of then-Pennsylvania representative Rick Santorum, a Pittsburgh native and huge sports fan.

Many of the Penguins—including superstar Mario Lemieux—were on long-planned vacations and had to adjust their schedules to make it to the White House on time. Some players didn't make it; defenseman Paul Coffey was hosting a charity golf tournament while Ulf Samuelsson and Jaromir Jagr couldn't find flights from homes abroad.

The players who could make it gathered in Pittsburgh the night before the ceremony—and decided to go out on the town.

"So of course, what do we do? We go out and keep celebrating," defenseman Grant Jennings told the *Athletic* in 2018. "We got to go to the White House tomorrow, but they're not going to put a curfew on us for that. The next day, we get up, we get to D.C. And they put us on buses, and we're kind of a little…*groggy*."

Jennings remembered that it was a hot and humid day in the nation's capital—what day in the summer in DC isn't?? "We're standing out there in our brand-new suits sweating out the beer. I'm like thinking, 'Keep a distance and don't breathe on him too much.'"

There was an awkward moment during the ceremony when Lemiuex, one of the most recognizable hockey players in the world, presented Bush with a Penguins jersey with the number 2—the number that Bush wore as a college baseball player at Yale—on the back.

"And you are?" Bush asked Lemiuex.

"Mario Lemieux," replied Lemiuex.

"I kind of had a feeling," responded the president.

Bush was a fan of many sports—but hockey was among the least of them.

One grace note from the Penguins visit: Tom Barrasso, the Penguins goaltender, had a young daughter named Ashley, who was battling neuroblastoma—brain cancer. The Barrassos got to meet Bush privately in the Oval Office before the ceremony. And, more important to Ashley, they got to hang out with Millie, the Bush's dog, and play on a swing at the White House that was frequented by the Bushes' grandchildren.

Two years earlier, Bush had made another first: welcoming a Little League team to the White House.

The team was from Trumbull, Connecticut—and featured a two-sport star named Chris Drury, who would go on to a long career in the National Hockey League that included a stint as the captain of the New York Rangers.

The way the tournament worked was that there were two brackets—an international one and an American one. The winner of each bracket played the other in the championship game in front of forty thousand fans at Howard J. Lamade Stadium in Williamsport, Pennsylvania.

For the previous two decades the championship had been dominated by teams from Taiwan; they had won thirteen of the previous twenty titles—often by lopsided scores. In the three years prior to 1989, the Taiwanese teams had outscored their American rivals by a combined 43–1 en route to the championship.

The 1989 game was different. The Trumbull team went down 1–0 early but rallied on the strength of a two-run single by Drury, who also pitched. Trumbull wound up winning 5–2.

Bush welcomed the Trumbull team to the White House in October of that year. And he shared with them his own personal experiences with Little League.

"All four of the Bush kids played it. I coached it," the president said. "And Barbara—well, back then there were tens of thousands of Texas kids in Little League. And as I've often said, she'd keep score, but there were times when I thought she was car-pooling each and every one of them. So, I think our family can sense your pride, and hope you can sense the pride we feel in you."

Bush also told the boys a story about his own personal hero—New York Yankee great Lou Gehrig. Recounted Bush:

He was a Hall of Fame first baseman in the twenties and thirties. But more than that, he was a good and decent man about whom a teammate said, "Every day, any day, he just went out and did his job." Fifty years ago, Lou Gehrig was stricken by a form of paralysis which now bears his name. And the disease ended Lou's record-consecutive-games-played streak and caused his retirement from baseball. And even so, he told that July 4th, 1939, crowd at Yankee Stadium: "I consider myself the luckiest man on the face of the Earth."

Bush added that Gehrig's life was an "American parable," adding: "He showed, like Little League, that what matters is how we conduct ourselves off as well as on the field. You kids here are proof of that."

———

That Bush would cite Lou Gehrig and Little League in the same sentence is fitting.

At root, he was a fundamentally decent man, a rule follower who believed deeply and passionately in the idea of fair play. He was a good sport—just as his mother had raised him to be.

That came with its own challenges, of course. Bush often operated under a sort of gentleman's agreement in politics and life that his opponents didn't heed. And his gentility often gave off the whiff of an out-of-touch elitism that his rivals used against him.

But history has also been kind to the Bush presidency because of the humbleness and team-first attitude built into his DNA. He did more in office than he initially got credit for—in part because he was averse to tooting his own horn and drawing too much attention to himself.

He could always hear his mother asking: "George, how did the *team* do?" in his head.

Clinton

Here's a tidbit that tells you everything you need to know about Bill Clinton: When he was governor, his jogging route included a McDonald's where he would regularly stop and place an order. So entrenched was the habit that the Little Rock McDonald's now carries a plaque commemorating the then governor's visits.

Clinton's McDonald's habit became the stuff of legend in the early 1990s when it was parodied by *Saturday Night Live*. Played by Phil Hartman, "Clinton" works his way around the restaurant—chatting with people, and eating their food.

Clinton's weight—and his often-unsuccessful efforts to lose it—had the effect of humanizing him for voters. Here was a big man with big appetites raised in the food-obsessed culture of the South. And even though he knew that eating healthy and exercising were what he *should* have been doing, Clinton couldn't help himself.

"Clinton, like many law-abiding Americans, is a fast-food addict," wrote Mike Littwin in a column for the *Baltimore Sun* shortly after Clinton's election in 1992. "We don't need support groups. We just need the occasional burger our way, large fry and Coke (OK, Diet Coke), and in a hurry. Bill 'Fry Guy' Clinton is our first fast-food president, born to the first fast-food generation."

But, running—and stopping to eat at McDonald's—was about more than just being a regular guy for Clinton. It spoke to his remarkable ability to compartmentalize the seemingly contradictory aspects of his personality.

Of his jogging, Clinton once told a female friend that "this running is a great deal. You can run for thirty minutes or so and then eat all you want and put on no weight."

Seen through that lens, running for Clinton was the "good" that canceled out the bad of his fast-food addiction. As long as he ran, it was OK for him to eat terrible food—it all worked out to a sort-of equilibrium in his mind.

That same balancing of the scales—pun intended—was at work throughout Clinton's presidency and life. This is a man, after all, with the most natural political gifts of his generation who was impeached for sleeping with a White House intern and lying about it.

Clinton spent his life desperately trying to cancel out his bad impulses with his good ones—keeping a running (ahem) tally of where he was in his account at any given moment.

Clinton had taken up jogging during his days at Georgetown to stay in shape. He kept up the habit—to keep the pounds off—during his time in the White House.

"Five days a week he got up at six a.m., donned blue shorts, a red T-shirt, a blue baseball cap and running shoes with the words 'Mr. President' inscribed on the sides and took a 3-mile run" around Washington, according to Paul Boller Jr., author of the book *Presidential Diversions*.

Clinton rarely did anything by himself—and running was no exception. In fact, the chance to be one of his running partners took on a prestige all its own.

"Jogging with the President is bigger than an audience in the Oval," Clinton White House aide Steve Rabinowitz told the *New York Times* in 1993.

And, despite his large frame—Clinton referred to himself as a youth as "the fat kid in band"—the president took his running seriously.

Again, the *Times*:

Many would-be runners underestimate the President's endurance and speed (he usually runs about three eight-minute miles). The White House now provides a "straggler van" to pick up people who conk out. And aides try to warn prospective runners that the President is no slug.

The straggler van picked up a number of Clinton's running companions, including Los Angeles mayor Richard Riordan and Georgia representative Cynthia McKinney, whose aides urged her to try to just make it to the first set of cameras snapshotting the president.

"I thought he'd chug along like a caboose," McKinney said of Clinton. "I thought it was an opportunity to see the President laid back and kicking back. But he was kicking up dust, and leaving me in the wind."

While Clinton was focused on the exercise, most of the politicians who ran (or tried to run) with him were more intent on getting a picture taken with the most powerful man in American politics.

"It's a status thing," explained then California representative Bob Filner. "I thought there'd be some interesting pictures taken that I could use to talk about in a fun way with my constituents." (Filner dropped out after the first mile.)

Clinton understood the transactional nature of his running partners—he would often give them a tour of the West Wing after they finished the jog.

Clinton's running habit was not without controversy. (Was anything Clinton did free from the whiff of scandal?)

Shortly after moving into the White House, construction began on the South Lawn. A quarter-mile running track was being installed—to allow the president to run within the secure confines of the White House complex.

The project, which cost $30,000, was briefly suspended amid questions of how it would be financed. See, Clinton was preparing a budget proposal that included tax increases—and the optics of the president calling for Americans to pay more to the government in order to fund a running track for him didn't look so good.

Ultimately the track was financed by private donations—with a cap of $1,000 per person. "The American people believe this is reasonable," Clinton press secretary Dee Dee Myers explained. "And they think this is perfectly acceptable, that the President have a place to run without leaving the grounds."

Despite the controversy over the track, Clinton never favored using it—preferring to get out into the streets of his adopted hometown.

Reported the *New York Times*: "Not one who likes to run around in circles, at least not when it comes to athletics, the President rarely uses the $30,000 jogging track built for him on the South Lawn with private donations."

Clinton, however, insisted the track wasn't wasted.

"The track is very good in bad weather," he said. "It's also very good for me at night or after dark, if I want to run. It's too much of a burden on the Service for me to run at night."

The burden on the Secret Service was very real. Protecting a president is hard enough. Trying to keep him safe while he runs through public streets in a major city is, well, damn near impossible.

"He dealt us this nightmare," said Dan Emmett, a former Secret Service officer who'd been on presidential protection duty. "The worst thing for the Secret Service is to take a sitting president into public when no one has been swept and anyone could be out there."

Like Ronald Reagan's need for Secret Service agents who could ride horses with him on his ranch, Clinton's running required special agents, too.

"Secret Service agents are generally fit, but we had to come up with a group of agents who were capable of running with the president," said Emmett. "You couldn't just run and look at the ground. We needed people with reserve energy to be able to fight if need be."

It wasn't just the Secret Service who struggled to adapt to Clinton's jogging habits. It was Washington, too.

As the *Washington Post* wrote in January 1993:

The new president's frequent jogs in the nation's capital threaten to become a major headache for morning commuters, D.C. police and the Secret Service agents assigned to protect his life, according to police and some members of the media assigned to keep tabs on him.

Helen Thomas, a longtime White House correspondent, told the *Post* that she "view[ed] this whole proposition of the jogging with dread," adding: "We'd like to know that he's nice and secure and safe and happy in the Oval Office. Not that we want to deprive him of human contact."

In response to the criticism of the president's running, CBS medical correspondent Bob Arnot wrote a letter to the *Washington Post* defending Clinton's running habits:

I was stunned by the press corps' negative reaction to the president's daily jog as reflected on the front page of the *Post*... Some past presidents smoked to excess, drank to excess, ate to excess and even smuggled mistresses into the White House with barely a whimper from the press. But God forbid that the president should jog on the streets of Washington.

Bill Clinton was a band kid.

In high school, while the likes of his boyhood friend—and eventual White House chief of staff—Mack McLarty was making the all-state team as a star quarterback, Clinton was playing saxophone. (He was good, too; he made first chair tenor saxophone in the all-state band.)

But, he wasn't *just* a band kid. As McClarty remembers, Clinton was "genuinely good friends with all athletes and vice versa" which was "not always the case between people who played football and people who played in the band."

Clinton might not have been a natural athlete, but he was a natural at people—understanding what made them get out of bed in the morning. And he grew up in Arkansas in the 1950s and early '60s—an environment marinated in a love for sports, especially football.

"You have to be an Arkansas football fan or you are exorcized from the state—and definitely not electable," said McLarty.

That's not to say Clinton's fandom was a put-on. Sports might not have been his first love—that was music, and he even contemplated pursuing a career in it—but Clinton was (and is) a full-blown fan.

During his time in the White House, Clinton would have Razorbacks football and basketball games piped into the theater room and invite fellow Arkansans to watch the games with him.

"If you happened to be in Washington, they would call and say 'Come over to the White House and watch the Arkansas game,'" said James "Skip" Rutherford, an Arkansas native who often marveled that the president of the United States knew he was in the capital city.

Rutherford remembers a time in 1999 when he was watching the Razorbacks basketball team with Clinton in the White House. Rutherford was in the back row of seats; Clinton was in the front. The president gestured to Rutherford to come and sit next to him.

"He said 'Tell me about this Joe Johnson,'" said Rutherford. "You knew him at Little Rock Central, right?"

(Johnson was the star freshman of the Razorbacks team. He averaged sixteen points his freshman year. Rutherford knew him because his daughter and Johnson had gone to the same high school.)

"Golly, he's just a freshman, he's going to be a star," Clinton told Rutherford. "I said 'You bet he is,'" said Rutherford. "I thought to myself here is the president of the United States calling me up to get a scouting report on Joe Johnson."

————

What did sports mean to—and do for—Bill Clinton?

They allowed him time to decompress and relax, according to Doug Sosnik, who spent most of the 1990s not just working for Clinton but oftentimes overseeing the president's schedule.

"He liked watching sports as a social activity whether he was in an arena or in a foursome," says Sosnik. "It was a shared experience. A way to unplug."

"He was a fanatic about sports," said Terry McAuliffe, the former governor of Virginia and a longtime friend of the former president. "He could give you any statistic. You always had a sports discussion when you were with him."

And yes, Clinton liked the competition of golf or cards, too. "There's a winner, there's a loser, there's competition," said Sosnik of sports' draw for the president.

But, he insisted that, for Clinton, sports and politics were best kept apart—a major difference from other presidents like Richard Nixon, Dwight Eisenhower, and, more recently, Donald Trump, who used the golf course to conduct political business.

"The moment you appear to be trying to politicize sports, the more toxic it is," said Sosnik.

———

As governor, Bill Clinton got very involved in the Hillcrest Softball League, a Little Rock–based league that was started more than three decades ago when there were virtually no team sports for girls to play.

Chelsea Clinton played in the league. One year, she and Skip Rutherford's daughter were on the same team.

"We spent a lot of time with the Clintons at the ballpark," remembered Rutherford. "People used to say to me, 'How did you get to know the Clintons?' I said, 'Through politics some, but where I really got to know them was sitting in the stands at the ballpark.'"

(Rutherford went on to work on Bill Clinton's 1992 presidential campaign and served as the first president of the Clinton Foundation in 1997. He also served as the dean of the Clinton School of Public Service at the University of Arkansas before retiring from that post in 2021.)

Rutherford said that Bill Clinton liked to watch the games from behind home plate, putting his hands in the fencing and coaching—politely—from there. (Rutherford recalled one time when Clinton, the sitting governor, was coaching up the players: "I said, 'You've got to be quiet because you're not the manager.'")

Hillary Clinton was a regular at the Hillcrest games, too. Rutherford remembered one time when a little girl was up to bat and kept missing the ball. "Come on, you can do this... You can hit that ball," said the Arkansas First Lady. "The little girl recognized that voice and turned around to the stands and had the biggest smile on her face," said Rutherford.

The games at Hillcrest had a way of "personalizing" the Clintons, explained Rutherford. "He was just an ordinary fan and ordinary dad." And he added that whenever Clinton was in town, he made sure to make the games. ("He probably made more games than I did," admitted Rutherford.)

And, Clinton—like any good team parent—liked to spoil the girls on the team after games. "At the end of the game he would pile a group of Chelsea's friends into the motorcade and then bring them home afterwards," said Rutherford.

————

A child of the south, Bill Clinton didn't play soccer growing up. Or even have a passing familiarity with the game until, that is, the United States hosted the World Cup—the sport's biggest showcase—in 1994.

That decision had been made six years prior—during the final days of the presidency of Ronald Reagan, with the U.S. beating out Brazil and Morocco for the honor.

Despite not being responsible for securing the World Cup for the United States, Clinton seized the opportunity that it presented—a massive world stage for nearly a month.

Bill and Hillary Clinton attended the opening ceremonies at Soldier Field in Chicago and he delivered remarks to kick off—ahem—the games.

"The World Cup has captured the imagination of our country, as has the game itself in the last few years," said Clinton. "The love of soccer is now a universal language that binds us all together. So I welcome all who have come from all countries and all continents and all who will watch these games in the United States for the next thirty days."

Germany went on to beat Bolivia in that first game.

(Sidebar: England soccer great Gary Lineker once described his sport thusly: "Football is a simple game. Twenty-two men chase a ball for ninety minutes, and at the end, the Germans always win.")

That same day—June 17, 1994—was one of the most momentous in American sports and pop culture history. On that same day—as Bill Clinton was opening the World Cup festivities in Chicago—Arnold Palmer was playing in his final round in a U.S. Open, the New York Knicks were battling the Houston Rockets in Game 5 of the NBA Finals, the New York Rangers were celebrating their Stanley Cup championship with a ticker tape parade in downtown Manhattan, and O. J. Simpson was in a white Ford Bronco driving very slowly away from police. All of that happened on one day! ESPN made a *30 for 30* documentary about it!

Clinton was not in attendance for the final game of the World Cup, in which Brazil beat Italy on penalty kicks. But his second-in-command— Vice President Al Gore—not only made the game but handed the World Cup trophy to Dunga, the Brazilian captain.

That taste of the beautiful game whetted Clinton's appetite for more. When the United States hosted the 1999 Women's World Cup, the forty-second president was at the quarterfinal game in Washington between the U.S. team and the Germans.

After watching the Americans go down 1–0 on an own goal by Brandi Chastain, Clinton witnessed the 3–2 come-from-behind victory for the U.S. side. He and Hillary made their way to the victorious locker room after the game. According to the *Los Angeles Times*, the security was so tight around the president that he nearly caused two U.S. players— including striker Cyndi Parlow—to miss their postgame drug tests, which would have led to the team being disqualified.

Two games later, Clinton was back in the team's locker room—holding the World Cup aloft following the team's 5–4 win in penalty kicks.

Clinton's interest in soccer continued well beyond his eight years in office. In fact, Clinton was "hugely involved" in the United States' 2010 bid to host the World Cup in 2022, according to soccer journalist Grant Wahl.

During the 2010 World Cup, which was played in June and July in South Africa, Clinton was in full salesman mode, recounted Wahl. He met with a group of journalists during the competition to pitch the U.S.'s bid and attended several games—including the fixture against England where the former president sat with none other than Sir Michael Philip Jagger (aka Mick Jagger of the Rolling Stones).

Following the U.S. team's stunning 1–0 win over Algeria in the last match of the group stage (Landon Donovan scored the game winner in the ninetieth minute), Clinton went to the team's locker room and had beers with the guys. (The United States went on to lose to Ghana 2–1 in the Round of 16.)

That December, FIFA held a ceremony in Zurich, Switzerland, to award the 2022 World Cup. Clinton was not only in attendance but was a major part of the United States' pitch to soccer's governing body. It, um, did not go well, according to Wahl.

"The whole thing was a disaster of epic proportions," he said—as Clinton used his speech as an ad for the Clinton Foundation rather than focusing on the U.S.'s bid. "Clinton spoke forever about things that had nothing to do with soccer," recalled Wahl, adding: "Morgan Freeman had been hired to give a speech and he screwed up his lines and announced 'I must have lost my page.'"

It's not clear whether the U.S.'s train-wreck presentation mattered in the end. Qatar won the right to host the 2022 World Cup. "It was embarrassing," said Wahl. "Clinton had given so much to host this initiative and it failed."

That failed bid did, however, spawn one deliciously devilish conspiracy theory, which goes like this: Pissed off at the FIFA snub, Clinton helped instigate the Department of Justice investigation into soccer's governing body, which led to the massive 2015 crackdown on the top officials at FIFA. My guess? This, like so many of the conspiracies that grew up around the Clintons, is more *National Enquirer* than *New York Times*.

Why was Clinton so drawn to soccer? After all, nothing in his upbringing—or in his own athletic pursuits—ever came close to the game. Wahl has an interesting theory: "He sees the rest of the world really connects with it and he realizes that's a way to connect with the rest of the world."

As president, Clinton became close with his Brazilian counterpart

Fernando Henrique Cardoso. In October 1997, the president traveled to Brazil.

Mack McLarty, who was serving as special envoy for the Americas at the time, arranged the visit. In the morning, Clinton would be in Sao Paolo to meet with business leaders. He would then fly to Rio and visit a Brazilian school. "We wanted to bookend prosperity and shared prosperity," McClarty explained.

On the way from the first event to the second, McLarty began to get nervous. Clinton was slated to play soccer—albeit on a miniature field—against Pele, the Brazilian legend and widely regarded as the best soccer player of all time.

"I just started having nightmares," said McClarty. "I started to think of Gerald Ford who hit someone in the crowd with a golf ball. I could just see President Clinton, who was not a natural athlete, against Pele, the best soccer player in history."

The moment was, in McClarty's memory, "scripted like you do a WWE wrestling event" so as to keep Clinton from embarrassing himself. But the president surprised his aide—booting the ball with his left foot into the goal. The kids assembled to see the president speak went wild.

The following summer, Cardoso and his wife visited the Clintons at Camp David. (The Cardosos were one of only two couples to be invited to Camp David; Tony and Cherie Blair were the others.)

The president noticed that the Brazilian seemed distracted and asked what was wrong. "I'm worried about how Brazil is going to do in the World Cup," admitted Cardoso. Clinton laughed. Cardoso was dead serious. "I'm up for reelection in six months, and if we don't do well in the World Cup that's going to affect my election."

(Brazil lost to France—3–0—in the World Cup final a month later. Cardoso fared far better, easily winning a second term later that year.)

Calling in to the *Mike and Mike* show on ESPN Radio in 2015, the former president reflected back on his basketball glory days. Or, maybe more accurately, basketball glory day.

"I was in a church league. I wasn't very good, I was too heavy. But I would run pretty well in short distances," Clinton said. "One night I was the leading scorer on our team. I scored sixteen points in a church league game, never have before or since. And I nearly dunked a ball! And I was only, at the time, six feet tall. I don't know what happened. It was just one of those magical nights. My hand got like right at the rim and I almost got the ball dunked in. I figured maybe every human being on earth is granted one good day in a sports game."

It's not entirely clear whether Clinton remembered the, um, "dunk" accurately. But at least none of his former teammates came out to say he was fibbing.

Clinton was, it seems, something of a basketball head. Which makes some sense given that his presidency dovetailed with a surge in the popularity of the NBA not just in America but worldwide, thanks in large part to one Michael Jeffrey Jordan. Jordan's Chicago Bulls won six NBA titles during the 1990s, with four of them—1993, 1996, 1997, and 1998—coming during Clinton's years in office. (Those years also gave us the "Crying Jordan" meme—a truly iconic moment in the history of the internet.)

The early 1990s coincided with the national rise of the University of Arkansas men's basketball team—led by coach Nolan Richardson and his famed "forty minutes of hell." (Richardson's teams would full-court press the opponent the entire game.)

In the 1993–1994 season, the Razorbacks were one of the top teams in the nation—led by Scotty Thurman and Corliss "Big Nasty" Williamson.

The squad manhandled its opponents in the NCAA tournament, making it all the way to the NCAA championship game against perennial powerhouse Duke—and its telegenic superstar Grant Hill.

The title game was played in Charlotte, and Clinton made the trip. (The president had a full sports day; he had been in Cleveland earlier to throw out the first pitch at Jacobs Field, the new stadium of the Cleveland Indians.)

Clinton had invited newly hired White House adviser David Gergen, a Duke alum, to join him in the box to watch the game. McLarty, a Razorback through and through, was there too. As he remembers it,

"Clinton became very agitated about the referees and started yelling from the box—expressing his discontent. And every time, the CBS cameras would pan to the box and here's the president waving his hands about a call. I said, 'Mr. President, you are going to be the first president in history to get a technical foul.'"

Clinton need not have worried. Arkansas beat Duke 76–72. The president made his way to the winning locker room to celebrate with Richardson and the team. He also stopped by the Duke locker room to console Hill; Clinton had gone to Yale Law School with both of the superstar's parents.

In the mid-1990s, Clinton, with Sosnik tagging along, decided to go to a Seattle Supersonics game. Prior to the game, Sosnik, who went on to work for the NBA after the Clinton presidency, briefed Clinton on the various players on the team and their stats.

After the game, Clinton and Sosnik made their way to the Sonics locker room. Gary Payton, a star of those teams, immediately approached Clinton and pigeonholed the president on the capital gains tax.

"He turned to me as we were walking out and said that was a great briefing you gave to me before the game," Sosnik recalled with a laugh.

Soon after he left the White House—and as he was working to acquaint himself with his new home of New York City—Clinton decided to stop at Rucker Park and its legendary pickup basketball game, where street cred was gained and lost. (Clinton's postpresidential office was, like Rucker Park, in Harlem.)

"He was very well received at Rucker Park," said Sosnik, who noted that the trip—in 2001—was long before the playground became the stuff of legend nationally. "Most people who weren't from the area didn't go to those games," he said.

Fat Joe, a Bronx-born rapper and frequenter of Rucker Park, said of the place: "When I coached at the Rucker, Bill Clinton was in the stands. David Stern was in the stands. White people before gentrification. That was the beginning of gentrification of the Rucker."

For all his hoops fandom—and the one phantom dunk—Clinton's baller credentials were *very* limited. "He didn't really play basketball. He didn't play football," said Bill Nichols, a longtime White House reporter who covered Clinton's presidency.

And yet, Clinton's decided lack of athleticism didn't stop him from giving some of the best athletes in the world advice. "Whenever we played with [golf] pros, Bill Clinton would invariably attempt to give them golf tips—on their grips [and] on their swings," said Terry McAuliffe.

McAuliffe recounted a visit to the U.S. Open tennis tournament in New York when Clinton met up with American tennis great John McEnroe. As they two men talked, McAuliffe looked over and saw Clinton giving McEnroe guidance on gripping the racket. And Clinton didn't even play tennis!

The sport that drew Clinton as he aged—and as more and more success came to him due to his natural charisma and deft political skills—was golf.

Unlike his struggles in basketball or football, golf was a sport where Clinton felt like he fit in. "There's a certain brand of masculinity associated with southern men that Clinton didn't have," said Nichols. "[Golf] was his way of checking that box. He could be on the golf course, could smoke cigars [and] could give off that vibe."

That's not to say Clinton was any standout on the golf course. "He was good," said Nichols. "He could have been much better…he was not as good as he wanted you to think he was."

Twice in 1993, Nichols played nine holes with Clinton at the Jackson Hole Golf and Tennis Club, a Robert Trent Jones–designed course, in Jackson Hole, Wyoming, where the Clintons often took summer vacations.

Nichols got a call from then White House press secretary Mike McCurry asking if he (a) wanted to golf with the president, and (b) whether he could be at the club in ninety minutes or less. "As with everything in the Clinton White House, there was no advance warning," said Nichols.

Nichols had brought his clubs with him on the trip—"We weren't in a 24/7 news cycle," he explained. "A group of us reporters, staff, and Secret Service guys would try to play when we could"—and hightailed it to the club.

The experience, according to Nichols was nerve-wracking. "There's a weird dynamic of 'do I try to play well' or 'do I not try to play well,'" he explained. (Nichols and Clinton tied the first time they played; the reporter beat the pol the second time out.)

Clinton on the golf course is a lot like Clinton off the golf course, according to Nichols. The foursome would rotate who would ride in the cart with the president—and in those moments you got the full Clinton treatment. "He is an incredibly engaging guy when you are in his line of vision," said Nichols. "When you're not, it's like you're not there."

While Clinton was competitive, he was not a gambling fiend on the course—with all sorts of side bets and complicated propositions. And he was not an inveterate bender of the rules although "he wouldn't hesitate to pick up a three-footer," says Nichols.

Nichols remembers an incident on a (theoretically) drivable par 4 with a water hazard guarding the front of the green. After all four men hit their first balls—each one laying up short of the water—the president suggested everyone hit a second ball to see if they could clear the water entirely. If they did it, they could play that second ball as their first. Three of them made it. The one who didn't was the president of the United States.

"We all just walked to the first ball we hit and pretended like none of it had ever happened," said Nichols.

———

Like so much with Clinton, pinpointing exactly how good (or not) he was at golf was extremely difficult. The reason? He took lots of mulligans or, in the president's parlance, "Billigans."

Like, a lot.

"Because he had trouble with the truth, he wanted the public to believe that he was a better golfer than he was," said Don Van Natta Jr., who wrote a book about presidents and golf called *First Off the Tee.*

Clinton had long held a private goal of breaking 80—a score on most courses of 8 over par. He went public with his dream during an August 1994 press conference when asked what he would wish for if he was granted three wishes.

His first wish was that Congress would pass his crime bill. (They did.) His second wish was for more civility in Washington. (Swing and a miss.) His third? "I still have dreams of breaking 80 on the golf course before I'm fifty," confessed Clinton.

In 1996 at the Coronado Golf Course near San Diego, Clinton claimed to have shot a 78 with "no freebies, no second drives, no nothing." Added Clinton: "I was hot. I was smoking them."

But that 78 started to look more suspect when the media analyzed the holes they had been able to see. On the first tee, for example, Clinton had hit two drives but counted only one. On another hole, Clinton took a gimme—a somewhat close putt usually conceded by a partner—but then putted it out, missed the putt, and scored himself for the gimme.

In August 1997, Clinton again claimed to break 80—at the Farm Neck course on Martha's Vineyard. And, again he was met with considerable skepticism.

Here's the UPI account of the round:

Clinton, known for his liberal use of the extra courtesy shot known as a "mulligan," had been seen that morning by reporters taking three opening shots off the first hole.

When they again were allowed visual sight of him at the end of the round, he reported the 79. Asked to explain as he began today's round, the president confirmed the authenticity of his score, adding, "The only reason I took two, three shots out here is because we didn't have time to go to the driving range."

Even the *Cape Cod Times* was skeptical. Under the headline "Clinton's 79: Not Seeing Is Believing," the paper said: "President Clinton reportedly shot a round of 79 earlier this week at Farm Neck Golf Club and cynics have been rolling their eyes ever since."

So, how good was Clinton? A round he played with two other presidents in 1995 may hold the key.

In February 1995, Clinton, Gerald Ford, and George H. W. Bush, along with comedian Bob Hope and pro golfer Scott Hoch, played in

Indian Wells at a pro-am organized by the always-golf-crazy Hope, who was in his early nineties by that time.

Bush and Ford—both better natural athletes (by a lot) than Clinton—put themselves down as 18 handicaps. (That means that on a par 72 course, they would shoot around 90.) Clinton wrote himself down as an 11 handicap.

The match was not without drama. On the first hole, Bush hit a shot that smashed a woman in the face—requiring stitches. That wasn't the only person Bush hit; later in the round he struck a man in the thigh with a ball.

Nor was Bush the only former president to strike a spectator. Ford, who had been mocked relentlessly during his time in office for his errant golf shots, hit a fan in the hand. Only Clinton kept the ball away from the crowd. (Clinton was up for a second term in 1996 and needed to stay in the good graces of the general public.)

As the *New York Times* reported of the golf:

> By the back nine holes, crowds were ducking right and left as Presidential shots went awry, with one of Mr. Clinton's shots landing in a yard adjoining the fairway, where a crowd of revelers urged him just to pick it up and drop it back on the fairway. (He did, but not before checking with tournament officials.)

As you might guess, none of the former presidents covered themselves in golf glory that day. Bush "won" with a 92 followed by a 93 for Clinton and an even 100 for Ford. (In Ford's defense, he was eighty-one years old!) Scott Hoch, the reigning champ at Indian Hills, shot a 70.

Clinton's 93—even with a gimme here and a mulligan there—suggests Clinton claiming an 11 handicap was more than a bit far-fetched. He was likely somewhere closer to a 20-ish handicap, which, coincidentally, was his regarded range at Chenal Country Club, his home course in Little Rock.

Clinton insisted in a 2000 interview that all the focus on his mulligans—and score—was overblown. "My mulligans are way overrated," he told *Golf Digest*. "I normally don't. I let everyone have one off the first tee, and then normally what I do when I'm playing with people is, I just play around and if somebody makes a terrible shot I say, 'Well, take one,' and then I give everybody else one. Otherwise there are never more than one a side."

While Clinton's score was the object of some fascination, it was the partners he chose to play with that drew even more attention.

As the *Times* noted: "A President who has been going out of his way to say he wants to work with Republicans seemed only too happy to pay his respects to his predecessors and to others in this valley of rich Republicans, where Presidents since Dwight D. Eisenhower have played golf and where Mr. Ford has a home."

And Clinton was careful to avoid being labeled an elitist for his very high-profile round of golf. "All kinds of people, all these new courses coming up, public courses, people able to play who never could have played 10, 20 years ago," Clinton told NBC's Dick Enberg in an interview. "And that's very rewarding, because it's a sport that you can play throughout your life and at all different skill levels. It's really a perfect sport for our people."

Clinton was right to worry about the politics of his golf game—and of the scores he claimed.

In November 1995, Clinton and congressional Republicans—led by Senate leader Bob Dole and House Speaker Newt Gingrich—were at loggerheads over the federal budget. Clinton lambasted the duo as "deeply irresponsible" in the morning and went to play golf that afternoon.

Gingrich and Dole leapt on the opportunity. As the *Washington Post* reported at the time, "At a late afternoon news conference, Gingrich and Dole strolled into the Senate Radio and TV press gallery twirling golf clubs, a la Bob Hope. 'We just wanted to get into the presidential mood,' Dole said. 'Do a little press conference, play a little golf, and don't worry about the government.'

" 'How can you all take seriously a man who says we should go into work and then goes to play golf?' the speaker asked."

In the fall of 1996, Dole, by then the Republican nominee for president, insisted that Clinton had not shot the 83 he claimed in a round on an Albuquerque, New Mexico, course the week prior.

"I don't know whether he shot an 83 or 283 or 483. You'll never really know," Dole said at a Florida rally. "You ought to be able to trust your president."

New Mexico governor Gary Johnson, a Republican, got in on the action, too. "He said he shot an 83," said Johnson. "I've asked fifty people...and nobody believes he shot an 83 while he was here."

Clinton spokesman Joe Lockhart hit back. "I think it's safe to assume that the president follows both the spirit and the letter of each and every rule and regulation as set forth...by the United States Golf Association," said Lockhart, insisting that Clinton had in fact, shot an 83—and had lost to Erskine Bowles, a top Clinton aide, who had shot a 79.

(Sidebar: Clinton had played golf in New Mexico prior to a debate with Dole. He kept that routine regularly during his debate prep. "You get beat up in the morning, you clear your head in the afternoon and get beat up again at night," Clinton explained fresh from the golf course in the fall of 1996. "It's a great way to do it.")

Dole's golf shot—ahem—was aimed not at Clinton's skill at the game but more at the notion that he was an inveterate cheat, someone always playing the angles and, therefore, not to be trusted. If Clinton cheated at golf, what else did he cheat at?

"It's mind-boggling, the number and persistence of scandals in this White House," Dole would say on the campaign trail. "Come on, Mr. President. Come clean, Mr. President."

Dole wasn't the only one making that argument. *New Yorker* writer Charles McGrath dedicated an entire column to Clinton's alleged exaggerations of his golf score—and suggested there was something more to it than just the strokes it took the president to get around the course.

What worries me about Clinton is that the other day, after finishing the round in which he'd taken his first drive over, he bragged about shooting an 82, and seemed to genuinely believe that he was only three strokes away from his grand, self-proclaimed goal of breaking into the seventies.

It was a little too reminiscent of that moment in the health-care debate when, after insisting that nothing less than

one-hundred-percent coverage would do, he settled for ninety-five—
or of the two or three or four mullies that he's already taken on the
Haiti issue.

The mulligan concept is one that this particular President might
be smart to stay away from.

Voters didn't seem to care about Clinton's transgression—golf related
or otherwise—electing him easily to a second term in 1996.

Two years later, of course, the scandal of the president's affair with
Monica Lewinsky—and his lies about it—had badly hampered Clinton's
second-term agenda. The solace of the golf course—away from prying
eyes and the ever-present questions from the media—was a rare respite for
Clinton.

In an interview with the *New York Times'* Tom Friedman, himself an
excellent golfer, for *Golf Digest* in the waning days of his presidency, Clinton seemed to acknowledge that fact.

"You can't play this game and think about anything else," he told
Friedman. "And also, it's a place where—even though you've got these
Secret Service people all around us—this is the nearest I ever am to being
like a normal person. I'm alone playing with friends. It reminds me of
everything I loved about my childhood and nature."

———————

No president since Eisenhower had played more golf than Clinton. While
he averaged a round a month while he was the governor of Arkansas in the
1980s, he usually played at least once a week while in the White House. And,
when he wasn't playing, he was often on the putting green outside the West
Wing. (Eisenhower had initially put in the putting surface but Nixon had
gotten rid of it. Clinton put it back.) The putting facility was designed by
legendary golf architect Robert Trent Jones Jr.

Sharon Farmer, the White House photographer during the Clinton
years, said that the president would play golf in virtually any circumstances. "We've had rain golf, snow golf, mud golf," she said. "Other than
reading and music, he'd rather be playing golf than anything."

For Clinton—as for a number of presidents—golf was a useful distraction from the rigors of the job. It allowed him space and time to think. ("What I like about golf is what other people dislike—it takes so long to play," Clinton once said. "Sometimes it takes me five or six holes to get into the game.")

"It's a think tank," former Clinton adviser George Stephanopoulos once said of the putting green. "It's quiet. It's quiet, there are no phones, and he can use the game to distract part of his mind and let the other part do its work."

Said Webb Hubbell, a longtime Clinton confidant: "Golf is an escape for Bill. He'll call and say 'I can get away, can you?' It's a chance to laugh and tell stories."

Clinton himself waxed poetic about why golf appealed to him.

"I love it," said the president. "It really is a lot like life. There is a lot of skill to it but it's mostly a head game once you reach whatever level you are swinging. If you don't concentrate or get upset or you do all the stuff I did, you make mistakes and pay for them. The other thing I like about it is, to some extent, it's an art, not a science. You do get breaks, both ways. You get some bad breaks, like when I hit the tree. And you get some good breaks—I hit another tree, and it went on the green. It's just a lot like life. I love it."

Tom Watson, a longtime pro golfer and occasional playing partner with the president, once offered him a bit of advice on his game.

"I tried to impress upon the president that if you grip the club with too strong a left hand, the ball goes left," said Watson. "If you use too strong a right hand, it goes right. The trick is to find a grip that hits it down the middle. When I told him that, the president laughed and said he tries to do that with everything, not just golf."

———————

Clinton, like so many kids who came of age in the 1950s, was a baseball fan. And, like so many Southern kids, he was a fan specifically of the St. Louis Cardinals.

(KMOX, the St. Louis station that carried Cardinal games, had a remarkably strong signal. That, plus the lack of a true Southern baseball team—the Braves didn't move to Atlanta until 1966—meant that the Cardinals were the favorite team of most Southerners.)

One day, when he was serving as chief of staff to Clinton, McClarty's phone rang. It was the president. "Mack, you have to come to the Oval Office right now," Clinton told him, with an urgent tone in his voice. Worried that some national crisis had broken out, McClarty asked the president what had happened. "Stan Musial is in the office," said Clinton. "Stan is in the office right now." "I said, 'It won't take me long to get there, Mr. President,'" remembered McClarty.

———————

Bill Clinton was, at heart, a bit of a gambler. And that came from where he was raised and who he was raised by.

While Clinton built a political story out of being born in Hope, Arkansas, he was raised in Hot Springs, Arkansas—a long way away, culturally speaking.

As Clinton writes in his autobiography, *My Life*:

The city's attraction was amplified by grand hotels, an opera house and, beginning in the mid-nineteenth century, gambling. By the 1880s, there were several open gambling houses, and Hot Springs was on its way to being both an attractive spa and a notorious town.

Clinton's mother, Virginia Kelley, took to the town—and its gambling traditions. Clinton says that his mother "usually got home by four or five, except when the racetrack was open." He adds, "Though she rarely bet more than two dollars across the board, she took it seriously, studying the racing form and the tout sheets, listening to the jockeys, trainers, and owners she got to know, debating her options with her racetrack friends."

It's impossible to miss the connection between his mother's love of having some skin in the game and the way that Clinton went on to live his professional and personal life.

Clinton's game of choice was hearts.

"Clinton is often photographed golfing or jogging," said the *Tampa Bay Times* in 1997. "But he probably spends as much or more leisure time playing hearts."

The paper went on to note: "Presidential hearts is most often played on late-night rides aboard Air Force One or during short hops on the Marine One helicopter. One marathon airborne session came on an overseas return flight and stretched six hours."

Hearts is an interesting game to love. The goal of the game is to avoid being saddled with points—effectively to keep yourself from losing as opposed to trying to win.

(Hillary Clinton hated the game for just this reason: "She believes you should play games to win, not to avoid losing," former deputy White House counsel Bruce Lindsey explained.)

It is, in some ways, the perfect game for the son of a woman who placed two-dollar bets. And a guy who smoked pot but famously/infamously didn't inhale.

But, built into Hearts is a go-for-broke strategy that runs counter to the entire rest of the game. Rather than try to get rid of hearts—and the dreaded queen of spades—a player can try to collect all of them. If he or she does, they "shoot the moon"—dumping twenty-six points on each of their opponents.

There's some of Clinton, the gambler, in that, too. His "comeback kid" New Hampshire primary campaign—amid widespread allegations of infidelity—was a shoot-the-moon moment. So too, his "I did not have sex with that woman, Miss Lewinsky," proclamation.

It wasn't every time in his political career that Clinton took that riskiest path. Usually he was placing a whole bunch of different two-dollar bets to see which ones paid off. But at crucial times, he was willing to take those big risks. And, like all gamblers, he won some and he lost some.

From the Mound of History

By the time George W. Bush came to the Texas Motor Speedway in March 1999, it was obvious to anyone paying attention that he was going to run for president the following year.

And Bush understood that NASCAR—and, more important, NASCAR fans—could help him get where he wanted to go.

"Bush recognized that NASCAR was a comet and he wanted to jump on the tail," said Eddie Gossage, a racing legend, who ran the speedway at the time. "And NASCAR welcomed him because they could see he was a star on the rise as well. It was a symbiotic relationship of the two helping each other out."

Gossage, by that point, had known Bush for years. They had first met in 1995 when Bush, as governor, had convened a meeting on, of all things, traffic patterns. The 150,000-seat speedway—"twice an NFL stadium," as Gossage likes to point out—was an economic boon to the state but also a traffic nightmare, with that many people coming and going every time there was a race.

NASCAR in the late 1990s was just coming into its own. It was growing out of its long past as a Southern regional sport and going national. A huge TV deal had been signed. Drivers were suddenly celebrities. Sponsorships were pouring in.

Suddenly, political consultants were talking about the importance of the NASCAR dad vote—Southern white men who happened to make up a not-insignificant portion of Bush's political base.

A brief word on NASCAR dads. The term was created by Democratic pollster Celinda Lake in advance of the 2004 election as a way to attempt to categorize young, blue-collar men who had begun voting in a bloc.

"It came out of a trend that we used to say that if you wanted to understand the public, you needed to go to a gun show, a NASCAR race, and an evangelical church," said Lake.

The notion came in response to the soccer moms of previous elections—upscale, largely white, and affluent women who leaned Republican on fiscal issues but were, generally speaking, more moderate on social issues.

Lake added that while Democrats could talk about issues forever, they couldn't reach NASCAR dads because they were culturally out of step with them. "They were under fifty, blue-collar men," she said. "Independent and not very political."

Gossage described the NASCAR fan this way: "It's a good cross section of America. There are a significant number of Democrats and liberals that are fans."

For Bush, these were his people. He had spent the better part of a decade cultivating an image as a Texas good ol' boy—a no-nonsense ass-kicker who would come to Washington and get things straightened out.

That, of course, was not how Bush was raised. He was the son and grandson of privilege. But if his family was all Connecticut, he wanted to be a Texan through and through—and NASCAR was a way to make that happen. Ricky Bobby. Don't overthink it. That's the Washington way. Just get stuff done. Shake and bake. That's the strategery.

Bush, unlike his father, didn't play sports in college. He wasn't particularly gifted in any one sport, but he was sporty—and competitive as hell. And he pursued athletic endeavors (and accomplishments) with an almost maniacal purpose—especially once he quit drinking in his forties.

In a 2002 interview with *Runner's World* magazine, Bush said that he began running in 1972 when he was in his midthirties.

"I was a man who was known to drink a beer or two," said Bush. "And over time, I'm convinced that running helped me quit drinking and smoking."

Do tell! Bush added this:

> As a runner, I quickly realized what it felt like to be healthy, and I already knew what it felt like to be unhealthy. If you're drinking too much, and you're running to cure a hangover, pretty soon you have to make a choice. Do you want to keep getting a hangover or do you want to feel the way you do after a run? Running is a way to heal people.

Which is pretty fascinating. Bush has previously attributed the end of his drinking to the aftermath of a particularly raucous fortieth birthday party; "I quit because at times I thought I like to drink too much," he once said. "Somebody said, 'Can you think of any day you hadn't had a beer?' And I couldn't." On a run the *very* next day, Bush pledged to quit drinking.

While in the White House, Bush said he ran six days a week—and rarely missed that schedule even while on foreign trips. "Even when I travel, there's always a treadmill in my room," he told *Runner's World*. "I have a treadmill on Air Force One. On long trips—for example when I went to Europe recently—I ran for ninety minutes on the flight over there. When I came back from China, I ran on the flight."

As the *New York Times* reported in April 2002 of Bush's exercise regimen while at his Crawford, Texas, ranch:

> President Bush ran on Saturday morning on his 1,600-acre ranch here, between phone calls from Secretary of State Colin L. Powell about Israeli tanks smashing into Yasir Arafat's compound in the West Bank city of Ramallah. He ran on Air Force One on his way

to Mexico last month, on a treadmill set up in the jet's conference room. Mr. Bush ran on the flight back to Washington from El Salvador too.

"I really like to run," Bush said in the spring of 2002 when announcing his pick—Richard Carmona—for U.S. surgeon general. "It makes me feel better."

Despite his penchant for running, Bush did only a single marathon—in Houston in 1993. And that wasn't even his initial plan.

Bush, who called himself "distraught" from his father's 1992 defeat at the hands of Bill Clinton, targeted the White Rock Marathon in Dallas as a "little project" for himself. The marathon, now known as the BMW Dallas Marathon, is run every year in early December.

"I gave myself a month to train for it, and pushed myself incredibly hard as this was after-election therapy," he recounted. "But I got sick, and it was really a foolish attempt on my part."

Bush eventually settled on the Houston Marathon—held in January 1993. He finished that race in three hours and forty-four minutes, proudly noting that he ran the first mile of the race in 8:30 and the final mile of the race in 8:30.

"It was one of the great experiences of my life," remembered Bush. "I learned that running can make you feel 10 years younger the day of the race and 10 years older the day after the race. I also learned not to be so compulsive."

As the marathon story makes clear, running, for Bush, wasn't simply for the exercise and the mind-clearing. He liked to keep track of how fast (or not) he was running. And he liked to use the sport as a way to signal toughness.

At his Crawford ranch, Bush had what was known as the "100 Degree Club," a group of (mostly) Secret Service agents and a few aides who would run with him in the searing temperatures of the Texas summers. "I had '100-Degree Club' T-shirts and certificates printed up and gave 'em away to everybody who went with me," he told *Runner's World* in 2002. Of course he did. Toughness! Perseverance! Machismo!

The *Times* reported back in 2002 that Bush's personal best was a 6:45 mile for three miles, which is a pretty fast pace for anyone—much less someone who, as of the early 2000s, was in his late fifties.

On the morning of September 11, 2001, in fact, Bush was on a run, with then-Bloomberg White House reporter (and all-American runner) Dick Keil. "We were running probably 7:15 miles and he was clipping along and talking very comfortably," said Keil. "If you're not in real good shape and running that fast, you can't carry on a conversation."

Bush's running speed even caused a bit of controversy. Dan Emmett, a former Secret Service agent, wrote in a memoir that the president "was not a jogger but an honest-to-God runner. He ran at a six-minute-per-mile pace normally for 3 miles, and there were even fewer agents who could run with him than with President Clinton."

Runner's World stepped in with a fact check. "Bear in mind that in the year of his first presidential inauguration, 2001, Bush turned 55," the magazine said. "We're not aware of many national-class masters in that age group, much less leaders of the free world, who regularly crank out sub-19:00 5Ks on their daily runs."

While Bush was able to run in public while he was governor of Texas, the Secret Service limited him while in the White House—a circumstance Bush chafed at.

"I try to go for longer runs, but it's tough here at the White House on the outdoor track," he said. "When I'm at my ranch in Crawford, I can do longer runs. It's sad I can't run longer. It's one of the saddest things about the presidency. There would be nothing better than to take off on a long run around the Mall, but I just can't. I really miss those long ones."

Years of running took their toll on Bush's knees. (In 2014, he had both knees replaced within two months of each other.)

"Like a lot of baby boomers, my knees gave out," Bush said while on a bike ride with journalists in 2005. "And I believe that mountain biking is going to be an outlet for a lot of people my age. I'm 59, and people are going to realize you get as much aerobic exercise—if not more—on the mountain bike, without being hobbled."

Aside from the physical gains (and avoidance of pains) from mountain biking, Bush clearly relished the mental health gains as well. "Riding helps clear my head, helps me deal with the stresses of the job," Bush said following a ride in hundred-degree heat shortly after turning sixty in 2006.

(Bush said around that time that he preferred mountain biking to road biking because "there are certain things that age brings with it, and not wearing the form-fitting Lycra shorts is one of them, if you know what I mean.")

As NBC said of Bush:

Bush does not ride quietly, constantly shouting out in his Texas twang the names of trees and geographic features and yelling at himself to pedal faster.

"Air assault!" he yelled as he started one of two major climbs, up Calichi Hill, which he named for the white limestone rock from which it is formed.

Ten years later, Bush celebrated his seventieth birthday on a mountain bike, too. "Celebrating 70 on the trails with wounded warriors," he wrote on Instagram next to a picture of himself traversing a hill.

Bush had been riding with wounded veterans for the better part of the previous five years. The idea germinated in 2011 when Bush was in San Antonio visiting Sgt. Maj. Chris Self at a rehab facility. Self had just been fitted for a prosthesis that allowed him to cycle—and Bush invited him to the Crawford ranch for a ride.

"He rode me into the ground with one leg," recalled Bush. "My day with Chris was so inspiring that I decided to host an annual bike ride for wounded vets, the Warrior 100K."

Yes, that's one hundred kilometers, or just over sixty-two miles, of mountain biking. The goal? "To honor our vets who have been wounded in combat, to thank their families and to thank the groups that have helped them recover from serious injury," explained Bush. (The most recent Warrior 100K was held in November 2019.)

When it came to mountain biking, Bush was also known for something far more ignominious during his time in office: falling off his bike.

In late May 2004, Bush was in mile 16 of a planned seventeen-mile biking foray when he fell—suffering a series of facial and knee scrapes in the process. "It's been raining a lot, and the topsoil is loose," explained White House spokesman Trent Duffy. "He likes to go all out. Suffice it to say he wasn't whistling show tunes."

(The previous year, Bush had fallen off a Segway—he was also holding a tennis racket at the time—during a visit to Kennebunkport, Maine.)

That wasn't the last time in Bush's presidency that he fell off a bike. A year later, while in Scotland for a Group of 8 meeting, Bush collided with a police officer. It was an hour into his ride, on wet asphalt, and the president was traveling at a "pretty good speed," according to a White House spokesman. Bush slid off the pavement and suffered scrapes and bruises but was otherwise unhurt.

(Bush had another scare in 2002—this time off a bike. He choked on a pretzel and briefly lost consciousness in the White House while doing what? Watching the Miami Dolphins–Baltimore Ravens game is what. "He said it [the pretzel] didn't seem to go down right," the White House physician later said. "The next thing he knew, he was on the floor.")

But not all of Bush's mountain biking stories ended in a fall. In August 2005, he rode with multitime Tour de France winner (and native Texan) Lance Armstrong. (This was years before Armstrong's 2013 confession that, despite decades of denials, he had blood doped to improve his cycling performance.)

"It's a dream scenario for me," Armstrong said at the time. "Now that President Bush doesn't run anymore, he rides his mountain bike fanatically. People wonder why he stays at the ranch so long; it might be the mountain bike trails."

Said Armstrong of Bush's approach to biking: "I can tell you he's one very competitive guy. Very competitive, there's no talking. A few minutes of warm up time, a little chitchat, then you go."

A reminder: George W. Bush doesn't do small things when it comes to physical activity. He is into major undertakings—pushing himself hard and far, to the point of exhaustion. He's not there to have fun. He's there to drive himself.

If you ain't first, you're last.

The two men biked for two hours and covered seventeen miles. Bush presented Armstrong with a "Tour de Crawford" shirt when they finished.

Armstrong later said that he spent much of the ride lobbying Bush to dedicate more federal dollars for cancer research. "I've never asked someone for so much money before," he said. Of Bush's performance on the bike, Armstrong said: "That old boy can go. I didn't think he would punish himself that much, but he did."

———————

Bush's competitiveness—and overall sportiness—wasn't limited to running and biking, however. He could pick up almost any sport quickly—and be pretty good at it.

Take duckpin bowling.

It was January 30, 2000. The next day Bush would compete in the New Hampshire primary. Win and the nomination was likely his—given his easy victory in the Iowa caucuses a week before and his strong standing in the still-to-come South Carolina primary.

After a day of campaigning, Bush made his way to Leda Lanes in Nashua to roll a few frames.

Now, if you're not from New England, you are likely, at this point asking something like: What the hell is duckpin bowling?

I, resident New Englander (and duckpin aficionado as a kid) will tell you. Duckpin—or, as some less cool people call it, candlepin bowling—is similar to the bowling you are likely familiar with—with three exceptions.

The first is that the ball is much smaller. Like the size of a large grapefruit. It has no holes for your fingers. Instead, you just sort of cradle it in your palm.

The second is that the pins are short and squat—an ogre-like cousin to the more sleek and slender pins used in tenpin bowling.

The third is that rather than getting two throws to knock down all the pins, you get three. The reason for this is because, contrary to what you might think, duckpin bowling is a hell of a lot harder than tenpin bowling.

While perfect games—twelve consecutive strikes—are somewhat commonplace in standard bowling, they are not just rare in duckpin bowling but nonexistent. That's right—there has never been a sanctioned perfect game in duckpin. Never!

Duckpin is a dying art—largely due to the proprietary technology of its pin-setting machine—developed by a guy named Kenneth Sherman in 1953. Sherman refused to sell the technology to Brunswick Equipment—the big boy on the bowling block—for fear they would use it to end duckpin.

Instead, his company went out of business, meaning that no new duckpin setters have been made in more than five decades, which kind of puts a pinch on the sport's expansion opportunities. (A 2016 *New York Times* article said that there were forty-one certified duckpin bowling alleys left in the country, down from almost 450 in 1963.)

Anyway, back to Bush. He goes to Leda Lanes, looking for one last opportunity to show Granite Staters that even though he's from Texas, he can speak their language. It went, um, only ok.

Here's the Associated Press report from Bush's night at the lanes:

As a Texan, Bush made a common beginner's mistake with his first roll of the palm-sized balls. By trying to muscle it down the lane, he ended up throwing a gutter shot.

He nearly had the same result on the second ball, but barely clipped the No. 10 pin, which netted him a score of one after two balls. Candlepinners get a third ball, but for Bush that made no difference. Again he rolled a gutter ball.

By the end of his third frame, Bush appeared to be getting the hang of the game. His first ball was a six, the second knocked down two pins and the third picked off one more, for nine within the frame.

The bowling was a foreshadowing of the 7-10 split—ahem—to come for Bush in New Hampshire. Then Arizona senator John McCain took 49 percent of the primary vote the next day to just 30 percent for Bush. That defeat signaled an extended fight between the two men for the nomination. While Bush ultimately won the nomination (and the presidency), New Hampshire did him no favors.

———————

The sport George W. Bush rode to political fame—and the one he inherited a love of from his father—was baseball.

"It's really part of the family legacy and for George W. Bush I think it was a little something to live up to," said Condoleezza Rice, Bush's national security adviser.

Bush began his long baseball journey as a Little Leaguer back in Midland, Texas. His favorite player growing up was Willie Mays. "I always thought I was going to be Mays but I couldn't hit the curveball," he said later.

A roster from 1955 includes Bush as one of fifteen players on the team—and the youngest. His address—1412 W. Ohio—is now a museum dedicated to his younger years. When Bush was inducted into the Little League Hall of Fame in 2001, he was presented with the framed original copy of that roster.

Bush was the first—and still only—president to play Little League. So, when he was elected president, Steve Keener, the head of Little League, traveled to Washington to meet with him.

Keener knew a good opportunity when he saw one. Out of that meeting came "Tee Ball on the South Lawn," a program designed to bring kids from all over the country to the White House for the chance to play. According to Keener, Little League held twenty-one games over the course of Bush's eight years in office—and the president was in attendance at every single one.

"You could just tell that what was important to him wasn't whether the kids were good baseball players," said Keener. "What the president would always tell me is that this is about communities and families. It's a chance for kids to have an opportunity to do something healthy and learn to be part of a team."

As historian John Sayle Watterson recounted of the first tee ball game held at the White House:

A seven-year-old hit a hard liner to right field. An extra base hit, the spectators thought, until an outfielder lunged and caught it. President Bush, seated near the first baseman, sprang to his feet. "What a catch," he yelled as he applauded the young prodigy. The president seemed more excited than the parents.

Decades before, the elder Bush—41—held an event of his own on the South Lawn to commemorate fifty years of Little League baseball.

At a reception before the event, Bush Sr. regaled then Little League president Creighton Hale with stories of his own days coaching in Midland, when Bush the younger was playing. First Lady Barbara Bush, never one to shy away when she thought the full story wasn't being told, injected herself into the conversation. "Creighton, if it weren't for women there wouldn't be a Little League," she told the organization's president. "I did more in that Midland little league than [the president] ever did. I drove [George W.] to practice and cleaned the uniforms. All [George Sr.] did was coach the team."

George W. Bush remembered his experience as a family affair, too, with his mother playing a front-and-center role. When he was inducted into the Little League Hall of Fame on September 1, 2001, he told the two teams assembled to play that day:

> When I played Little League I played on this dusty old little field down in Texas. And my mother would pull her lawn chair behind home plate and she would keep score. And every time I came up to bat, she would tell me what to do. And she is still telling me what to do.

(Sidebar: Barbara Bush watched a whole lot of baseball in her life. From watching her husband play at Yale—while pregnant with George W., she sat in William Howard Taft's double-wide seat—to throwing out the first pitch [a strike!] at a Rangers game in 1989, the former First Lady spent a whole lot of time at the ballpark as well.)

That was a fateful trip. After the ceremony inducting Bush, the president went into the stands to watch the game. As Keener remembers it, former Pennsylvania governor Tom Ridge was on the aisle, then Keener, then the president.

"People kept handing Governor Ridge baseball programs and baseballs to get the president to sign them," said Keener. "After about the 2nd inning they shut that off [and] Bush leaned over to Ridge and said 'I've got a job for you in DC: Official presidential autograph handler.'"

Ten days later came the attacks of September 11, 2001. And Bush did tap Ridge—but as director of a newly created Department of Homeland Security.

––––––––––

It was September 11—and baseball—that marked another seminal moment in the Bush presidency.

In the immediate aftermath of the terror attacks, there were questions about whether normal life could—or should—continue.

That included sports. "We're talking about life and death. We're not talking about wins and losses," said Arizona Diamondbacks pitcher Randy Johnson. "It's completely understandable if all sports shut down for a while."

The decision on whether to play or not to play was particularly acute for baseball; the season had only two and a half weeks remaining, and pennant races were happening all over the country. After football canceled its planned games for the coming weekend, Major League Baseball followed suit—announcing that baseball would return September 17. (It was the first time since the death of Franklin Delano Roosevelt that all baseball games had been canceled.)

The remainder of the season felt like it happened in a haze. The country was shocked, scared, and on the defensive. Sports—especially the daily rhythms of baseball—helped the notion of normality but no one was fooled: We had, collectively, gone through the looking glass.

But the playoffs were played and, as was inevitable in those days, the New York Yankees made the World Series. They faced off against the Arizona Diamondbacks—led by star pitchers Randy Johnson and Curt Schilling.

MLB Commissioner Bud Selig offered Bush the chance to throw out the first pitch of the series—on October 27 in Arizona. Bush rejected the offer, insisting that if he was going to throw out a first pitch in the 2001 World Series, it needed to be at Yankee Stadium, a way to symbolically show the country (and the world) that the United States was unbowed and unafraid in the face of the terror attacks.

"I knew baseball could be a part of the recovery after 9/11," explained Bush.

That meant Bush would throw out the first pitch at Game 3 on October 30 in New York City, forty-nine days after the attacks on September 11. Days before, the threat level had been raised, with the intelligence community warning of another terror attack—this one potentially larger than 9/11. Spectators had to go through not one but two magnetometers to get into the stadium. There was a general fear of another attack—and a more specific worry that the president himself might be targeted.

(Sidebar: It was not the first first pitch Bush had thrown that season. He had thrown the first pitch to open the Milwaukee Brewers' season back in April 2001. He had bounced that one in—which had been a disappointment to him. "I don't know why it matters but it did matter," Bush said later. "I wanted to throw a strike.")

In Marine One on the way to the Bronx, Bush flew over the World Trade Center site and grew visibly emotional. When he arrived at Yankee Stadium, Bush and his team snaked their way through the tunnels under the ballpark. Bush was fitted with a bulletproof vest. (He wore it, deferring to the wishes of the Secret Service, but worried about its impact on his ability to throw a strike, he admitted.) And then he began to warm up off of a mound under the stadium.

As Bush was throwing, Derek Jeter, the captain, star, and face of the Yankees, stopped by. "He's taking it pretty serious," Jeter later recalled of Bush. "Trying to get loose."

The two men talked. Jeter suggested that Bush throw off the actual mound rather than in front of it—to avoid being booed by the tough Yankees crowd. Jeter also gave the president another piece of advice: Don't bounce the throw.

When Bush emerged from the Yankee dugout, it was to a monstrous ovation. (It's hard to imagine in these fractious times, but the aftermath of September 11 led to a putting aside of partisanship the likes of which the country hadn't seen in a generation—and isn't likely to see again.)

"The gravity of the moment never really hit me until that first step coming out of that dugout," recalled Bush, who strode to the mound and took a long look around the stadium before offering his signature thumbs-up.

He then threw the pitch—a strike, right down the middle of the plate. The roar was deafening. It felt like we had all just watched the president of the United States give the terrorists the finger. Bush has stood firm in the face of very real concerns about his life and not just thrown out the first pitch but thrown a damn strike. America was going to be all right after all. It was a bookend to Bush's bullhorn moment atop the rubble of 9/11 when he told first responders (and the country) that: "I can hear you. The rest of the world hears you. And the people who knocked these buildings down will hear all of us soon."

"Even people who later despised him would not in any way subtract from the grace under pressure he showed," said historian Curt Smith.

It was, in retrospect, a high point of the Bush presidency. "He spoke to the American people in a way no speech could have ever done," said Condoleezza Rice.

————

Decades before Bush walked to that mound in Yankee Stadium, baseball changed his life in a hugely meaningful way.

Bush was just an executive in Texas primarily recognized—to the extent he was recognized at all—as the son of Vice President George H. W. Bush. "My biggest liability in Texas is the question, 'What's the boy ever done?'" Bush said in 1989. "He could be riding on Daddy's name." (Bush had lost a race for Congress in 1978.)

But Bush the younger, like his dad, had always loved baseball—and spoke about it in glowing terms.

"Baseball is a 162-game season," Bush once said. "You have ups and downs during the season. It's a marathon. It kind of reminds me of life."

For Bush, opportunity knocked when, in the late 1980s, the Texas Rangers, a franchise largely defined by its lack of success, went up for sale.

Bush didn't have the money—or anywhere close to the money—to buy even this middling team. But what he had was (a) a famous last name, and (b) the connections to wealthy and influential people that went with that name.

The sale went through in April 1989—for $86 million. Bush's total stake in that sum? A meager $500,000—giving him a 1.8 percent ownership stake. (The investor group upped Bush's stake to 10 percent once the deal went through; when the team sold in 1998 for $250 million, Bush personally made $14.9 million, a twenty-five-fold increase on his original investment.)

But the investors were savvy. They knew Bush could be the face of the franchise, a chance to rebrand what Texas Rangers baseball meant. Young, good-looking, and with a recognizable last name, Bush could make the Rangers into winners—or at least make them profitable.

"He had a well-known name, and that created interest in the franchise," Tom Schieffer, the Rangers' former president, admitted in 1999. "It gave us a little celebrity."

And Bush played his role to the hilt. He was a regular presence at games, oftentimes with his wife, Laura, and their young family.

"George, Laura and their twin daughters, Barbara and Jenna, according to his count, logged fifty to sixty games each year, sitting in their box next to the dugout," wrote historian John Sayle Watterson in his book *The Games Presidents Play*. "Here Bush kidded with the players and conversed with fans, always giving them autographed copies of his own specially designed baseball cards. He learned the names of the ticket-takers and the hot-dog vendors. He sat proudly beside Bart Giamatti, the new commissioner of baseball and former president of Yale, as Nolan Ryan struck out batter number 5,000."

The Rangers did show some improvement. After finishing twenty-one games under .500 in 1988, the team won more than they lost over the next two seasons—finishing 83-79 in both 1989 and 1990. In 1991, the Rangers went 85-77.

If the Rangers benefited from Bush as their head cheerleader (a return to a role he had played at Phillips Andover, the tony prep school he attended for high school) he also got something out of the deal.

In an April 1992 cover story for *D* magazine (a Dallas glossy), Ruth Miller Fitzgibbons wrote these prescient words:

> His role as front man for the Rangers has given him the perfect entree into all echelons of Texas society, not incidentally paving the way for an eventual political career of his own. In fact, it is Texas that has given form to George W. Bush's emerging political persona. By the time the younger Bush gets around to running for office, not even cartoonist Garry Trudeau will accuse him of laying a false claim to being a Texan.

In fact, Bush so enjoyed his role as the face of the Rangers—and was, by all accounts, very good at it—that his life almost headed in a very different direction.

In 1992, Milwaukee Brewers owner Bud Selig had led the efforts to oust then commissioner Faye Vincent who, following a no confidence vote among the owners, resigned in September of that year. (Bush had been on the other side, arguing for keeping Vincent, a family friend, in the job.) Selig effectively became the acting commissioner while a search for a permanent replacement commenced.

Vincent, in a memoir in the early 2000s, said that he and Bush talked about the next commissioner in the months following his ouster.

"Faye, what do you think about me becoming commissioner?" Bush asked.

"I think it's a great idea," Vincent said.

"Do you think I'd make a good commissioner?" Bush asked.

"Absolutely," Vincent answered. "You're smart. You love baseball. Is it something you want?"

"Well, I've been thinking about it," responded Bush. "Selig tells me that he would love to have me be commissioner and he tells me that he can deliver it."

That account by Vincent largely gibes with how Selig explained the situation in his own 2019 memoir *For the Good of the Game*:

> George was intrigued by the possibility of being commissioner. He and I talked about it.
>
> I told him at the time that I didn't want to be commissioner, and I really didn't…
>
> George would have done a great job. He had a great personality and he loved the game.

So, why didn't it happen?

Vincent insisted it was Selig's ambition.

"George, I'm worried. I think Selig wants the job for himself," Vincent recounted of a conversation with Bush.

Replied Bush: "He told me that I'm still his man but that it will take some time to work out."

To which Vincent responded: "George, he can't tell you the truth because the truth is painful and telling painful truths is not his strength. He has never been able to tell people what they don't want to hear."

Selig had his own story. The owners, according to Selig, were wary about bringing in a new commissioner until a new labor agreement with the players had been worked out. The players ultimately went on strike in August 1994—and the work stoppage caused the cancellation of the playoffs and World Series. The strike didn't formally end until April 1995.

Regardless of the reason why, the timing didn't work out for Bush. By the time the strike ended, Bush had decided on another career path.

In the spring of 1995, as baseball resumed, he was the governor of Texas, having ousted incumbent Democrat Ann Richards in 1994. Four years later, he crushed middling Democratic competition to win a second term. On March 7, 1999, he announced he was running for president—just seven years removed from his dream of becoming the commissioner of baseball.

In retrospect, Bush might have chosen the easier route. Selig, who had the "acting" taken from his title in 1998, had to negotiate a labor dispute that cost the sport the World Series, and he also had to navigate the steroid era in baseball—a black mark that left asterisks all over the record books.

Since Bush left office, there have been occasional whispers that he might finally get the job he quite clearly wanted in the early 1990s.

A childhood friend of Bush's, Doug Hannah, told *Vanity Fair* in 2000 that the former president "wanted to be [MLB's 1st commissioner] Kenesaw Mountain Landis," adding: "I would have guessed that when George grew up he would be the commissioner of baseball. I am still convinced that that is his goal."

Wrote Democratic strategist Bruce Reed in 2007: "It's also remotely possible that Selig and the owners are still grooming Bush for the commissioner's job but think he's too toxic to take a chance on until 2012 or later. That would be the ultimate irony of the Bush presidency: Serving as president didn't help his résumé any more than it helped the country."

In 2013, *Bleacher Report* listed ten candidates to replace Selig. Of Bush, they wrote:

> Bush is known to owners, can handle the public relations part of the job and wouldn't be someone who needed to put his fingerprints all over the game the way that Selig has. Bush's legacy is solid and being commissioner would be largely symbolic, giving the ex-President something to do...Bush wouldn't campaign for the position, but it seems that if he were asked, Bush would serve.

The current commissioner of baseball—in case you were wondering—is Rob Manfred, who has had the job since 2014. (He beat out Red Sox chairman Tom Werner.) He is decidedly unpopular, and the internet is filled with suggestions of who could replace him—from former executive Theo Epstein to super-agent Scott Boras, to, yes, Bush.

Bush, though, has been supportive of Manfred. "I really believe the owners made a really wise choice in picking Rob," he said in 2015 at an event in which he interviewed the newly minted commish. (The conversation was part of an exhibit at the Bush library called: "America's Presidents, America's Pastime.")

In the summer of 2022, the rumor mill began churning, again, when a photo of Bush at MLB headquarters in New York City made the social media rounds.

"President George W. Bush, former Texas Rangers owner, big baseball fan and noted strike thrower, entering MLB headquarters today," teased *New York Post* baseball columnist Jon Heyman.

Bush, at seventy-six, is probably past his prime as a commissioner of major league baseball or any other sport. Although, Joe Biden did get elected president in his late seventies, so . . .

Unlike the men who preceded and followed him in office, George W. Bush played very little golf in the eight years that he occupied the White House.

He gave up the sport in August 2003 following the bombing of the United Nations headquarters in Baghdad, which led to the death of Sergio Vieria de Mello, who was the top U.N. official in Iraq at the time.

"I remember when de Mello, who was at the U.N., got killed in Baghdad as a result of these murderers taking this good man's life," Bush told *Politico* later. "I was playing golf—I think I was in central Texas—and they pulled me off the golf course and I said, 'It's just not worth it anymore to do.'"

Bush never played golf once the wars in Iraq and Afghanistan began in earnest. "I don't want some mom whose son may have recently died to see the commander in chief playing golf," Bush explained. "I feel I owe it to the families to be in solidarity as best I can with them. And I think playing golf during a war just sends the wrong signal."

Not everyone was pleased with Bush's decision. "Thousands of Americans have given up a lot more than golf for this war," said Brandon Friedman, the vice chair of VoteVets, a veterans organization. "For President Bush to imply that he somehow stands in solidarity with families of American soldiers by giving up golf is disgraceful. It's an insult to all Americans and a slap in the face to our troops' families."

Before Bush formally gave up the sport, he made a faux pas that became a viral moment and dogged his presidency.

He was on vacation in Maine and set to play a round of golf with his father, former president George H. W. Bush. A suicide bomber had just killed multiple civilians by blowing up a bus in Israel. Bush thought he could handle both of these events in a single set of remarks.

"I call upon all nations to do everything they can to stop these terrorist killings," he said—and then, without missing a beat: "Thank you. Now watch this drive."

Uh, yeah. The statement felt rote—and utterly devoid of any empathy or passion. Bush seemed to be trying to joke about his driving prowess—he had a slight smirk as he said it—but the whole thing just fell utterly flat.

In 2004, liberal filmmaker Michael Moore released *Fahrenheit 9/11*, a critical look at Bush and his administration's response to the September 11 terror attacks. Moore's broad point was that Bush and his top allies couldn't get their story straight. One day, the threat level had been moved from orange to red—signaling the possibility of an imminent attack. The next Bush was urging people to enjoy themselves, and even take a trip to Disney World.

The central image of that confusing set of messages was Bush's "now watch this drive" moment. One minute Bush was condemning terrorism, the next he was mashing a drive down the fairway. What were the American people supposed to take from that?

Once Bush left office, his press coverage—and his golf game—improved.

On March 20, 2019, Bush, at age seventy-two, made his first hole in one—on the twelfth hole at Trinity Forest Golf Club in Dallas. The twelfth is a 164-yard par 3—from the white tees—that is the easiest hole on the course. Posting a photo of himself on the green, Bush commented: "Next golf goal: live to 100 so I can shoot my age."

In 2021, playing at Cape Arundel Golf Club in Kennebunkport on his seventy-fifth birthday, Bush shot a scalding 74—just 5 over par. "Feeling good on my 75th birthday," Bush posted on Instagram. "Thanks for all the well wishes. And thanks to (par-69) Cape Arundel Golf Club for giving me a chance to finally shoot my age—with a stroke to spare."

———————

It is impossible to write about the physical activities and exertions of George W. Bush while in the White House and not cover his obsession with clearing brush from his ranch in Crawford.

The removal of (primarily) cedar is not a sport per se. It was, however, a form of recreation for Bush, who took to it with maniacal dedication.

"'Clearing brush' is, hands down, George W.'s most cherished form of recreation, at least as measured by how often you hear about it," wrote Mark Leibovich in the *Washington Post* in 2002.

What, exactly, is clearing brush, you ask? Well, in Texas, cedar trees are everywhere—and a threat to all other plant life as they suck up moisture like a Hoover vacuum. In order to ensure the plants and trees you want to live get enough water, you have to get rid of the cedar.

Which Bush did. And did. And did.

As the *Washington Post* wrote in December 2005:

> For five straight days since Monday, when Bush retreated to the ranch for his Christmas sojourn, a spokesman has announced that the president, in between intelligence briefings, phone calls to advisers and bicycling, has spent much of his day clearing brush.

Why was the president drawn to such a thankless task? (There is, after all, always more brush to clear.)

"It's therapeutic for him, I guess," White House counselor Dan Bartlett told the *Washington Post*. "There's very few things he gets to do hands-on."

Historian Robert Dallek had a different take: "This is part of his macho image. Obviously this is nothing Bush has to do. He is the son of a rich man who doesn't have to spend his time cutting underbrush."

The way Bush took to clearing brush was, occasionally, a contact sport. Trent Duffy, a spokesman for the president said that Bush "clears brush like he rides his bike . . . he goes at it."

During his Christmas trip to Crawford in 2005, Bush tangled with some cedar. As he explained: "I have an injury myself—not here at the hospital, but in combat with a cedar. I eventually won. The cedar gave me a little scratch."

So much of the Bush persona has to be understood through the lens of his famous father. He worshipped his dad and aimed to be that same sort of good sport and decent human.

At the same time, the attacks of wimpiness against his dad had stung, and so Bush the younger sought to create a more macho, bro-y image—Texas vs. Connecticut—that would insulate him, both politically and personally, from that same caricature.

"You gotta win to get love, everyone knows that, I mean that's just life," poet-philosopher Ricky Bobby once said. And that became George W. Bush's credo.

Take Your Shot

He Got Game

Presidential Shooting Guard

If you asked anyone in Barack Obama's White House to tell you a "fun" fact that people might not know about the president, nine times out of ten they would tell you that he was a sports fan. And a big one at that.

In profile after profile of Obama, his sports fandom crept in. Like this *New York Times* piece from May 2012 about Obama's plans for reelection, which included these lines:

> In a contest increasingly guided by factors beyond the direct control of either candidate, Mr. Obama has gradually increased the attention he has devoted to the race. Yet aides say he still spends far more time on his iPad checking scores on ESPN than obsessively reading up on Mr. Romney, or digging into the weeds of his own polls or campaign metrics.

He looks at ESPN! He's just like us!

The positioning was simple: Obama—born to a Kenyan father and a white mother and raised in Indonesia and Hawaii—didn't have the background of the average American. Or, really, almost *any* American. But he loved and followed sports just like they did—so how bad could he be, really?

"When Obama talks sports, he shows America his birth certificate," wrote Bryan Curtis in a piece for *Grantland* in 2012.

———————

Barack Obama's connection to basketball—both the way the sport drew him in and the ways in which he used it to identify culturally with Black Americans—began, oddly enough, with his father.

Obama's father was barely a presence in his life, but, when the future president was eleven, both his mother and father came to stay with him and his grandparents in Hawaii for Christmas.

"He was much thinner than I had expected, the bones of his knees cutting the legs of his trousers at sharp angles" Obama wrote in *Dreams of My Father*, adding: "There was a fragility about his frame, I thought, a caution when he a lit a cigarette or reached for his beer."

His father stayed with the family for a month—and was even invited to the young Obama's classroom to share his experiences about living in Africa. ("The other kids looked at me as my father stood up, and I held my head stiffly, trying to focus on a vacant point on the blackboard behind him," Obama wrote. "He had been speaking for some time before I could finally bring myself back to the moment.")

The only picture Obama has of himself and his father came from that trip. In it, the older Obama holds a tie his son has given him, while the younger Obama holds an "orange basketball," a gift from his father.

It is, on one level, an odd gift. Prior to being gifted the basketball, Barry Obama, as he was known then, did not have a basketball jones. And basketball was not some sort of cultural currency in the elder Obama's native Africa, either. (Earlier in the trip, Obama's father had given him something of that sort—three wooden carved figurines of "a lion, an elephant and an ebony man in tribal dress beating a drum," according to Obama.)

Did the elder Obama understand the role basketball was playing in defining Black culture in America? Did he mean to hand a key to that culture to his son? Or did he simply grab a ball as a gift because little boys tend to like balls?

We'll never know. The elder Obama died in a car crash in Kenya at age forty-eight in 1982.

What we *do* know is that as Obama came of age, basketball increasingly came to help him define who he was in America—a Black man, with all that entailed. The story of Obama's young life is one of a search for identity; he was forever caught between worlds and cultures, never feeling fully a part of any of them. Basketball helped him feel less other, helped him find a place and a vibe where he fit—naturally and without having to "be" anything other than himself.

As Alexander Wolff wrote in his book *The Audacity of Hoop*: "There's no accounting for exactly why a native of a country where the game was hardly played chose this particular present, but Barry would come to regard that basketball as a charge as much as a gift."

Wolff notes that Obama—just weeks after his father left—went to a University of Hawaii basketball game with his grandfather. "He was totally smitten by the Afros on these guys," said Wolff. "To see 5 big black guys in Hawaii just didn't happen."

(Sidebar: The Rainbows were a perennially weak hoops team—except for the years Obama saw them play. Between 1970 and 1972, the so-called Fabulous Five—decades before Michigan's own "Fab Five"!—went 47-9 and made the NIT and NCAA tournaments, the first of each in the history of the program. "With aloha-print shorts and bountiful Afros, junior-college transfers Al Davis, Jerome 'Hook' Freeman, Dwight Holiday and Bob Nash, joined by John Penebackeer, an Air Force vet discovered in a local Armed Forces league, averaged more than 90 points a game as the pep band played *Jesus Christ Superstar* and fans spilled raucously into the aisles," wrote Wolff.)

What ultimately sealed Obama's love of the game? No one can be quite sure. Reggie Love, the former Obama aide, suggests that the democratizing nature of the game was what drew him in. "In theory, it's a low cost of entry and tons of opportunities to play," he explained. "You don't need a lot of resources to do it."

Wolff offers something similar. "He was not playing decorous pickup in the University of Chicago gym," he said of Obama. "The gyms where he played weren't in gated communities."

There's also this: Basketball functioned effectively as a bridge between Obama's two worlds. Kansas, where his mother's family was from, was (and is) basketball crazy. And hoops has long been a feature of Black American culture. The ability to fuse the two into a singular experience was, for Obama, revelatory.

Love sees the same traits present in basketball—pickup, in particular—that Obama valued in his first career as a community organizer. "There is an element of being connected to people and having connecting plays," said Love. "If you get beat on defense, someone helps and recovers and then you do the same for them. You make a great assist. There is a community to the game of basketball that you don't always have in other sports. You don't have those moments in golf."

———————

Love, a former Duke basketball (and football) star, smiles when I bring up the origins of the Obama pickup basketball games. "It started in New Hampshire," he recalled. "It was just a tactical way for the state director [Matt Rodriguez] to get more hours of the day out of the candidate."

See, Obama liked to work out and eat breakfast in (relative) peace. Which meant that his mornings—until 7:30 or 8 a.m.—were blocked off. But Rodriguez soon realized that if he could schedule Obama to play pickup hoops with an influential New Hampshire pol early in the morning, he could get around that schedule block.

Love, Obama's body man during the campaign, orchestrated the games along with the candidate's advance staff—but he said that, at least initially, they were something short of glamorous. "When we were traveling during the campaign, beggars can't be choosers," he noted. "We got whatever gym we could and found some warm bodies to play 3 on 3 or 5 on 5."

The candidate had played pickup on the day of the Iowa caucus—in which he beat Hillary Clinton and former North Carolina senator John Edwards. But, he skipped a game in New Hampshire less than a week later, with polls showing he would win the Granite State comfortably.

When Clinton stunned Obama in the New Hampshire primary, the superstitious Obama decided that he had to play pickup hoops on every primary and caucus day going forward. He said it was for "good luck," remembered Love.

David Axelrod, Obama's top consultant and political Svengali, said the games were a "way to calm everyone down" on stressful days.

Except when it wasn't. In October 2007, Obama was playing a pickup game in Philadelphia—hours before he was set to debate Hillary Clinton and the rest of the Democratic primary field. Axelrod had drawn the assignment of covering the boss.

"He was a little quicker than me and he cut past me," Axelrod said. "I did the matador defense thing and raked him on the nose. I hit him pretty hard and he went down clutching his face. The Secret Service came running over. And I'm thinking 'I broke my candidate's nose three hours before the debate.'"

Obama, slowly, sat up. Then he stood up. "And," Axelrod said, "he said to me, 'Ax, we have a debate in three hours, what are we doing here?'"

The candidate made the debate—and Axelrod kept his top spot at the campaign.

Axelrod used basketball—and Obama's competitiveness at it—to describe how he became convinced this guy could be president.

"Every time he played, he played to win," Axelrod said of Obama on the court. "When we were talking about him running for president, I said, 'I don't know if you are pathological enough to run for president.' He said, 'I understand that, and yes, I would rather flop down and watch ESPN with friends. But you know this from playing ball with me, I am competitive. If I get in the game, I get in to win.' Whether it's a game of horse or a pickup game, he was always in the game to win."

How was—and is—Obama as a player? Love offered a quick scouting report: "If you're guarding him, late contest on the jumper. He'll make it if he's wide open. You'd rather him be a shooter than a driver. He's a strong right-handed driver even though he's left-handed. He likes to come back to finish [at the rim] with his left hand."

Obama is, according to Love, largely retired from playing in pickup games—worried about suffering a knee or an Achilles' tendon injury that could lay him up for a year or more. I asked Love about when he last remembered Obama being really "on" in a pickup run. Love immediately says that they played on election day 2016—"the day Donald Trump won"—at Fort McNair. The soon to be former president had it all working that day, according to Love. "He said to himself, 'At this age, that's about as well as I am going to play.'"

Wolff ascribes Obama's unlikely wins in Indiana and North Carolina in the 2008 campaign directly to the pickup games.

"The two reddest states he flipped to blue are North Carolina and Indiana," Wolff said. "They are both basketball states where he used the game in campaigning."

In Indiana, Wolff added, Obama's campaign organized 3 on 3 tournaments where voters would have the chance to play with (and against) the candidate. In North Carolina, Obama played pickup with the Tarheels basketball team, which included stars Tywon Lawson and Tyler Hansborough. Obama, at one point drove hard into the lane and put up a shot over the outstretched arm of the six-nine Hansborough. But the shot hit the rim and bounced off. (Obama soon took a seat on the sidelines with legendary coach Roy Williams: "These guys are a lot better than I am," he told reporters of the team.)

When Obama won, the pickup venues got nicer but the game was still central to who Obama was, according to Love.

"In the White House, we had more flexibility," said Love, recounting that the games would usually be played at the FBI building ("They have a nice gym in the basement," according to Love), at Fort McNair, or at the Department of the Interior ("Small gym but nice").

Obama also installed a basketball court on top of the tennis courts so that he could shoot around on the grounds. (He had basketball lines drawn on the court so it served a dual function; First Lady Melania Trump did away with the hoops lines and built a tennis pavilion.)

That court became the site of a considerable amount of hoops diplomacy over Obama's time in the White House. Love remembered that during the legislative fight to pass the Affordable Care Act—the signature legislative achievement of Obama's presidency—the president would host members of Congress at the White House for a shoot-around (and some light cajoling).

Wolff goes even further—theorizing that without basketball Obama might never have seen the ACA succeed.

"The ACA was going nowhere, it was in deep shit," said Wolff. "But the NBA season overlapped with the critical sign up period. And the demographic groups they had to get into the exchanges overlapped with NBA fandom... Young, male, black and Latino. Someone in the White House figured out that they could drive signups by enlisting the NBA."

One such event took place in Los Angeles in October 2013, with NBA stars Chris Paul (then of the Los Angeles Clippers) and Steph Curry (of the Golden State Warriors) using their platform and prominence to encourage enrollment in the national health care exchanges the ACA established.

"We can reach young adults," Paul said at the time. "We're with kids all day, every day, and they're watching our games, and we have an influence, so we have an opportunity to use our voice."

Speaking of Paul, he was one of a number of NBA luminaries on hand at the White House for Obama's forty-ninth birthday party. The group, which included LeBron James, Carmelo Anthony, Derrick Rose, and Joakim Noah—among other professional ballers—gathered at Fort McNair in southwest Washington to play pickup as part of the party. Kobe Bryant was in attendance, but didn't play.

"I was shocked at how good he was," Paul said of Obama. "Nice lefty jump shot. But he got lucky one time on the break. I sort of jumped out, made him guess which way to go and he made the right play, crossed over, made it look like he crossed me up. It'll never happen again."

Obama was, in Axelrod's telling, "finding himself remarkably free to shoot." That didn't sit well with Bryant, who called over Chris Paul midgame and said, "You are one of the meanest motherfuckers in basketball and you won't get within ten feet of that guy! Play some fucking defense!"

Obama doomed himself that day, however. He was talking junk to Noah—a gifted defender with limited offensive skills. "He said 'Where'd you get that ugly shot,'" said Axelrod. Noah took it upon himself to guard the president for the rest of the game. "[Noah] put a strangulating defense on Obama to where [the president] couldn't even move," said Axelrod. "He didn't score a point after that."

Shane Battier, a Duke star and longtime NBA player, remembered it differently.

"We won," said Battier, who was on Obama's team. "And in fitting fashion, the President hit the game-winning shot. It was point-game, and we gave him the ball, and it all cleared out. He took two dribbles, got to the elbow, raised up, and knocked it down. And he walked it off the court like he knew he was going to hit it. I wouldn't say it was MJ-esque, but I'm sure in his mind it was MJ-esque."

That willingness to get into it—verbally—on the court wasn't an isolated incident. He wasn't afraid to dip into the bag of trash talk," said Wolff. "He knew how to get into peoples' heads if that's what it took. Whether in Chicago or pickup in Hawaii in some of those more untidy precincts of the islands, he was absolutely exposed to it."

———————

Obama didn't just play basketball—he followed it religiously, too. So it was that one day in March 2009, a special guest was quietly escorted into the White House—his mission known only to a select few. Secrecy was the name of the game.

An international incident? Some domestic policy snafu that needed cleaning up? Nope! The president of the United States was picking college basketball games.

A hoops addict and regular watcher of ESPN offerings like *Pardon the Interruption* and *SportsCenter*, Obama played the role of fan-in-chief—filling out a college basketball tournament bracket every spring alongside then-ESPN reporter Andy Katz.

Obama's picks were not only covered live by the Worldwide Leader but also pored over by every sports (and politics) junkie in the country. Was he picking schools to win because they were in swing states (North Carolina, e.g.) and he wanted to cozy up to those constituencies? Did he actually know what he was talking about, or was some aide just briefing him on who to pick? In short: Was this real or a put-on? Was Obama a real fan or just another politician trying to leverage sports to reach the common man?

To hear Katz tell it, Obama's fandom—and the bracket picking that rose from it—was very much authentic.

"He always had an interest," said Katz of Obama and college hoops. "That's why I knew it would work."

Wolff notes that the president and his White House saw a golden opportunity in the brackets. "It seemed to be that everyone in America is doing it, so I am going to do it, too," Wolff said of Obama, noting that the White House helped "blow it up into this springtime ritual [and] ESPN didn't mind it either."

So, how did it happen? Katz was working on a piece on Obama's basketball pickup habits during the 2008 campaign.

Just nine days before the election—the Sunday before the final Sunday of the campaign—Katz got a call that he would get time with Obama. He rushed to a Hampton Inn in Dunn, North Carolina—Obama was doing an event at nearby Fort Bragg—where he and the candidate spent twenty minutes or so chatting on camera.

Unbeknownst to both men, former secretary of state Colin Powell had just endorsed Obama on *Meet the Press*. Axelrod and Robert Gibbs, the campaign's press secretary, came into the room where the interview had taken place and told Obama to stay put while they reworked the speech he would be giving to include the Powell endorsement.

"For some period of time, it's me and Obama in the room," Katz recalled. "Just hanging out." Then, suddenly, Katz had what he called an "epiphany": "I stand up and say 'Senator, I have a great idea. If you win, how about I come to the White House and we do the NCAA tournament bracket.'" Obama immediately agreed.

During the transition, Katz followed up with Tommy Vietor, one of the young press operatives on the campaign, to make sure the deal was still on. It was. "They were committed," says Katz.

That first year—2009—Obama and Katz picked only the men's NCAA bracket. For the next seven years of Obama's presidency, they filled out a men's and women's bracket.

"The first day we went in 2009, we snuck the bracket boards in and out," recounts Katz. "There was such a buzz we were doing this on year one . . . reporters were trying to lean underneath [the bracket boards] to see who he picked."

───────

For all of Obama's much-discussed grace on the court and flair for big moments (how many times have you seen him hit a jump shot—on camera—before walking out of a gym?), there's another side to Obama, the athlete. Call it Obama, the awkward.

Perhaps the most famous sporting fail of Obama's presidency came in the runup to Pennsylvania's Democratic primary in 2008. Axelrod thought it would be a good idea for the then Illinois senator to head to a bowling alley in Altoona for some glad-handing. (Only one person bowls while four or five sit around—a prime chance for the candidate to shake some hands, as Axelrod explained his thinking.)

"It never occurred to me he would actually bowl," said Axelrod. "Some advance guy said they thought it would be a good photo op."

It, um, was not. Obama's first ball landed in the gutter. Through seven frames, he had scored a 37—the sort of score that your eight-year-old might be embarrassed by. "The man was a scholar in school," the owner of the alley told a local newspaper later. "He didn't have time to bowl."

For Axelrod, Obama's disastrous performance on the lanes wasn't explained away so easily. "I got a call saying, 'We have a problem. The Senator bowled.' I said, 'That's great!' 'They said he bowled a 37.' He was so embarrassed by it."

Obama took that embarrassment with him into the White House, which not only has its own bowling alley—thanks, Richard Nixon!—but also has lanes at the official presidential retreat: Camp David.

"I found out that he was spending time on his own bowling while he was president so that if it comes up again and he is in a public venue, he wouldn't embarrass himself," said Axelrod. "He felt personally challenged by it. By the end he was bowling 200 games."

Then there was baseball—another sport that didn't come all that naturally to Obama. During his 2004 Illinois Senate campaign, Obama was invited to throw out the first pitch at a Kane County Cougars game, a minor league affiliate of the Oakland A's.

"I didn't think to ask him if he knew how to throw a baseball," recounts Axelrod. "He gets on the mound and throws a pitch that could generously be described as a parabola." Obama's toss, as Axelrod remembers it, earned him lots of, er, colorful language and razzing from the Cougars dugout.

The following year, after he was elected to the Senate and was riding mounds of positive buzz about his potential on the national stage, Obama was asked to throw out the first pitch of Game 2 of the 2005 AL Championship Series, in which the Senator's favorite team, the Chicago White Sox, were taking on the Los Angeles Angels.

According to Axelrod, Obama and his body man, David Katz, himself a hugely accomplished golfer at the University of Michigan, "borrowed" Wrigley Field for a few hours so the senator could ensure he wouldn't have a repeat performance of the year prior. "He wanted to make sure there wasn't another incident," said Axelrod. (The White Sox won that game—and went on to win the series three games to two. They then swept the Houston Astros to win the World Series.)

In 2009, Obama threw out the first pitch at the All-Star Game in St. Louis—and made headlines not for the pitch, but for his outfit.

Obama wore a Chicago White Sox jacket on top, which was fine. But he also wore very high-waisted jeans, which came to be the stuff of internet legend—and not in a good way.

"I suppose President Obama is indeed a father, so we should allow him such a strike against humanity," Tanner Stransky wrote in *Entertainment Weekly* of the so-called dad jeans. "And I guess he couldn't have come out in skin-tight baseball pants (or, rather, why not?) or the suit pants that he normally dons. But my, oh my. I wasn't ready to see him in such an ill-fitting pair of what look like 501s. I thought he was cooler than that, somehow. This humanizing of the President doesn't sit so well with me."

Obama, in later years, defended his choice of legwear. "There was one episode like four years ago, in which I was wearing some loose jeans, mainly because I was out on the pitcher's mound and I didn't want to feel confined while I was pitching," Obama said in 2014. "I've paid my penance for that. I got whacked pretty good. Since that time, my jeans fit very well."

For Obama, golf is the game that he has pursued most passionately—both during and after the presidency.

He started playing during his days in Springfield, Illinois. "He was stuck in Springfield and there's not a lot to do there," said David Axelrod. "There's only so many times you can visit the Lincoln sites...it was his way to socialize."

Don Van Natta recounted an early Obama golf outing when he showed up in a "black silk shirt" and "didn't play well. He got a lot of ribbing for it—and became pretty good, pretty quickly."

(Obama also played in a poker game with a small group of fellow legislators during his Springfield days.)

David Katz, the Obama body man, said that the future president "used poker and golf as a way to connect with downstate Illinois legislators" who loved both. "He needed to find a way in," and golf was it.

During the 2004 campaign, when the two men would spend twelve hours a day together, they would often finish at 6 or 7 p.m.—and then head to the course. "I distinctly remember him changing from his suit into his golf clothes in the back of a car while I was driving to a golf course," recalled Katz.

The candidate played a fair amount of golf during that race. "I called [Obama] during the Senate race in 2004," Axelrod remembered. "He told me, 'Hey Ax, can I call you back...Katz and I are playing golf for money.' So, when he called me back I said, 'I signed up with you because I thought you were the smartest guy, but you are playing against Katz for money?'" The candidate replied: "Don't be ridiculous, he's on my team."

Obama and Katz frequented courses around the state capital of Springfield as well as the Jackson Park course in downtown Chicago. "I grew up playing there and we all lived seven blocks from there," said Katz. "It's a city course—a little rough around the edges."

That course now abuts the location of the Obama presidential library. The course has long been tagged for major overhaul by none other than Tiger Woods; the project, first approved in 2017, remains stuck.

As the *Chicago Sun-Times* reported in August 2021:

> Whatever happened to the golf course idea? The one that was to involve Tiger Woods and was pushed in tandem with Obama's project, promising public works with star power? Obama called Woods to get him on board, the *Chicago Tribune* said.
>
> The idea appears to be in hibernation, like a fairway that never gets water. Signs of life are hard to find, although advocates say the project is still viable. Robert Markionni, executive director of the Chicago District Golf Association, said now that the Obama buildings are underway, "we hope the golf course project will be more front and center. Tiger Woods is still ready."

When Obama won, Katz joined him in the Senate. But the golf stopped. "Playing golf was not a priority," said Katz. Shortly after winning the Senate seat, Obama began running for president. For four years then, Obama barely played, with the exception of an occasional holiday trip to Hawaii.

Once he was president, Obama started to play again—regularly.

Katz recalled that he would get a text from Obama body man (and fellow golfer) Marvin Nicholson every Sunday around 12 or 1 p.m.—after the president had watched his girls play basketball or some other sport—asking whether he wanted to play with the president.

"We would always play skins game," explained Katz. "We always played two on two...I can count the number of times I wasn't on his team."

(In skins game play, each hole is worth a "skin." Usually the skin is tied to a specific amount of money. If the two teams tie on a hole, as is common, the skins—and the money—carry over to the next hole until someone wins outright.)

Obama, unlike other presidents—such as his successor, Donald Trump, for one—would rarely play golf with heads of state and other luminaries. "He would typically play with staffers," said Katz. "It would often be two staffers, [Health and Human Services Secretary Kathleen] Sebelius and the president."

During his first term, the president played almost exclusively at two courses: Fort Belvoir in northern Virginia and the course at Andrews Air Force Base in Maryland. There are two eighteen-hole courses and a nine-hole setup at Andrews; Fort Belvoir has a single eighteen-hole loop. Both are public courses.

According to *Golf Digest*, Obama logged more than three hundred rounds during his two terms. (White House unofficial historian and resident number cruncher Mark Knoller pegged it at 333 rounds, to be exact.) As the magazine noted on Obama's last full day in office in January 2017:

> In the last hours of his presidency, it's time we pause to celebrate Barack Obama's many admirable qualities: his eloquence, his measured temperament, his nimble grasp of complex issues. At *Golf Digest*, it only makes sense that we also commend him for his deep commitment to supporting the golf industry.

The amount of golf that Obama played was a regular point of interest for then billionaire businessman Donald Trump. "Can you believe that, with all of the problems and difficulties facing the U.S., President Obama spent the day playing golf," Trump tweeted in 2014.

Of course, once Trump became president in 2017, he hit the links on the regular, too. In fact, a PolitiFact analysis of the golfing habits of Obama and Trump found that Trump had played on nineteen more occasions than Obama had in their first years or so in office.

Obama also came under criticism in 2014 for playing golf immediately following the beheading of American journalist James Foley by Islamic State militants.

"Every day we find new evidence that he'd rather be on the golf course than he would be dealing with a crisis that's developing rapidly in the Middle East," said former vice president Dick Cheney.

(Cheney's former boss, President George W. Bush, was far more supportive of Obama's golfing habit. "I know what it's like to be in the bubble and I know the pressures of the job, and to be able to get outside and play golf with some of your pals is important for the president," Bush said in Obama's defense. "It gives you an outlet.")

The White House, unsurprisingly, defended Obama's right to free time. "I will say that, generally, I think that, you know, sports and leisure activities are a good way for release and clearing of the mind for a lot of us," said spokesman Eric Schultz.

Looking back through the lens of history, the critique of Obama's golf playing feels, well, lame. Compared to the likes of Dwight Eisenhower or Donald Trump, Obama was a casual golfer at most.

On to lighter fare—what kind of golfer is Obama? A strict rule follower, according to Katz. If Obama hit the ball into a hazard, rather than just throw another ball down, he would execute a drop from over his head—above and beyond what the average duffer does.

"I used to say, 'You don't have to do that,'" said Katz. "In his mind, he wanted to over-emphasize that he was a rules follower and respected the game."

The other thing to know about Obama on the golf course was that he was fiercely competitive. "He knew the scores," said Katz. "We would come to the green and he would know what we all lie. Who knows that?

"He is just the most competitive person," added Katz. "Whether he lost or won, he loved the competition of the game and the moment. It was almost like a political race [to him]."

The rule following and the competitiveness are traits that lie deep in Obama's psyche. As a kid who always felt caught between two worlds, never totally fitting in, he learned the rules and learned how to follow the rules as a way of being accepted. The competitiveness was born of years of feeling other—and wanting to prove to anyone asking that he was not just up to the challenge but overqualified for it.

The president worked at his game. Katz took lessons from a guy named Henry Young, who split his time between Michigan in the summers and Florida in the winter. Katz said to Obama that he probably should take lessons but not from just anybody. So, when Young was driving in between Florida and Michigan, he would stop off in Washington and give the president a lesson.

Katz told Young, "You get to teach him but really don't go nuts on this"—that is, don't go bragging around that you are teaching the president. Young, who taught the guy who taught Phil Mickelson, wound up giving Obama five or six lessons, estimates Katz.

Obama's natural strength in golf is his short game. "He's a good putter and a good chipper," said Katz. "His drive wasn't the longest. He wanted to improve that."

(For you technical golfers out there, Obama's swing was plagued by what is called a "chicken wing." His right arm—and, specifically, his elbow, would bend when he impacted the ball. That would lead to him hitting behind the ball or topping it—hitting only the top half of the ball. By straightening his right arm at impact, Obama was able to improve his ball striking and add twenty to thirty yards to his drives.)

Michael Jordan—yes, that Michael Jordan—was, um, slightly more critical of Obama's game than Katz. Jordan called Obama "a shitty golfer," adding: "He's a hack, man, I'd be all day playing with him."

Obama quickly hit back on a Wisconsin radio station. "There is no doubt that Michael is a better golfer than I am," he said. "Of course if I was playing twice a day for the last fifteen years, then that might not be the case. He might want to spend more time thinking about the Bobcats—or the Hornets."

That both men decided to engage with one another is revealing. Jordan, the übercompetitor, feels as though it's necessary for him to offer up his unvarnished critique of the former president because, well, he's Michael Jordan.

And why the hell not? Obama, while trying to play it off as no big deal, can't resist getting in his own gibe—while also displaying his utter fluency with the NBA's inner workings.

The more Obama played—and the more lessons he took—the better he got. And the better he got, the more he wanted to play. "Those lessons got him slightly more addicted" to the game, said Katz.

Why did—and does—golf appeal to Obama? Katz believes the game reminds Obama of earlier—and simpler—times. "If he is surrounded with people who also happen to be from an earlier time, he could act like someone who is not the president for those four hours," said Katz.

Acting like someone who isn't president very much includes some gamesmanship. "He talked a little bit of trash when we were playing skins game," said Katz. "He could joke around with the people he trusts."

Golf's hold over Obama is also tied to his desire to find things at which he can improve. "He's good at so many things—so to be in an area that he's not as strong but knows he can get better" appeals to Obama's nature, explained Katz. "The challenge of it is very important to him."

How to explain Obama's twin sports passions? Easy. "There is a direct through line from basketball to golf," said Van Natta. "Obama kept getting injured playing pickup basketball so Michelle suggested he start playing golf."

Alexander Wolff, who wrote *The Audacity of Hoop* about Obama's basketball addiction, tells a similar story.

"He played until he took an elbow [to the face] in a pickup game. Suddenly he starts playing a lot more golf. The First Lady brought the hammer down—she said it was ridiculous that given his age and his position that he was putting himself in danger of giving a 'State of the Union' speech with a shiner."

The Obama on the golf course was also similar to Obama the hoops player and Obama the politician: cool and competitive as hell.

"Obama is unflappable on the golf course," said Van Natta. "Even on a bad day he would roll with it and string three good holes together."

"As with politics and everything else, once he got into it he wanted to be good at it," noted Axelrod.

Obama, like Reagan, used the White House as a landing spot for championship teams—especially NBA teams. Obama was, in many ways, our first NBA president.

There was an element of peacocking that he brought to these visits—a confident guy who was in the know. It wasn't just that Obama was celebrating teams at the White House. He knew these guys and this game— and he wanted you to know he knew.

In January 2010 when the Los Angeles Lakers came to the White House to celebrate their championship the previous summer, Obama turned to Lakers legend Magic Johnson and made reference to Michael Jordan's infamous changing-hands layup in the 1991 NBA finals. "You remember that, Magic," the President said.

That December, after the Lakers had won the title again and returned to Washington to celebrate, Obama joked that "Kobe [Bryant] and Derek [Fisher] have been here so many times they could lead tours themselves. Same for Coach [Phil] Jackson."

In 2012, the Dallas Mavericks, led by Dirk Nowitzki, won the NBA title—and instead of giving Obama a jersey with a #1 or a #44 on it, they gave him one with #23—which Obama loved. "Actually, I was No. 23 before Jordan. I think he got the number from me," said the president.

In 2013, it was the star-studded Miami Heat—LeBron James, Dwyane Wade, and Chris Bosh—who came to the White House as champs. Referencing their victory over the Oklahoma City Thunder in the finals (and with a little self-promotion thrown in), Obama joked: "I think it's clear that going up against me prepared them to take on Kevin Durant and Russell Westbrook. It sharpened their skills and gave them the competitive edge they needed. I think that part of the reason they came back today is they want another shot at the old guy."

In 2015, Obama again flashed his knowledge as the fan-in-chief making a sly reference to San Antonio Spurs coach Gregg Popovich's notorious one-word answers during in-game interviews. "I want the coach to know that he is not contractually obligated to take questions after the first quarter of my remarks," teased Obama. Then, again, he flashed that Obama confidence: "If you guys need any tips on winning back-to-back, you know where to find me."

In 2016, his final year in the White House, Obama welcomed the Golden State Warriors as champions. And, again, he made it a little bit about himself. "You defied the cynics, accomplished big things, racked up a great record," he told the team. "You don't get enough credit. I can't imagine how that feels."

Obama also honored two NBA greats—Michael Jordan and Kareem Abdul-Jabbar—with Presidential Medals of Freedom in 2016. (Obama gave out twelve Medals of Freedom to athletes, the most of any president.)

Of Jordan, Obama said, "There is a reason you call somebody 'the Michael Jordan of'—the Michael Jordan of neurosurgery or the Michael Jordan of rabbis or the Michael Jordan of outrigger canoeing, and they know what you're talking about, because Michael Jordan is the Michael Jordan of greatness. He is the definition of somebody so good at what they do that everybody recognizes it. That's pretty rare."

In praising Abdul-Jabbar, Obama noted that the NCAA banned the dunk for nine years because of him. "They didn't say it was about Kareem, but it was about Kareem," said Obama. "When a sport changes its rules to make it harder just for you, you are really good." (Obama, comically, struggled to hang the actual medal around the seven-foot-two Abdul-Jabbar's neck.)

Of the recipients, Obama said: "These are folks who have helped make me who I am."

And while Obama hosted a lot of NBA teams, he also invited a slew of other sports teams through the White House as well. He brought in every team that won the NCAA basketball tournament during his years in office. He invited the winners of the Little League World Series. He paid homage to the undefeated season of the 1972 Miami Dolphins!

In 2015, the year after they had won the World Cup, the U.S. Women's Soccer team visited the White House. "This team taught all of America's children that playing like a girl means you're a badass," Obama said.

In 2016, celebrating the eleventh UConn women's basketball national title, Obama said, "When I called Coach Geno [Auriemma] to congratulate him for winning the title—again—I told him we'd have his room ready for him when he gets here. It's a small room, with a cot. He doesn't get the Lincoln Bedroom. But he does seem to spend an awful lot of time here."

That same year, the Chicago Cubs won their first World Series since

1908—and Obama quickly invited them to celebrate at the White House before he had to vacate the premises. The Cubs brought along gifts—including a "44" tile from the Wrigley field scoreboard and a "W" pennant (which flies over the stadium after every Cub win) signed by the entire team. "Best swag I've gotten as president," said Obama.

Altogether, Obama hosted eighty-six teams at the White House over his eight years in office, according to Mark Knoller. That's twice as many as the forty teams that George W. Bush, no slouch when it came to sports fandom, had at the White House during his two terms.

———————

Obama, in addition to being president, tried his hand at coaching hoops during his time in Washington. (Coaching runs in his extended family. Michelle Obama's brother, Craig, coached the Oregon State men's basketball team.)

Obama's daughter, Sasha, was in fourth grade and playing on a rec league basketball team called the Vipers. The team's practices were, um, chaotic and not terribly heavy on basketball tactics and strategy.

So, Obama and Reggie Love, the former Duke baller and Obama body man, stepped in. They volunteered to run a few extra practices on Sunday to help the girls get more familiar with the game. "Dribbling, passing, making sure your shoelaces were tied," Obama wrote of what they covered in the training sessions.

The Vipers wound up winning the championship. (It was a low-scoring affair—an 18–16 final.) The victory was a little less than sweet, however, as parents on the other teams complained that they didn't get the special attention and treatment that the Vipers had.

"A few of the parents from a rival Sidwell [Friends] team started complaining to the Vipers' coaches, and presumably the school, that Reggie and I weren't offering training sessions to their kids, too," Obama wrote in his memoir *A Promised Land*. "We explained that there was nothing special about our practices, that it was just an excuse for me to spend extra time with Sasha, and offered to help other parents organize extra practices of their own. But when it became clear that the complaints had nothing to do with basketball—'They must think being coached by you is something they can put on a Harvard application,' Reggie scoffed—and that the Vipers' coaches were feeling squeezed, I decided that it would be simpler for all concerned if I went back to just being a fan."

Obama's run as a quasi coach was over. But he did win that championship . . .

Smackdown!

Presidential Heel

In January 1984, a new figure showed up at the USFL's annual owners' meeting in New Orleans: Donald J. Trump. And he had a message: The league needed to change—and fast.

"I guarantee you folks in this room that I will produce NBC and that I will produce ABC, guaranteed, and for a hell of a lot more money than the horseshit you're getting right now," Trump told the owners, as recounted in Jeff Pearlman's terrific book *Football for a Buck* on the rise and fall of the USFL. "Every team in this room suffers from one thing: people don't watch to watch spring football... you watch what happens you challenge the NFL... I don't want to be a loser. I've never been a loser before and if we're losers in this, fellas, I will tell you what, it's going to haunt us... Every time there's an article written about you, it's going to be you owned this goddamn team which failed... and I am not going to be a failure."

Sound familiar?

"You can cut and paste the USFL and the GOP and it's the same damn story," Charley Steiner, the radio voice of the USFL's New Jersey Generals, told *Esquire* in 2016. "It's all about him and the brand and moving on to the next thing if it doesn't work out."

The USFL, which launched in 1983, was envisioned by its founders as a way to challenge the NFL's monopoly on American football. Whereas the NFL was old and boring, the USFL would be young and fun. Touchdown celebrations would be encouraged. Replay would be used to make sure refs got the calls right. Teams could go for two-point conversions after scoring a touchdown. And so on.

But the USFL owners weren't idiots. The NFL owned the fall—and had a massive TV deal that made competing on that turf all but impossible. So, the USFL launched its season in the spring at a time when, in theory, people would be hungry for more football—and the NFL season would be a long way off. The USFL secured broadcasting contracts with ABC and a fledgling sports network known as ESPN.

The first season was, generally speaking, seen as a success. Heisman Trophy winner Herschel Walker had spurned the NFL to sign with the Generals and rushed for more than 1,800 yards and 17 touchdowns.

Then along came Trump, who had something the USFL owners lacked: star power. Trump bought the Generals from J. Walter Duncan, an Oklahoma oilman who didn't like spending his weekend traveling to and from the East Coast. Trump paid $10 million for the team, which was $1.5 million more than Duncan was asking.

Shortly after buying the Generals, Trump secured a meeting with then–NFL commissioner Pete Rozelle—and made it clear that he would happily give up his current team for an NFL one in exchange.

"As long as I or my heirs are involved in the NFL, you will never be a franchise owner," Rozelle reportedly told Trump.

Trump later testified that Rozelle told him in that meeting, "You will have a good chance of an NFL franchise and, in fact, you will have an NFL franchise."

Soooo...

Trump wasn't bothered by Rozelle's dismissal. As Pearlman writes:

The New Jersey owner...had a specific strategy. He would purchase the Generals, build them into the class of the USFL, watch the upstart league either fold or merge with the NFL, and eventually relocate to Shea Stadium until his new facility was constructed in Manhattan. The end result: The NFL's New

York Generals, hosting 80,000 red-and-white clad fans in the state-of-the-art Trump stadium.

Trump was already knee-deep in the mythmaking that has defined his life in and out of politics. The focus then and now wasn't on how things really were but on how they looked.

In the near term, Trump set out building the best team money could buy. He tried to hire Miami Dolphins legendary coach Don Shula and, when that failed, recruited former New York Jets coach Walt Michaels to lead the Generals. He signed Brian Sipe, the starting quarterback for the Cleveland Browns, to play the same position for his team. The following year, he inked quarterback Doug Flutie, who had just won the Heisman Trophy at Boston College, to a six-year deal worth more than $8 million. He helped spread the rumor that he would sign New York Giants star linebacker Lawrence Taylor when LT's deal with the Giants expired. "No one knows if we signed him—actually only three people know, that's Lawrence, his agent, and me," Trump told the *New York Times*. "All I can tell you is, 'no comment.'" (He hadn't signed LT.)

In 1984, Trump even said that he could have bought the NFL's Dallas Cowboys—if he had wanted to. "I could have bought an N.F.L. team," he told the *New York Times*. "There were three or four available—that still are available, including, of course, the Dallas Cowboys."

Why didn't he? Not enough room for growth. "I could have bought an N.F.L. club for $40 million or $50 million, but it's established and you would just see it move laterally," explained Trump. "Not enough to create there."

(Sidebar: The Cowboys, as of August 2022, are worth $7.64 billion. That makes them the most valuable sports franchise in the world. Whoops!)

At the end of the 1986 season, Trump played his, um, trump card. He began pushing the USFL owners to move their season to the fall, promising them TV contracts that were, in fact, a chimera.

"If God wanted football in the spring," said Trump, "he wouldn't have created baseball." (Less than two years prior, Trump, asked about whether spring football could succeed, had responded: "What I like is for people to tell me that something can't be done, when I think it can.")

And Trump bullied the other owners into going along with his plan.

"I think he became a Pied Piper," onetime USFL commissioner Chet Simmons told Pearlman. "He spun a web of stories to the rest of the owners that all this could be accomplished, and it could be accomplished if you followed what he believed in and the people that he knew and his ability to get to people we couldn't in order to raise the level of income from the networks, to get the interest of Pete Rozelle and the rest of the National Football League in terms of the accommodation of a few teams. And away he'd go being the savior of what was the United States Football League."

The USFL—led by Trump—also filed a $1.5 billion antitrust lawsuit against the NFL. The trial, which played out in the spring and summer of 1986, turned into a debacle for Trump.

"The more I developed the strategy, the more I wanted Donald Trump as my fall guy," said Frank Rothman, who served as the NFL's lead lawyer. "I would call it Donald versus Goliath. I would make their scheme Donald's plan, which it was. I would show that Donald Trump is not a little lightweight; he is one of the richest men in America... He was such a lousy witness for them, and a great one for us."

Rothman's strategy worked. While the court found that the NFL did, in fact, have a fall TV monopoly and had colluded to kill the USFL, it awarded the upstart league only a single dollar in damages—arguing that the USFL had done itself far more damage than the NFL had been able to inflict.

As the *Los Angeles Times* reported of the verdict:

Without a large judgment to go along with an otherwise favorable verdict—the kind of judgment that would enable the USFL, which has lost nearly $200 million in its three years of existence, to continue, or without the injunctive relief that would strip one of the three networks from the NFL and make it available to the USFL—the "victory" is hollow.

Less than a week after the court decision, the USFL owners made the decision to suspend the 1986 season. "Without a damage award from the suit, and without a network television contract, play for the eight-team league—which was to have started on Sept. 13—was not feasible," said the *New York Times*.

Trump, decades later, dismissed the league as "small potatoes."

But Trump never gave up his dream of owning an NFL franchise. In 2014, he went public with his interest in buying the Buffalo Bills following the death of longtime owner Ralph Wilson. (Wilson had bought the Bills for $25,000 in 1959.)

"I'm going to give it a heavy shot," he told a reporter for the *Buffalo News*. "I would love to do it, and if I can do it I'm keeping it in Buffalo."

He added in an interview on a local Buffalo radio station: "People have actually talked to me about the Bills. I mean, the group of people called me—would I be interested in investing, and I'll take a look at it. I mean, I look at a lot of things. I'll take a look at it."

Trump wound up being one of three finalists for the teams—alongside Terry and Kim Pegula, who owned the Buffalo Sabres, and an investment group led by rocker Jon Bon Jovi. In September 2014, the NFL awarded the franchise to the Pegulas for the price of $1.4 billion. (Trump reportedly bid in the mid–$800 millions.)

"Even though I refused to pay a ridiculous price for the Buffalo Bills, I would have produced a winner," Trump, in his usual classy manner, tweeted in October 2014. "Now that won't happen."

On that same day, he offered this take: "The @nfl games are so boring now that actually, I'm glad I didn't get the Bills. Boring games, too many flags, too soft!"

Which is, of course, utter bunk. Trump has long wanted to be a member of the exclusive club of thirty-two team owners—some of the most rarefied air in the country. His interest in being president developed only after he had been spurned from being an NFL owner at least twice.

Why does football appeal so much to Trump? Well, it's a uniquely American sport, for one—not really played anywhere else in the world. It's also extremely popular and extremely violent, two other traits he is drawn to in life.

It will surprise you not at all that Donald Trump had a very high opinion of his own athletic ability.

"I've always enjoyed sports, starting from the time I was a kid," Trump told the *New York Times* all the way back in the mid-1980s. "I was always the captain of the teams in high school. I liked baseball, golf, tennis, football, all the sports."

In 2004, he wrote: "I was supposed to be a pro baseball player. At the New York Military Academy, I was captain of the baseball team. I worked hard like everyone else, but I had good talent."

In 2010, Trump told MTV that he "was supposed to be a professional baseball player. Fortunately, I decided to go into real estate instead."

And in 2013, Trump tweeted this: "I played football and baseball, sorry, but said to be best bball player in N.Y. State—ask coach Ted Dobias—said best he ever coached."

OK, so there is a lot to unpack there.

What isn't up for debate is that Trump was a pretty good baseball player. He started off playing catcher but eventually wound up as a first baseman.

(Sidebar: When he was in sixth grade, Trump wrote a poem about baseball. "I like to see a baseball hit and the fielder catch it in his mitt," it began. It got worse from there.)

"He was big and tall," said Marc Fisher, a *Washington Post* reporter who wrote a 2016 biography of Trump. "And he could hit—that was the main thing."

Fisher also noted that Trump had a built-in aggression—this will surprise you not at all—that worked in his favor on the athletic field. "His classmates always talked about it going back to his elementary school years," said Fisher. "Trump was always the dirtiest guy on the field—literally. He was sliding all over the place, plowing into people. He had this notion of sports as combat."

Trump also had a very tight relationship with Dobias, who, in addition to being a baseball coach, was the school's "drill sergeant and disciplinarian," according to Fisher. "Trump was always getting in trouble, so he was always sucking up to Dobias."

Dobias, in 2015, told the *Daily Mail* that scouts from the Philadelphia Phillies and Boston Red Sox had their eye on the young Trump, although it's extremely hard to verify that being the case.

(Trump did also play football at NYMA. He was a tight end but wasn't terribly good, and he quit the team as a junior after a long-running feud with the coach, who did not find him as charming as Dobias did.)

Even way back in the mid-1960s, Trump was showing the tendency for exaggeration and outright lying that came to define his life and presidency.

As NYMA classmate Sandy McIntosh recounted in 2017:

My last conversation with Donald Trump was at the New York Military Academy, where we were both cadets. It was 1964, the year he graduated. We were walking together near the baseball field where, he reminded me, he'd played exceptionally well. He demanded that I tell him the story of one of his greatest games.

"The bases were loaded," I told him. "We were losing by three. You hit the ball just over the third baseman's head. Neither the third baseman nor the left fielder could get to the ball in time. All four of our runs came in; we won the game."

"No," he said. "That's not the way it happened. I want you to remember this: I hit the ball out of the ballpark! Remember that. I hit it out of the ballpark!"

Ballpark? I thought. We were talking about a high school practice field. There was no park to hit a ball out of. And anyway, his hit was a blooper the fielders misplayed.

So, yeah. Some things never change.

In May 2020, *Slate* did a deep dive into just how good Trump actually was—going all the way to old Hudson Valley newspapers in search of box scores from the NYMA baseball team from the years Trump was on the diamond.

What did the reporter—Leander Schaerlaeckens—find? This:

Combined, the nine box scores I unearthed give Trump a 4 for 29 batting record in his sophomore, junior, and senior seasons, with three runs batted in and a single run scored. Trump's batting average in those nine games: an underwhelming .138. (I found one additional mention of a hit and another of a hitless game in games that didn't have box scores.)

Nine games may seem like a small sample size, but NYMA played only a dozen or so games per baseball season, suggesting that Trump's entire high school career spanned between 30 and 40 games.

It's perhaps unfair to draw conclusions from a fraction of those games, but the box scores showed that in his sophomore year, Trump's .100 batting average in those games was the lowest of any of the five players who had at least eight at-bats. As a junior, he did a tad better, hitting .200, albeit on a team that mustered a mere 11 hits over three games. Trump's senior year, four teammates had more hits than he did.

Which is, as the author notes, a decidedly partial sample. But also that partial look does not suggest the gaudy numbers of someone who was (a) the best baseball player in a large state like New York, or (b) a pro prospect scouted by the Phillies and BoSox.

It's also worth noting that Trump never played baseball at the collegiate level—either at Fordham, where he started school, or at Penn, where he finished it.

Trump did play a sport at Fordham, however. Squash. "He was known to his teammates as an extremely aggressive player," said Fisher. "He never had the patience to outlast someone in rallies so he would just try to smash the ball past his opponents." (The symbolism there is a little on the nose—even for me!)

According to Fisher, Trump would bring his friends on the team to and from games in his sports car. (No lowly team bus for Trump.) Despite the fact that the coach would give him travel money for transporting the team, Trump would ask the guys to pony up for gas and tolls anyway.

On one trip—following a particularly bad loss at the Naval Academy in Annapolis, Maryland—Trump pulled off the road and into a Montgomery Ward department store. He emerged minutes later with a new set of golf clubs as well as tees and balls. The group proceeded to a bluff overlooking the Chesapeake Bay where they blasted ball after ball into the water. When they got bored, they hopped back in the car, leaving the golf clubs by the side of the road.

———————

Almost no one—and no president (with the possible exception of George W. Bush)—*likes* to exercise. You do it because you know it's good for you.

But what if it wasn't, in fact, good for you? What if it was actively bad for you? That is what Donald Trump believes.

"He believed all his life that the human body is like a battery," said Marc Fisher. "You have a finite amount of energy. You are an idiot if you exercise because you are depleting your stock of energy."

In a 2015 *New York Times* profile of Trump, he was openly dismissive of the benefits of exercise.

"All my friends who work out all the time, they're going for knee replacements, hip replacements—they're a disaster," he said. He exerts himself fully by standing in front of an audience for an hour, as he just did. "That's exercise."

There is, um, no medical science to back this up. I did find one study from 2015 published in *Circulation* magazine (yes, that is a real magazine) that suggested people who exercised strenuously four to seven times a week were at increased risk for vascular disease when compared to those who exercise strenuously two to three times a week.

But, Trump doesn't exercise strenuously two to three times a week. Aside from golf—where he always rides in a cart—he appears to get no actual exercise.

In a 2018 interview with Reuters, Trump was somewhat defensive about his exercise regiment. "I get exercise," he said. "I mean I walk, I this,

I that. I run over to a building next door. I get more exercise than people think."

"I this, I that." Incredible.

Trump's battery theory of life force was made all the more remarkable by his decided lack of transparency about his physical health.

Unlike past presidential candidates, Trump released no detailed information about his medical history. Instead, his longtime personal doctor—Dr. Harold Bornstein—released a letter in December 2015 that made the outrageous claim that "if elected, Mr. Trump, I can state unequivocally, will be the healthiest individual ever elected to the presidency." (Bornstein later admitted that Trump had dictated that letter to him.)

Trump received a physical in 2018 by then White House physician Ronny Jackson (now a member of Congress from Texas). Jackson pronounced Trump, who is six foot three and then weighed 239 pounds—right on the edge of obese—in good health. Asked how that could be the case given Trump's penchant for cheeseburgers, Diet Cokes, and vanilla ice cream, Jackson responded, "He has incredible genes, I just assume."

Jackson did advise that Trump needed to—wait for it—exercise more regularly, advice that the president appears to have ignored. "The President received a diet and exercise plan last year after his annual physical, but the President admits he has not followed it religiously," said deputy White House press secretary Hogan Gidley in 2019.

In October 2020, Trump announced that he had contracted COVID. He was taken to Walter Reed National Military Medical Center for treatment, and his condition was more serious than the White House let on at the time.

As the *New York Times* reported in February 2021:

President Donald J. Trump was sicker with Covid-19 in October than publicly acknowledged at the time, with extremely depressed blood oxygen levels at one point and a lung problem associated with pneumonia caused by the coronavirus, according to four people familiar with his condition.

His prognosis became so worrisome before he was taken to Walter Reed National Military Medical Center that officials believed he would need to be put on a ventilator, two of the people familiar with his condition said.

Trump eventually recovered and took to Twitter to tell people they had nothing to fear from it. "Don't be afraid of Covid," he wrote. "Don't let it dominate your life."

_____

When Donald Trump came into the White House in 2017, the tradition of winning sports teams visiting after their championship seasons was almost one hundred years old.

It all began in 1924 when the Washington Senators were feted at the White House by President Calvin Coolidge.

"While President Coolidge has not, perhaps, shown as great a fondness for baseball as some of his predecessors, that he has the welfare of the Nationals at heart was demonstrated yesterday when, at his request, Manager Stanley Harris and the whole team visited the White House," the *Washington Post* reported at the time. "The chief executive not only shook hands with all of the players but told them he was mighty proud of the showing the Nationals have made to date and was confident they would keep up the good work and return to the Capital in October for the world's series."

While baseball was first, other sports followed. The Boston Celtics became the first NBA team to visit the White House following their 1963 championship. The Pittsburgh Steelers, fresh off their Super Bowl win, stopped by the White House in 1980. And the Pittsburgh Penguins became the first NHL team at the White House after winning the Stanley Cup in 1991.

It was a win-win proposition. The athletes loved the chance to walk the halls of power, meet the president, and take some pictures. The presidents— some more than others—loved the opportunity to rub elbows with larger-than-life sports heroes, throwing a pass, and getting a jersey with their name on the back.

(It's no surprise that winning teams visiting the White House became standardized during the presidency of Ronald Reagan. The former movie star understood that how things looked *always* mattered.)

It was a feel-good moment all around. And, even as partisanship in Washington increased as the decades went along, the visits of championship teams to the White House always had something of a carve-out: a politics-free zone.

That is, until Donald Trump came to the White House. Like so many traditions and norms, Trump broke this one, too.

It began in the fall of 2017 when, after leading the Golden State Warriors to the NBA championship, star guard Stephen Curry said that he would not be going with his team to the White House.

Explained Curry of his decision:

That we don't stand for basically what our President has—the things that he's said and the things that he hasn't said in the right times, that we won't stand for it.

The day after Curry's comments went public, Trump took to Twitter to disinvite him. "Going to the White House is considered a great honor for a championship team," Trump tweeted. "Stephen Curry is hesitating; therefore invitation is withdrawn!"

(Sidebar: Curry wasn't hesitating. He had said flatly he had no interest in going; Tweeted LeBron James to Trump: "U bum @StephenCurry30 already said he ain't going! So therefore ain't no invite. Going to White House was a great honor until you showed up!")

When the Warriors schedule brought them to Washington the following February to play the Wizards, the team used their day off to tour the National Museum of African American History and Culture with a group of local kids in lieu of going to visit the White House.

"The White House is a great honor but there are some other circumstances that we felt uncomfortable going," forward Klay Thompson told the *Washington Post*. "We're not going to politicize anything. We're going to hang out with some kids, take them to the African American museum, and hopefully teach them some things we learned along the way, and life lessons, and hopefully give them some great memories."

That same year Trump did more disinviting—this time of the Super

Bowl–winning Philadelphia Eagles after it became clear that a large number of players on the team would not be in attendance. Said Trump.

> The Eagles wanted to send a smaller delegation, but the 1,000 fans planning to attend the event deserve better. These fans are still invited to the White House to be part of a different type of ceremony—one that will honor our great country, pay tribute to the heroes who fight to protect it, and loudly and proudly play the National Anthem. I will be there at 3:00 p.m. with the United States Marine Band and the United States Army Chorus to celebrate America.

In 2019, Megan Rapinoe, star of the U.S. Women's soccer team, was blunt about her interest in visiting the White House if the team won the World Cup. "I'm not going to the fucking White House," she said. "No. I'm not going to the White House. We're not gonna be invited. I doubt it."

Trump, of course, responded—telling Rapinoe to "WIN first before she TALKS! Finish the job!" Trump added that he was planning to invite the team to the White House whether they won or lost.

Shortly after that tweet, the U.S. team played France in the tournament's quarterfinals. Rapinoe scored a goal and celebrated with an arms-flung-out gesture that was widely seen as a response—and rebuke—to Trump.

"It was kind of like a 'Fuck you,' but with a big smile and a shit-eating grin," Rapinoe said of the goal celebration. "You are *not* going to steal any of our joy."

The team did win the World Cup in 2019, beating the Netherlands 2–0 in the final. Rapinoe was named the most valuable player of the tournament and also won the Golden Boot for most goals scored—six—in the tournament.

They did not celebrate at the White House.

Not everyone turned down the Trump invitation to the White House, of course.

The 2019 Clemson football team, which crushed Alabama 44–16 in the

national championship game came to the White House—and were greeted
with a fast-food bonanza that included delicacies from McDonald's, Wen-
dy's, Burger King, and Domino's. Trump tweeted that there were more
than one thousand "hamberders" and that he had paid for all of it.

"We have some very large people that like eating," said Trump at the
event. "So I think we're going to have a little fun."

Golf tells you so much about Donald Trump. It's the sport he has played
the most in his life—and the only one he played regularly as an adult. It's
the sport he has long been best at and, if you believe his official handicap—
which most people don't—he is the best golfing president ever. His epony-
mous golf resorts are at the center of his real estate empire. In short: It's
impossible to see where Trump ends and his golfing bullshit begins. Everything in his personal and professional life has golf intertwined in it.

So, where to start?

This is as good a place as any: Trump played a massive amount of golf
during his four years as president.

According to the website Trumpgolfcount.com, Trump made 298
trips to golf clubs during his term in office—a number that includes evidence of him actually playing golf on at least 150 occasions.

(Sidebar: The Trump White House was very tight-lipped about
Trump's golf playing. He would often travel on the weekends to his golf
course in Virginia, but his press office would not confirm that he was
actually playing golf at the club. Only when photos emerged on social
media of Trump riding in a cart or swinging a club did we get confirma-
tion that he was actually playing.)

Philip Bump of the *Washington Post*, who closely tracked Trump's golf
playing throughout his term, estimated that Trump played 261 rounds of
golf as president. Wrote Bump: "If accurate, though, that's a round every
5.6 days. By contrast, [Barack] Obama played 333 rounds of golf—over
twice as many years. That's about once every 8.8 days."

Which is ironic. Because Trump was a regular critic of how much
Obama played golf while in office.

"Can you believe that, with all of the problems and difficulties facing the U.S., President Obama spent the day playing golf," Trump tweeted in 2014. "Worse than Carter."

And this in 2016: "While our wonderful president was out playing golf all day, the TSA is falling apart, just like our government! Airports a total disaster!"

Trump, while on the campaign trail, insisted golf wouldn't be a priority for him. "If I win I may never see my property—I may never see these places again," Trump said at an August 2016 campaign event. "But because I'm going to be working for you, I'm not going to have time to go golfing, believe me. Believe me. Believe me, folks."

Um, well, no.

He also insisted that when he did play golf, he would be doing so with foreign leaders and other powerful dignitaries—working while on the course.

In 2018, White House press secretary Sarah Sanders was asked what, specifically, Trump had accomplished during his rounds of golf to date. Here's how she responded:

> I think it would certainly be developing deeper and better relationships with members of Congress in which those relationships have helped push forward the President's agenda, specifically when it comes to helping get the tax reform and tax cuts passed. A lot of that, I think, and the success of that came from the strong relationships that the President has. And he's played golf with a number of senators and used that time, certainly, to accomplish that.

I crunched the numbers and, at that point in his presidency, less than 10 percent of the total rounds Trump had played were with members of Congress. All of his known playing partners from Congress were Republicans.

In 2020, Trump defended his regular rounds. "My 'exercise' is playing, almost never during the week, a quick round of golf," Trump tweeted. "Obama played more and much longer rounds, no problem." (Fact check: He did not!)

In a subsequent tweet, Trump added: "I play VERY fast, get a lot of work done on the golf course, and also get a 'tiny' bit of exercise. Not bad!"

The other central—and basic—question when it comes to Trump and golf is how good he actually is. Which turns out to be a harder question to answer than you might think—due in large part to Trump's widely reported tendency to cheat.

Rick Reilly, who wrote an entire book about Trump and golf (Title: *Commander in Cheat: How Golf Explains Trump*), says that Trump "cheats like a mafia accountant."

In his 2016 biography of Trump, Marc Fisher said that when the president played golf "the people who played with him would notice that he wrote down phony scores, moved his ball and called a 'gimme' when his ball was yards away from the hole." Added Fisher: "A lot of people who played golf [with him] say that on a scale of cheating from 1 to 10, Donald was an 11."

One example among many: In 2018, while Trump was, you know, serving as president of the United States, he also managed to win the club championship at his Trump course in West Palm Beach, Florida. Which is a pretty amazing accomplishment!

(Sidebar: Trump has also won the 1999, 2001, and 2009 club championships as well as the 2012 and 2013 senior club championships at the course. Pretty good run!)

The story goes like this: A man named Ted Virtue (not making him up), the CEO of MidOcean Partners, played in and won the club championship in 2018. (Virtue helped finance the movie *Green Book*, which won the Oscar for best picture in 2019.) Sometime after Virtue's win, Trump bumped into him at the club and somewhat jokingly told him, "The only reason you won is because I couldn't play." Trump proposed that he and Virtue play a nine-hole match for the title of club champ. Trump won. Hence the plaque on the wall.

Trump claims that he has won twenty club championships in his lifetime. "Pretty much a natural golfer," he told *Golf Digest* in 2014. "I've won a lot of club championships. Anytime I win a club championship, I'm proud of those rounds. Club championships are like our majors."

But according to Reilly, there's lots and lots of fibbing built in there. "Whenever he opens a new golf course that he buys, he simply plays the first round by himself and all of a sudden he's the champion, he's the king. Give him the crown," said Reilly.

And, no, in case you were wondering, that is not at all how the awarding of club championships works.

With all that said, there's not much debate that Trump is a good golfer—and a very good one for his age. His official handicap—2.8, meaning he usually shoots three-ish strokes over par in a round—may oversell it slightly, but people who have played with him and those who have analyzed his swing and ball-striking ability have come away generally impressed.

"He hits the ball a long way off the tee," said Luke Kerr-Dineen, the game improvement editor at *Golf* magazine. "And he focuses singularly on hitting the ball off the tee. To him that's the sign of a good golfer. Putting and all these other details are not as telling as your ability to hit the ball."

Dineen said that Trump's real handicap is like "somewhere between a 5 and an 8" when you factor in "lots of gimmes" that he tends to take.

Jaime Diaz, writing—somewhat too credulously—in 2017 in *Golf Digest* of his own experience of playing with Trump, said:

Trump was 67 when I played with him in 2013 at his course outside Charlotte and in early 2014 at Doral, but he still possessed a significant remnant of big-man athleticism. He was not particularly long off the tee—averaging about 230 yards—but a big reason was a steep downswing that produced a low fade and was better suited to good iron play. Trump had clearly made a calculation that being exceedingly straight—he was rarely in the rough and never in chip-out or penalty trouble—works better than long and (too often) wrong.

When I asked Trump about this, he said he hadn't given it a lot of thought. He's basically self-taught, never consistently working with an instructor. "I think of golf as a very natural game," he said.

"I never really wanted to know a lot about my technique. I really trust instinct a lot, in golf and a lot of things."

So, Trump is good. But not as good as he says—or as his many club championships would suggest.

Which, when you think about it, it's a pretty apt analogy for Trump's broader life. Yes, he was born into money—his father gave him a $1 million loan when he turned twenty-one—but by any account he has made lots and lots more money. He has had success on television. And, hell, he was elected president of the United States in his first run for any elected office!

And yet, none of that is good enough for Trump. He can't just be wealthy. He has to exaggerate his wealth by several degrees. He can't just have been successful on TV. He has to have had the biggest hit in the history of the NBC network in *The Apprentice*. He can't have just won a single term as president. He has to have actually won a second term only to be cheated out of it by (nonexistent) voter fraud in swing states.

Nothing is ever enough. He can never be good or even great. He must always be the best.

"In the world of sports as in politics as in business as in his personal life, the same rules apply," said Fisher. "You are either a winner or a loser. If you are a loser you barely have any reason to live."

Loser, is, in fact, Trump's preferred putdown. He's called the late senator John McCain a loser, Anthony Scaramucci a loser, Chris Cuomo a loser, Mike Bloomberg a loser, George Conway a loser, CNN a loser, Bill Kristol a loser, Karl Rove a loser—and that's just on Twitter!

For Trump, winning wasn't—and isn't—about putting more points on the board or more goals in the net or even more votes in the ballot box. It's about crushing anyone who dares to challenge you.

"He defines winning as beating some guy—showing up some fancy person," said Fisher. "In every one of those fields, he finds a way to declare himself a winner and moves on to the next thing."

Seen through that lens, Trump's relentless acquisition and promotion of his own golf course—splashed with the Trump name everywhere— makes perfect sense.

The fact is that someone like Donald Trump—garish, publicity-seeking—would never be offered the chance to join the old-money clubs that represent the pillars of the golf establishment: Augusta National, Cypress Point, Pine Valley, Seminole, and the like.

"His bombastic nature doesn't fit those clubs," said Ron Sirak, a long-time golf writer. "If he wants to be at a club where he wants to be a big deal, that's not any of those clubs."

Think here of Al Czervik (aka Rodney Dangerfield) in *Caddyshack*. Trump is a perfect comp for Czervik. He's rich, sure. But so are lots of people. He dresses loud, talks loud—hell, he probably thinks loud. He wants to play the "naked lady" balls. He insults the hat of one of the leading members. He's into real estate and nouveau riche in every possible way. Like Trump, Czervik is impossible to ignore. He stands out in a crowd. And that makes them both utterly unpalatable at the finer golf clubs in America—whether it be Augusta National or Bushwood.

Trump, deep down, knew that. So what did he do? He found a way to win on his own terms. He not only bought his own courses but he also declared himself the club champion of many of them. That'll stick it to those tight-ass fuddy-duddies! To quote Czervik: "A member? You think I actually want to join this scumatorium? The only reason I'm here is because I might buy it!"

"He built his own clubs and wanted people to be in his club," said Sirak. Trump officially owns seventeen courses—twelve of which are in the United States, including three in his adopted home state of Florida.

(Sidebar: While Trump's desire to buy up a bunch of clubs—and name them after himself—was largely driven by selfish reasons, it wound up being a very smart business decision. According to *Forbes*, Trump's clubs were worth $650 million in 2021—the second most valuable thing he owned. Trump's New York City real estate was valued at $1.1 billion.)

According to Sirak, Trump "weaseled" his way into the U.S. Golf Association by buying several distressed properties—including Turnberry in Scotland and Doral in Florida—during the teeth of the Great Recession.

In the wake of the September 11, 2001, terrorist attacks, Trump went to then–USGA executive director David Fay and told him that the organization needed a permanent backup course on which to hold the U.S. Open tournament. Trump offered up his Bedminster, New Jersey, club, which just so happened to be quite close to the USGA headquarters in Far Hills, New Jersey.

In 2014, the Bedminster course was awarded the PGA Championship. Hosting a major championship was for Trump, at long last, an invitation into the club from which he had long been excluded.

Then the January 6, 2021, riot in the U.S. Capitol happened. Within four days, the PGA announced that it was moving the 2022 U.S. Open from Trump's course to Southern Hills in Tulsa, Oklahoma.

"I won't be watching it, no," Trump said of the tournament. "I will not watch it. The only thing I like about it is that I love Oklahoma where, as you pointed out brilliantly, I have won seventy-seven outta seventy-seven counties. But I will not be watching it. No."

That snub by the PGA explains why Trump has been so willing to play host to the LIV Golf tour, a rival entity funded, in large part, by money from Saudi Arabia's sovereign wealth fund.

(Sidebar: LIV Golf, thanks to a virtually unlimited pot of money, successfully lured several big-name golfers away from the PGA tour including Phil Mickelson, Dustin Johnson, Brooks Koepka, and Sergio Garcia.)

Trump hosted two events in LIV Golf's first season—one at Bedminster in late July 2022 and the season finale in late October at his West Palm Beach course.

And he seemed to have zero ethical concerns with working hand in hand with the Saudis who, among other things, have been directly linked to the brutal murder of *Washington Post* journalist Jamal Khashoggi in 2018.

"I've known these people for a long time in Saudi Arabia, they've been friends of mine for a long time," Trump told ESPN. "They've invested in many American companies, they own big percentages of many, many American companies, and frankly what they're doing for golf is so great."

Yes, he has known the Saudis "for a long time." In fact, the first foreign trip Trump made as president was to Saudi Arabia where he was—to put it mildly—feted. They rolled out the red carpet for him, literally, at the airport. They projected an image of Trump's face on the Ritz Carlton in Riyadh. They hung American flags from the lampposts that lined the highway. They included him in a traditional sword dance. And, of course, there was the picture of Trump, King Salman of Saudi Arabia, and Abdel Fattah el-Sisi of Egypt putting their hands on that glowing orb. (If you don't know the picture, you have apparently not been on the internet for the past five or so years.)

As the *New York Times* noted of the visit, "The attention lavished on Mr. Trump laid the groundwork for the cozy ties the Saudis were seeking, an investment that paid off for the kingdom throughout Mr. Trump's presidency."

When asked in advance of the LIV Golf event about protests from families of victims of the September 11, 2001, attacks—fifteen of the nineteen hijackers were Saudi citizens—Trump was similarly dismissive.

"Well, nobody's gotten to the bottom of 9/11, unfortunately, and they should have, as to the maniacs that did that horrible thing to our city, to our country, to the world, so nobody's really been there," he said. "But I can tell you there are a lot of really great people that are out here today and we're going to have a lot of fun and we're going to celebrate."

Whether it's the USFL, the PGA tour, or the presidency, the end with Trump is always the same: ruin, with a healthy helping of blame to go with it. Things *always* end badly when Trump is involved. And he *never* takes blame for even a small part of those problems, choosing instead to lean into unfounded conspiracy theories and try to keep the stench of defeat off of himself. And always he is looking to divide, putting himself on one side and his supposed enemies and, er, haters on the other.

You may not think of professional wrestling as a sport—it is, spoiler alert, fake, after all—but if you are looking for a way to understand how Donald Trump both views and interacts with the world there is no better decoder than grappling.

Trump has long had close ties to the world of pro wrestling.

He hosted the sport's marquee event—*Wrestlemania*—at his Atlantic

City casino in 1988 and 1989. He was in attendance at *Wrestlemania VII* in Las Vegas in 1991. He was again in the crowd at *Wrestlemania XX* in 2008, and was interviewed by former wrestler Jesse "the Body" Ventura, who had also done a stint as the governor of Minnesota. "I think that we may need a wrestler in the White House in 2000," Ventura told Trump. *Oh, how right you were, Jesse!*

Trump was also prominently featured in story lines within the company.

In the spring of 2007, Trump was set against WWE owner Vince McMahon in what was billed as the "battle of the billionaires." (Both men were, in fact, billionaires.) In signing the contract for the match—each billionaire chose a wrestler to represent them—Trump was accompanied to the ring by two, um, buxom women. The deal was this: Whoever's wrestler won got to shave the head of the other guy.

During the match, which took place at *Wrestlemania 23*, Trump was on hand to watch his pick—and hopefully keep his hair. Hijinks ensued—as they always do—and Trump wound up clotheslining McMahon and landing a series of less-than-realistic punches to his face. Trump's wrestler also managed to win—and the real estate mogul got to shave McMahon's head.

Two years later, Trump was back in the WWE story line. This time he had "bought" the wrestling operation from McMahon and decided to run the flagship show *Monday Night Raw* without commercials. Within a week, McMahon panicked—and bought it back from Trump at double the price. "I can do whatever the hell I want," Trump told McMahon. *Foreshadowing!*

In 2022, an internal investigation by the WWE showed that Mc-Mahon had made $5 million in unreported contributions to Trump's charity that lined up with those two story lines—one for $4 million in 2007 and another for $1 million in 2009.

Trump was inducted into the celebrity wing of the WWE Hall of Fame in 2013. "I consider this to be my greatest honor of all," he said. "I do."

Less than four years later—in a script no wrestling writer could come up with—Trump was elected president and named Linda McMahon, Vince's wife, to lead the Small Business Administration. (Oh yeah, in between those two events, McMahon ran unsuccessfully for the Senate from Connecticut twice—spending lots and lots of that wrestling money in the process.)

The over-the-top showmanship and outlandish story lines of pro wrestling clearly influenced Trump's political persona when he ran for president in 2016—and how he acted as president.

One episode stands out. As Trump was recovering from COVID-19, he floated the idea of leaving the hospital looking frail but then suddenly ripping open his button-down shirt to reveal a Superman logo shirt underneath.

Yes, you read that right. Trump ultimately decided against the move—although he did, in a grand gesture, rip his mask off once he returned to the White House from the hospital.

What Trump learned from his years of watching and participating in pro wrestling is that people like their world painted in black-and-white. Good guys and bad guys. Heroes and villains. Babyfaces and heels. They don't want gray area. They want to know who to root for and who to root against.

As Josh Moon put it in a 2016 column in the *Montgomery Advertiser* of Trump's wrestling-like appeal to voters:

> It is macho. It is primal. And it is satisfying.
>
> The screaming fans in those arenas mostly know that the action is staged, that the arguments are scripted and that the whole thing is a big show, but dammit, it's a lot of fun to watch.
>
> Trump has used the same formula on America.
>
> He is the hero brazenly taking on the establishment. He's saying the politically incorrect things they won't. He's going to solve problems with brute force and ego.

What Trump understood is that people didn't really care if he was telling them the truth. They wanted to believe in a version of reality that he was shopping because it made things simpler. They knew who they should cheer and, more important, who they should boo.

Presidents and Pickleball

Something AARP

Fighting Irish

Underdog

J oe Biden's childhood struggle with a stutter is well known. What's far less well known is how sports became Biden's way to express himself in those difficult years.

"From a young age, he was physically capable and verbally paralyzed," explained Evan Osnos, whose biography of Biden was published in 2020. "The stutter was the defining fact of his intellectual and mental life. It made him feel off balance. But he could get out on the court or the field and he didn't have to say a word and his performance spoke for him."

For as halting as Biden was in conversation, he was that fluid on the field. And the ease with which he picked up and played sports—football, basketball, and baseball—came with something else: a daredevil streak.

"As much as I lacked confidence in my ability to communicate verbally, I always had confidence in my athletic ability," Biden wrote in his 2007 memoir *Promises to Keep*. "Sports was as natural for me as speaking was unnatural."

While Biden was able, he wasn't elite. He was an outfielder who struggled to hit the curve. (Presidents—they're just like us.) Biden's best sport was probably football; he was part of an undefeated team in 1960 at Archmere Academy.

It was a remarkable turnaround, as the Auks had finished 1-6 in Biden's junior year and hadn't had a winning season since 1946.

The quarterback of that team—William Peterman—credits Biden with his success. "I didn't have a chance to be first string. But I saw this kid and he was tall and he looked like he could catch the ball. So I said, 'Go long, Joe,'" Peterman recalled to the *Los Angeles Times* in 2022. "And he went long, I threw him a bomb. And he caught it. And then, they made me the first-string quarterback."

That was the first of many connections between the two. Biden caught nineteen touchdown passes that year; "I knew where he was going to be," Peterman said, "and I could always hit him."

E. John Walsh, who coached Biden's team at Archmere, spoke highly of his athletic ability in an interview with the *New York Times* in 2008. "He was a skinny kid," said Walsh, "but he was one of the best pass receivers I had in 16 years as a coach."

Biden's sportiness was apparent in his high school yearbook entry. "Joe is another one of our all-around athletes," it read. "For three years, he played on both the football and basketball team, contributing his fine personality and hard work to each...Whenever a sport was being played that he was not in, Joe was right there cheering the rest of the team on."

Years later, Richard Ben Cramer, in his seminal book *What It Takes*, would draw a direct comparison between politics and football:

What he wanted [politics] to feel like was the organized emotion of a football play—practiced for months, until it was clockwork—where he knew, where he *saw* in his mind, before the snap of the ball, how he'd run, exactly, twenty yards down the field, where he'd feint for the goalpost and cut to the sideline...like it had already *happened*.

Fifty-one years after the heroics of Peterman and Biden, the Archmere Academy Auks went undefeated again—winning the Delaware state championship in the process. Days after the win, Biden recorded a message that played over the school's public address system.

"Fellas, it's a tradition for the President of the United States to host championship teams," Biden said. "Tom Brady and the Buccaneers came to celebrate the Super Bowl at the White House. I had them here. I think it's only right I host all of you to celebrate your title as well. Consider this an invite."

The team visited the White House in July 2022. They were scheduled to spend fifteen minutes but—on Biden time—it lasted thirty.

"The kids were laughing at a bunch of things he was saying," recounted coach John Bellace. "They asked him 'Who was your favorite rival?' and he said 'We used to play [Salesianum] and we would play it like it was a real game.' So I think he meant that it was a scrimmage. But he said he was getting ready to return a kick and he looked over at the [Salesianum] sideline and they had 40 guys, and he looked at the Archmere sideline and they had seven. Our guys laughed at that."

Biden tried on the state championship ring of one of the players and the team gave him a framed #30 jersey, the number he wore when he played for the Auks way back when.

Back then, Biden's success on the football field translated into social success, too. "He was emerging as a young athlete which, in the ways of high school, bled over to general social competence," explained Osnos. "He was elected to student government."

Biden served as class president at Archmere his junior and senior years. (His sister, Valerie, who would become his longtime political consigliere, helped her brother win those first elections, too.) "The only election Biden lost was for captain of the football team," Michael Fay, a classmate, told the Wilmington *News Journal* in 2019. (Fay was the guy Biden lost to.)

(In 1960, when another Irish Catholic—John F. Kennedy—was elected president, Biden went into the school library and looked up "what does it take to become a U.S. Senator," according to Osnos. The conclusion? Go to law school—which Biden eventually did at Syracuse University.)

Biden, later in life, spoke of his time playing football as broadly instructive about how to live.

"I remember the first time I walked out on the practice field as a freshman and I was an 18-year-old kid," he said. "And it didn't take me long to realize that much more is expected of me and all those who walked out that day onto that practice field than our athletic ability. We are expected to be gentlemen. We are expected to conduct ourselves on the field and off the field the same way."

Which is a nice quote if a bit odd, since Biden's gridiron glory didn't extend beyond high school.

"When he got to college, he didn't have a football career to speak of," said Osnos, noting that Biden played club football at the University of Delaware.

That's an interesting story, too. And comes with a bit of controversy.

As a freshman, Biden was expecting to go out for the team at the University of Delaware but doomed himself with poor grades. "When my first semester grades came out, my mom and dad told me I wouldn't be playing spring football," wrote Biden in *Promises to Keep*.

Entering the spring of his junior year, when he returned to football with improved grades, Biden wrote that he was on track to make the team.

"I hadn't played for two years, but I surprised the coaches by moving up the depth chart fast," he wrote. "After the annual spring game that April, it looked like I had a shot to start at defensive back. I couldn't wait until next September; I could almost see the fall season unfold in my head."

Then Biden went on spring break to Florida. While there he met a Syracuse University undergrad named Neilia Hunter—and, in Biden's words—fell "ass over tin cup" in love.

As his sister, Valerie, wrote in her memoir *Growing Up Biden*:

The [University of Delaware] football coach told Joe there was a spot for him on the team. He just needed to commit. Joe was thrilled; he'd played all his life, starting with touch football in Mayfield when we were kids…

But then Neilia happened and everything changed. The choice became clear: He could either drive five hours every weekend to Neilia's home on the Finger Lakes in Skaneateles, or he could follow his lifelong dream to play football and stay on the Delaware campus. He chose Neilia. It wasn't even a choice.

Biden went to Syracuse Law School, and he and Neilia Hunter were married in August 1966. Six and a half years later, she and their young daughter were killed in a car accident. The couple's two other children—Beau and Hunter—survived.

And now for the controversy...

During the 2008 and 2012 campaigns, Biden, as vice president, made a campaign stop in Athens, Ohio—home of the Ohio University Bobcats. And, in both visits, he told a similar story.

"I was a football player," Biden said during the 2012 campaign stop. "I came here in 1963, and I had to go back, I just double-checked my memory—you know, you get my age and you're not so sure of it, you know, your glory days look more glorious than they really were and all that, so we went back on the internet and I just want you to know, I came here in October 1963 and we beat you Bobcats 29–12."

Conservatives blogs went crazy—scanning through yearbooks from Delaware to note that nowhere did Biden appear on the roster of the school's football team.

So, here's the thing. In 1962, the Delaware Blue Hens *did* beat the Ohio U. Bobcats by a score of 29–12. But, Joe Biden wasn't there—or, if he was, he wasn't on the football team. "We don't have him as lettering for freshman football or varsity," the assistant sports information director at Delaware told NBC News in 2012. "We don't have the freshman team playing Ohio University in 1963. We don't have any record of the freshman team playing there."

Biden, in short, fibbed.

Although his football career ended in high school, the confidence-bordering-on-bravado that his gridiron heroics had produced in Biden never really left him. "Once a football star, always a football star in the mind," said Osnos.

Richard Ben Cramer put it even more succinctly: "Joe Biden had balls. Lot of times, more balls than sense."

The death of his eldest son, Beau, changed something fundamental about Biden. It made him more vulnerable—and more identifiable to voters.

"Late stage Biden—the one electable to the presidency—was a slightly more muted figure," said Osnos. "The one some Americans chafed against in 1987 and 2007 was a guy who was a little too chesty."

————————

Later in life, Biden, like lots of middle-aged men, picked up golf. It was the late 1970s and Biden was approaching forty. "He hadn't played golf before that," said Osnos.

Which, of course, draws a sharp contrast with some of the other to-the-manor-born pols who had preceded Biden in office—most notably the George Bushes, whose father and grandfather, respectively, were club champions at the Round Hill Country Club in tony Greenwich, Connecticut.

"Biden did not grow up with the aristocracy," said Osnos. "He was always peering in through the window and wanted to figure out what that was like."

In 2011, Biden was part of a foursome at the so-called golf summit, playing alongside Obama, then–House Speaker John Boehner, and then Ohio governor John Kasich at Joint Base Andrews in Maryland.

On the first hole, Obama, Boehner, and Kasich all made par. Biden rolled in a fifteen-foot putt to salvage a bogey. Dropping that stroke came back to haunt the Biden-Kasich team, however, as they lost to Obama-Boehner by a single stroke on the eighteenth hole.

Multiple news sites pointed out the irony of Biden playing the worst of the four on the first hole as, by handicap, he was the best golfer of the group. In an August 2016 piece in *Golf Digest*, Biden tied for the sixty-eighth best golfer in the Washington area, with a 10 handicap. (Obama was 113th within a 13 handicap; Donald Trump, who would go on, later that year, to win the presidency, ranked twelfth with a 2.8 handicap.)

"After finishing their round, the president, Speaker Boehner, the vice president and Gov. Kasich went to the patio of the clubhouse where they enjoyed a cold drink, some of the U.S. Open coverage and visited with service members," said the White House of the round.

During the 2012 campaign, Biden's golf game became a controversial subject. In a speech at the Republican National Convention that year, Kasich suggested that Biden wasn't entirely truthful about his scores.

"Folks, let me tell you this—Joe Biden disputes a lot of those facts, but Joe Biden told me that he was a good golfer," said Kasich. "And I've played golf with Joe Biden, I can tell you that's not true, as well as all of the other things that he says."

(Sidebar: It is more than a little ironic that four years after Kasich gave that speech, Republicans nominated Donald Trump, a notorious golf cheat, as their party's presidential nominee.)

As Biden considered a third run for president in the 2016 election, he noted that if he ran, it would likely be detrimental to his golf game. At a 2014 event, Irish prime minister Enda Kenny extended an offer for Biden to come to the country and play a round. "If you want to keep your handicap in golf don't run for President. So I expect strokes," Biden said.

After he won the White House in 2020, Biden waited three months to play his first round. The setting was his home course—the Wilmington Country Club. Biden joined the club—where his late son, Beau, had also been a member. His playing partners were longtime aide Steve Ricchetti and Ron Olivere, Beau's father-in-law. "The course record is still intact," Biden joked after the round.

According to Mark Knoller, a former CBS News reporter who keeps detailed statistics on every president, Biden had played just fifteen rounds of golf through July 20, 2022, a far cry from the ninety-one rounds Donald Trump had played by that point in his presidency or even the forty-two played by Obama.

Still, Biden and his team have gone out of their way to make it hard to know when (and with whom) he plays as president.

"He doesn't seem to want people to know he golfs," Rick Reilly told *Politico* of Biden. Reilly noted that Biden hasn't posted an official golf score since 2018 and that "they won't even acknowledge he plays."

Why? Likely for the same reason so many presidents are weird about golf. It remains a sport regarded as for and by elites. And no politician—especially not one who touts his blue-collar roots at every turn like Joe Biden—wants to be seen as elitist or out of touch with the average joe.

———————

Joe Biden loves the role of underdog. His entire life story—Joe from Scranton, up from the bootstraps, and all that—is built around the notion that no one ever gave him anything and that he was always underestimated.

That story line also happens to be at the heart of a whole hell of a lot of really good sports movies. Hollywood is rife with underdogs who simply can't win—right up until they do. *Yes, some of these are moral victories, but they are victories nonetheless!*

So, let's rank some of the greatest sports movie underdogs (that Joe Biden would be proud of)!

8. **Jimmy Chitwood in *Hoosiers*:** It's a little bit hard to be an underdog when you are an unguardable sharpshooter who may well be the best basketball player in the entire state of Indiana. Nevertheless, Chitwood sells it! His parents aren't around—never explained!—and he's being raised by an administrator from the local high school. She hates basketball and wants Jimmy who, again, is the greatest shooter the world has ever seen, to focus on his studies. But then haggard and scandal-plagued coach Norman Dale appears in the town and somehow wins over both Jimmy and his guardian. Jimmy leads the team all the way to Indianapolis where he makes the winning shot to hand tiny Hickory High the victory over South Bend Central.

7. **Shane Falco in *The Replacements*:** Falco was an All American QB at Ohio State, but his career is in tatters after getting crushed in the Super Bowl. Now he fixes rich people's boats. That is, until he gets a call from Coach Jimmy McGinty, who offers him a second chance. Did I mention that the regular players of this fictional league are on strike and there are only four games left in the season? Well,

yeah, that is happening, too. The team manages to win three of the four games, securing a playoff bid when Falco—played by master thespian Keanu Reeves—throws a touchdown bomb to a deaf wide receiver. The strike is ending, so the replacements won't be around for the playoffs, but they accomplished what they came to do (or something).

6. **Danny Noonan in *Caddyshack*:** Danny is caddying at Bushwood Country Club after his senior year of high school to try to scrounge up enough money to pay for college. He thinks he's solved all of his problems when he wins the caddy tournament and the college scholarship that goes with it. But then he finds out his Irish girlfriend (with one of the worst Irish accents in filmmaking history) is pregnant. And he's called on to play in a grudge match between members of the club that could cost him the scholarship. He plays anyway and sinks the match-winning putt for the good guys—thanks to the surprise detonation of a massive amount of explosives. No word on where—or whether—Danny actually went to college.

5. **Rudy Ruettiger in *Rudy*:** Rudy doesn't have the money or the grades to get into Notre Dame. Also, did I mention he's tiny? But he has a dream to play football for the Golden Domers. So he enrolls at a nearby college to get his grades up and befriends a groundskeeper at the university. Rudy eventually gets into Notre Dame and is allowed to suit up for the final game against Georgia Tech. The coach doesn't want to let him on the field but his teammates intervene, and he sacks the quarterback to end the game—and is carried off the field. It's all a bit maudlin but, hey.

4. **Ricky Vaughn in *Major League*:** It's a pretty big leap from the California Penal League to the Cleveland Indians but Vaughn somehow makes it (mostly) seamlessly. He can throw a ball through a wall but can't seem to put it anywhere near the strike zone until the coaches realize he needs glasses and get him fitted with a pair of thick-rimmed black ones. Oh, also, he sleeps with the star third baseman's wife as her revenge for her husband cheating on her. But it all works out in the end when the Indians win a one-game playoff

(on a Tom Berenger slash bunt, no less) against the New York Yankees to win the pennant.

3. **Kit Keller in *A League of Their Own*:** Mention *A League of Their Own* and most people will remember Geena Davis's character, Dottie. But Dottie was a classic overdog: hugely talented and, let's be honest, a little entitled. The real hero of the movie is her little sister, Kit, who wasn't as naturally gifted but who ground out a career in the pros anyway. Plus, Kit wins the World Series for the Racine Belles. (She was traded from Dottie's Rockford Peaches earlier in the season.) She runs through a stop sign at third base and crashes into her sister (the catcher for the Rockford Peaches) who drops the ball in the collision. Also, THERE'S NO CRYING IN BASEBALL!!!!

2. **Daniel LaRusso in *Karate Kid*:** First, Daniel is forced to move from the paradise that is Newark, New Jersey, all the way across the country to Los Angeles. Yuck! Then he starts getting bullied by some teenage toughs who train with a psycho sensei at a local dojo. (BOW TO YOUR SENSEI!) Luckily (also very conveniently) an old man who fixes things in the apartment complex where Daniel and his single mom live also happens to be a karate master who takes the kid under his wing. Wax on, wax off, and all that. Fast-forward to the big karate tournament where Daniel crushes his bullies—and employs the rarely seen crane kick directly to the face of the biggest jerk of them all to win the competition. Yes, there are more *Karate Kid* movies but they all stink, so let's stick to the original.

1. **Rocky Balboa in *Rocky*:** One minute Rocky is playing the heavy for some local crime boss and fighting palookas for peanuts. The next minute he's battling the world heavyweight champion—and lover of American flag paraphernalia—Apollo Creed! What a story arc! And I didn't even mention that in between all of that Rocky meets his future wife, gets a dog, runs very fast through the streets of Philadelphia, catches a chicken in an alleyway, and pounds on a bunch of frozen meat. Only downside? He winds up being related to Paulie.

Joe Biden is part of Peloton Nation.

That's right, the septuagenarian president gets his sweat on with—maybe—your favorite Peloton instructor. (Jezebel—bless them—tried to figure out who Biden's preferred instructor would be. Their investigation led them to Jess Sims.)

The *New York Times* wrote that Biden and his wife "engage in regular morning negotiations" over who gets to ride their Peloton first. The *Washington Post* added this:

> During the 2020 campaign, he biked regularly on both a traditional bike and a Peloton. His current Peloton preferences are something of a state secret, however; West Wing aides would not even reveal whether he had brought the interactive stationary bike with him to the White House.

The key word in all of that is *interactive*. See, a Peloton has a microphone and a video camera built into it. It ups the whole experience for the average ride; you can see and hear other people struggling up that hill right along with you.

The problem is that those sorts of interactive elements pose a security risk when the rider is the leader of the free world. As the *Times* noted: "The last thing the C.I.A. wants is the Russians and the Chinese peering or listening into the White House gymnasium."

A skit on *The Late Show with Stephen Colbert* imagined a Peloton instructor named "USA Mike," with a strong Russian accent, telling Biden to set the resistance on his bike to "first digit of nuclear code then second digit of nuclear code and so on." Then, for working his bicep, the instructor recommends "grabbing something heavy like maybe the intelligence report you were given today. Lift up and to the camera."

Back to the serious stuff. Biden is balancing two competing interests here.

On the one hand, Peloton bikes cost upward of $2,500—meaning that they are out of reach for most Americans. Much like playing golf regularly, riding a Peloton is a sort of cultural indicator of wealth and elite status—a signal that Scranton Joe most definitely does not want to send.

On the other hand, Joe Biden is in his late seventies. And poll after poll shows that people—Republicans, yes, but Democrats and independents, too—are concerned that he is too old to be president and certainly to serve a second term. (Biden would be in his mideighties by the time his second term ended in 2028.)

It is absolutely imperative then that Biden be seen as hale and hearty. (When Biden contracted COVID-19 in the summer of 2022, the White House was very careful to ensure that, on a daily basis, images and videos of Biden hard at work—and not at all laid up!—were distributed to the media.)

As Claire Malone wrote for *Esquire* in January 2021:

> We want leaders, especially older ones, who are making every effort to stay sharp. That takes on even greater meaning when the oldest-ever president takes office during a pandemic. We find death at the forefront of our minds all the time now, and understand more viscerally than ever before the precious commodity that is time on earth. Biden's campaign line was that there was lots for him to fix and that he was particularly well-suited to do the fixing. What went unspoken was how, statistically, his time on earth would be running out.

The White House is mum on whether Biden is still riding a Peloton in the White House. But, every once in a while I search "Biden" or "Joey B" or even "JRB" on my own Peloton just to see if the president is lurking. No luck yet.

———

Everyone knows that Joe Biden is the most famous person from Delaware. (Sorry. Pierre du Pont! And Aubrey Plaza!) But, he is definitely not the most famous—or best—athlete from the First State.

Below, an alphabetical list of the ten best athletes the second smallest state in the country—I see you, Rhode Island!—has produced.

* **Elena Della Donne:** Della Donne is, without question, the best basketball player—male or female—to ever come out of Delaware. In her high school career at Ursuline Academy in Wilmington, she was the three-time Gatorade player of the year in the state, scored more than 2,000 points, and led her team to three straight Delaware state championships.

Della Donne committed to play for the powerhouse University of Connecticut women's basketball team out of high school but left the school after just a few days on campus and returned to Delaware, enrolling at the University of Delaware. (Della Donne is very close to her family, including her older sister Lizzie, who has special needs.) She stopped playing basketball entirely for a year. "As hard as it was to go through, I'm glad I went through it," Delle Donne told the *Washington Post* in 2017. "Because it's made me into the person I am and taught me so much about following my heart, what's important to me. It just helped me to grow."

When she did start playing again, she shone. As a junior she led the country in scoring. As a senior, she led the Blue Hens to the Sweet Sixteen. She wound up as a three-time All American.

Her WNBA career is just as lauded with accomplishments. She has been the league MVP twice and an all-star four times. In 2016, she helped Team USA win the gold medal at the Brazil Summer Olympics.

* **Delino DeShields:** DeShields is from Seaford, a city in the far southwestern part of Delaware. He was a standout baseball and basketball player in high school and had committed to play hoops at nearby Villanova University. (BOOOO!)

But, he was drafted twelfth in the 1987 Major League Baseball draft by the Montreal Expos—and chose baseball as his career instead. He came up to the big leagues in 1990 at the age of twenty-one and hit .289 in 129 games. (He finished second in rookie of the year voting; Atlanta Braves slugger Dave Justice, who is not from Delaware, won the award.) DeShields played thirteen seasons, finishing with a .268 lifetime average and 463 stolen bases.

He has stayed in baseball as the first base coach for the Cincinnati

Reds. He is also the father of two professional athletes; his son, Delino DeShields Jr., is an outfielder for the Reds, while his daughter, Diamond DeShields, is a WNBA standout for the Phoenix Mercury.

* **Margaret Osborne duPont:** DuPont was a dominant figure in doubles tennis in the middle of the twentieth century, winning thirty-one(!) Grand Slam titles. (She also won six Grand Slams in singles.) From 1947 to 1950, duPont was ranked number one in the world in women's singles. Her reign at an elite level in tennis lasted for an incredible two decades.

"A poised and canny playmaker, DuPont wielded a dazzling arsenal of shots, including low-flying spin volleys and gravity-defying lobs, often executed in sensible shorts rather than the billowy tennis skirts customary in her day," read the *New York Times* obituary of duPont, who died in 2012.

She was married to William duPont Jr., a tennis lover who also happened to be the heir to the duPont chemical fortune. (He was twenty-two years her senior.) She skipped the Australian Open every year because her husband, in frail health, insisted that the family needed to winter in California. What a life!

* **Paul Goldschmidt:** The star St. Louis Cardinals slugger was born in Wilmington but raised in Texas. Doesn't matter! We are claiming him for Delaware! Goldy was drafted directly out of high school (in Houston) by the Los Angeles Dodgers in the forty-ninth round of the 2006 draft. Goldschmidt wound up going to college, playing for Texas State.

He was eventually selected in the eighth round of the 2009 draft by the Arizona Diamondbacks. He spent eight seasons with the Diamondbacks and was an All Star in six of those seasons. In December 2018, he was traded to the St. Louis Cardinals. He has a lifetime batting average of .295 with more than 300 home runs and more than 1,000 RBIs.

* **Dallas Green:** Green was a star baseball player in high school and at the University of Delaware; he still holds the ERA record at the school—0.88. He hung on in the majors for more than a decade as, primarily, a relief pitcher.

But Green is best known for his years as a manager. In 1980, in his first full season as manager, Green led the Philadelphia Phillies—Delaware's adopted baseball team—to the World Series. "There's very few people who were more synonymous with the Phillies than Dallas," Phillies chairman David Montgomery told the Wilmington *News Journal* when Green died in 2017.

That first season was Green's best. He finished with a lifetime 454-478 record as a manager in stints with the Phillies, Yankees, and Mets.

* **Judy Johnson:** Johnson—full name William Julius Johnson—was a star in the Negro League. He played third base and hit over .300 seven times during his years in the league. (He never got the chance to play major league baseball.) "If Judy were only white, he could name his own price," said legendary manager Connie Mack of Johnson.

Johnson was inducted into the Baseball Hall of Fame in 1975, only the sixth Negro League player to earn that distinction. (The previous five: Satchel Paige, Buck Leonard, Monte Irvin, James "Cool Papa" Bell, and Josh Gibson.)

"I felt so good, I could have cried," Johnson said of being elected to the Hall. "I've been to the Hall of Fame before, but this time it will be different."

Johnson died in 1989 at eighty-nine years old.

* **Johnny Weir:** OK, so technically, the skater (and fashion icon) was born in Pennsylvania. But, he moved to Delaware at twelve and trained there, too. He also now lives in the state—Greenville, to be exact—and his house was the first Delaware house ever to make it on an episode of MTV's *Cribs*. I mean . . .

Weir is a two-time Olympian in figure skating and has a load of other accolades in the sport, including being a three-time U.S. national champion. After he retired, he made his name as a color—and colorful—commentator on the sport.

* **Randy White:** The legendary footballer went to high school just outside of Wilmington before going on to play at the University of Maryland.

White, a defensive lineman, was picked number two overall in the 1975 NFL draft by the Dallas Cowboys. He went on to play fourteen seasons with the team, making nine Pro Bowls, and he helped the Cowboys win Super Bowl XII, where he was named most valuable player. His own teammate once crashed into White's midsection and broke his own helmet. He ended his career with 111 sacks and was chosen to the Pro Football Hall of Fame in 1994.

In his induction speech, White shouted out his high school coach, Blaine Tanner, who he said was "the first guy that put in my head that I may have a chance to go to college and have the opportunity to play pro football, and I thank him for that."

* **Val Whiting:** Whiting, like Della Donne, played high school basketball at Ursuline Academy in Wilmington. She then went on to star at Stanford University, where she was named freshman of the year in the PAC-10 conference.

Whiting was an All American at Stanford and was part of two national championship teams. She also played in the early years of the WNBA. In 2006, she was named by ESPN as one of the top twenty-five players in the history of NCAA women's basketball.

* **Vic Willis:** Willis was born near Newark, Delaware, in 1876. Known as the "Delaware Peach," Willis played for the University of Delaware in 1897.

He pitched for twelve seasons in the major leagues for the Boston Beaneaters (amazing name), the Pittsburgh Pirates, and the St. Louis Cardinals.

Of his 471 career starts, Willis pitched 388 complete games and 50 shutouts. He won twenty or more games in eight seasons. He had a lifetime ERA of 2.63.

"Willis has speed and the most elusive curves," the *Boston Sunday Journal* said. "His 'drop' is so wonderful that, if anyone hits it, it is generally considered a fluke."

Willis was inducted into the Baseball Hall of Fame in 1995.

———

One sport that Joe Biden doesn't play—yet—but *literally* everyone else his age does is pickleball.

You know, the sport that's sort of like Ping-Pong and sort of like tennis and sort of like badminton all rolled into one? And that old people are playing like it's the twenty-first-century version of shuffleboard?

Actor Jeff Daniels has called pickleball "half-court basketball for elderly people."

Go to any country club or any big public park and you're likely to see it—a court smaller than a tennis court, a net slightly lower than a tennis net and a racket slightly smaller than a tennis racket. And the ball? The same one you played wiffle ball with with your friends when you were a kid.

The game has actually been around since the mid-1960s. It was invented on Bainbridge Island in the Pacific Northwest by Republican congressman Joel Pritchard (yes, everything comes back to politics!) and friends named Bill Bell and Barney McCallum. (At the time he created Pickleball, Pritchard was a state representative.)

One afternoon, after playing golf that morning, the two men were looking for something to keep the kids entertained. (Welcome to my life!) They had Ping-Pong paddles, a wiffle ball, and a net. Voilà!

"We had it pretty much worked out in four or five days," Pritchard said in 1990. "What makes it such a great game is that the serve isn't so dominant, like it is in tennis." (In pickleball you have to serve underhand.)

The name, which is, um, odd, is a point of some disagreement. Pritchard's wife, Joan, has said it comes from the fact that "the combination of different sports reminded me of the pickle boat in crew where oarsmen were chosen from the leftovers of other boats." But, the Pritchards also had a dog that liked to run after errant balls. And that dog's name was Pickles. So . . .

Within two years the first permanent pickleball court had been built at the house of a friend of Pritchard's. (U.S. senator Slade Gorton had pickleball courts built at his homes in Olympia and on Whidbey Island.) By 1976, pickleball tournaments were being held.

The sport only grew from there. (Pritchard's political career grew too; he served as the lieutenant governor of Washington from 1988 to 1996.)

But, it was during the COVID-19 pandemic that pickleball really took off.

"Pickleball is the fastest-growing sport in America," declared a January 2021 *Economist* headline.

"Last March, when quarantines went into effect and gyms closed, portable pickleball nets temporarily sold out," said the story. "Players set up courts, which are half the size of tennis courts, in driveways. 'It's the new thing,' says Derek Heil, an employee at Dick's Sporting Goods in Dallas, who has seen a sales spike for pickleball equipment over the last year, including for higher-end paddles which sell for around $100."

(Confession: For Father's Day 2021, my wife got me a set of pickleball rackets. They have a polymer honeycomb core. So I've got that going for me...)

In November 2021, the *Today* show did a segment on pickleball—the surest sign yet that it has arrived as a cultural phenomenon. In a pickleball tournament between the show's hosts, Hoda Kotb and Jenna Bush Hager won. (On a related note: Hoda is the best.)

That same year nearly 5 million people played pickleball, according to *Deadspin*, an 11.5 percent average annual growth rate for the sport over the last five years. There are now three—yes, three—professional pickleball leagues.

The sport has even become a sort of signifier of class. As the *New York Post* reported in June 2022:

Don't expect to visit the Hamptons this summer, for example, without encountering a waitlist for the three new courts at Dune Deck Beach Club, open only to members.

"If you walk into any of our clubs between the hours of 8 a.m. and 12 p.m. the courts are packed," said Mike Meldman, founder and chairman of Discovery Land Company, owner of the exclusive Hamptons beach club residences...

Pickleball is infiltrating other tony ZIP codes, too. All of Discovery's luxury resort communities—from Barbuda to Portugal—now have pickleball courts.

And it's even being cast as a potential societal savior. "Can Pickleball Save America?" asked a lengthy July 2022 *New Yorker* story on the sport. The piece posits the notion that the friendliness built into the DNA of the game—and the sheer proximity of the players (the court is only fourteen feet long) may be the cure for what ails our body politic.

Wrote Sarah Larson:

Robert D. Putnam's book *Bowling Alone*, from 2000, mourns the loss of beloved community groups—a bridge club in Pennsylvania, an N.A.A.C.P. chapter in Roanoke, a sewing charity league in Dallas—which, for decades, fostered norms of reciprocity, trustworthiness, and general good will. A craving for such feelings is a key part of pickleball's popularity. At one tournament, a senior pro told me, "The most important thing about this sport is the friendships. I just lost my husband a week ago, and the only reason I'm here today is because of my pickleball community lifting me up." She got teary. "There's no other sport like that. Tennis isn't like that. You go to a tennis tournament, it's them against you."

Which is a lot to put on pickleball!

Pickleball has also become something of a political football—see what I did there—as well.

In a May 2002 speech on the floor of the Senate, Mitch McConnell attacked Joe Biden's American Rescue Plan for doling out money for "localities seeking to build or upgrade their pickleball amenities." Added McConnell: "If the Hoover Dam and the Lincoln Tunnel are enduring monuments to the New Deal's infrastructure spending, well, perhaps pickleball courts will become the lasting legacy of the $1.9 trillion American Rescue Plan."

Perhaps!

Or maybe there's a growing pickleball vote out there? What would that voter look like?

"Middle aged moms who want to continue to be athletic and competitive, but don't want to: 1) injure themselves; 2) run too much," speculated Amy Walter, the editor of a nonpartisan political handicapping tip sheet in Washington. "I suspect the sport is super-duper white, suburban, and middle-aged/older. But I also think it is more economically diverse than golf or tennis or people who buy Pelotons."

What Biden's entire candidacy—and presidency—seem to be premised on is the same notion that pickleball is pushing: that everyone can not only participate but can find ways to get along, too. That things don't *have* to be as ugly as they are right now. That we have lots more in common than we have that makes us different. That rooting for the Golden State Warriors or Serena Williams is not just OK but should be encouraged. That there is a collective national good out there, and sports helps us not only remember it but tap into it.

Acknowledgments

This book would not exist without the unique brain and Herculean patience of Sean Desmond, my editor at Twelve. I've written two books now with Sean, and I would have written zero without him. Attention must be paid.

My wife, Gia, was—and is—the sun around which I orbit. My two boys, Charlie and Will, served as a constant reminder that play sits at the heart of who we are as humans.

Byrd Leavell at UTA was the book's Sherpa to the publishing world. Two other agents at UTA—Jerry Silbowitz and Ryan Hayden—were sounding boards as I tried to imagine what the book could—and should—be.

My longtime collaborator and one-time colleague Brooke Brower also deserves mention; Brooke encouraged me from the start and helped guide me through the at-times confusing process of turning a book idea into an actual book.

My friends Julie Tate and Carlos Lozada were always there to offer a word of encouragement or a bit of advice.

This is a book that has been rattling around in my brain for the better part of the last five years. I am just so damn proud of it.

Works Cited

Books I Used Throughout

Games Presidents Play: Sports and the American Presidency by John Sayle Watterson

Presidential Diversions: Presidents at Play from George Washington to George W. Bush by Paul F. Boller Jr.

Presidential Lies: The Illustrated History of White House Golf by Shephard Campbell and Peter Landau

You Gotta Have Heart by Frederic J. Frommer

Eisenhower

Arnold Palmer: A Life Well Played by Arnold Palmer

Eisenhower by Geoffrey Perret

Ike & Dick: Portrait of a Strange Political Marriage by Jeffrey Frank

Kennedy

JFK: Coming of Age in the American Century 1917–1956 by Fredrik Logevall

Victura: The Kennedys a Sailboat and the Sea by James Graham

The Complete Guide to Golf on Cape Cod, Nantucket and Martha's Vineyard by Paul Harber

LBJ

Lyndon Johnson: Master of the Senate by Robert Caro

Lyndon Johnson: The Path to Power by Robert Caro

The Vantage Point by Lyndon Baines Johnson

Lone Star Rising: Lyndon Johnson and his Times by Robert Dallek

In the Arena by Chuck Robb

Nixon

The Memoirs of Richard Nixon by Richard Nixon

Fan in Chief: Richard Nixon and American Sports 1969–1974 by Nicholas Evan Sarantakes

The President's Man: The Memoirs of Nixon's Trusted Aide by Dwight Chapin

Richard Nixon: The Life by John Farrell

Ford

Gerald R. Ford by Douglas Brinkley

An Ordinary Man: The Surprising Life and Historic Presidency of Gerald R. Ford by Richard Norton Smith

Carter

Keeping Faith: Memoirs of a President by Jimmy Carter

An Hour Before Daylight: Memoirs of a Rural Boyhood by Jimmy Carter

His Very Best: Jimmy Carter, a Life by Jonathan Alter

Reagan

An American Life by Ronald Reagan

President Reagan: The Role of a Lifetime by Lou Cannon

George H. W. Bush

The Quiet Man: The Indispensable Presidency of George H. W. Bush by John H. Sununu

My Father, My President by Doro Bush Koch

Bill Clinton

First in His Class by David Maraniss

My Life by Bill Clinton

George W. Bush

Decision Points by George W. Bush

For the Good of the Game by Bud Selig

Barack Obama

Dreams from my Father by Barack Obama

Barack Obama by David Maraniss

A Promised Land by Barack Obama

The Audacity of Hoop by Alexander Wolff

Donald Trump

Trump Revealed by Marc Fisher and Michael Kranish

Football for a Buck by Jeff Pearlman

Commander in Cheat by Rick Reilly

Confidence Man by Maggie Haberman

Joe Biden

Promises to Keep by Joe Biden

Growing Up Biden by Valerie Biden Owens

Joe Biden: The Life, the Run, and What Matters Now by Evan Osnos